Cheaper,
Better,
Faster

Other books by Mary Hunt

Seven Money Rules for Life
Raising Financially Confident Kids
Debt-Proof Your Christmas

Cheaper, Better, *Faster*

Over 2,000 Tips and Tricks
to Save You Time and Money
Every Day

Mary Hunt

Revell

a division of Baker Publishing Group
Grand Rapids, Michigan

© 2013 by Mary Hunt

Published by Revell
a division of Baker Publishing Group
P.O. Box 6287, Grand Rapids, MI 49516-6287
www.revellbooks.com

Printed in the United States of America

Library of Congress Cataloging-in-Publication Data
Hunt, Mary, 1948-
    Cheaper, better, faster : over 2,000 tips and tricks to save you time and
money every day / Mary Hunt.
      p. cm.
    ISBN 978-0-8007-2144-2 (pbk.)
    1. Home economics. I. Title.
  TX158.H78 2013
  646.7—dc23   2012032499

Published in association with the literary agency of The Steve Laube Agency, 5025 N.
Central Ave., #635, Phoenix, Arizona 85012-1502.

The internet addresses, email addresses, and phone numbers in this book are accurate
at the time of publication. They are provided as a resource. Baker Publishing Group
does not endorse them or vouch for their content or permanence.

13   14   15   16   17   18   19   8   7   6   5   4

In keeping with biblical principles of
creation stewardship, Baker Publishing Group advocates the responsible
use of our natural resources. As a
member of the Green Press Initia-
tive, our company uses recycled
paper when possible. The text paper
of this book is composed in part of
post-consumer waste.

Contents

Introduction

I didn't actually set out to become a tip aficionado. But that's exactly what's happened since the day I began publishing *Debt-Proof Living* newsletter (formerly *Cheapskate Monthly*) and invited readers to share with me their best money- and time-saving tips.

Three or four fascinating tips came pouring in those first few months (two or three more than I expected), and because they were great, I shared them with my readers. The more tips I published in subsequent months, the more readers responded with new and better tips. In time, I began to go out of my way looking for tips and was amazed at how many turned up. I'm not sure if I was more attracted to the tips or the tips to me (sometimes I feel like a tip magnet), but the result was clear: I loved tips. I can read a tip, digest it quickly, mentally file it for future use, move on to the next one, and never get bored.

Before long, tips began arriving at my office faster than I could figure out what to do with them. I couldn't throw them away. And because of the way they arrived (and still do)—printed on napkins; buried in the recesses of long, detailed letters; salvaged on snippets torn from newspapers; phone, fax, and email messages—I had a logistical challenge from the very start.

I was able to stick with a simple filing system for about three days until I discovered a much easier method: piling—which took hardly any time at all. And then piles began to grow and spill into each other at an unprecedented rate into what I would eventually name Mt. Tip.

I knew I was headed for trouble the day I spent hours searching for one wonderful tip I knew was in there somewhere. And that was the day I conceded that I had to either find a way to move mountains or call a rubbish-removal contractor. I couldn't go on living like this.

First published in 1997 under the title *Tiptionary*, this book was a big hit. Apparently I wasn't the only one who loved handy tips! Readers told me that reading the book was a lot like being faced with a bag of potato chips: It was almost impossible to stop with just one tip.

In the years since *Tiptionary* was released, the world has changed a lot! And that meant this book needed a radical update to make it current. Sections on banking, computers, and travel, for example, needed overhauls.

Enter Revell Books. All I had to do was mention the availability of a really awesome collection of handy tips to my editor, Vicki Crumpton, and the best publishing team in the world was mobilized into action.

What you have here is a revised and updated, fabulously fun collection of tips—short, to-the-point suggestions for ways to do things cheaper, better, and faster. Many of these tips are timeless; others we know were current and relevant five minutes ago, but who knows about next month!

Some of the best tips you will read have completely unknown origins because they've been passed from generation to generation, and someone along the line sent them my way. Some tips were left out because they turned out to be nothing more than myths—legends people believe with all their hearts, but when put to the test, fail.

One rejected tip had to do with bread and wallpaper. No foolin'. The tip was to discard the crust from a piece of bread, wad it up into a tight dough ball, and use it like an eraser to clean dirt and marks from wallpaper. I tried it and "erased" with all my might, but that little dirty spot on my wallpaper would not budge. I threw the bread ball in the trash, grabbed a bottle of laundry stain remover, and took care of the smudge in a flash.

Some entries were discovered quite by accident. I think of the woman who wrote to me so excited because she no longer needed to scrub the toilet on Saturday since her husband had started dumping his denture-soaking liquid into the commode each morning. Bingo! A great household tip (page 63).

Surely there's a long story that goes along with the tip that arrived on a postcard without a return address or signature, simply a postmark from somewhere in Alaska: "Have your head examined before you attempt to build your own home. Unless you are a developer or professional contractor, you are in for a few surprises, not the least of which is that it will take twice as long as promised and cost twice as much as estimated." There you go, for what it's worth.

The criteria for whether a tip made it into this collection were fairly simple: If it didn't insult my intelligence, included a reasonable expectation that it saved time or money, and prompted a response anything close to *Wow! What a great idea!*—it was in. This means you won't be reading any tips that tell you to brush and floss your teeth, because we're smart and we already know we should do that every day. But floss a turkey? Now that's a great tip (page 125). Or floss that winter coat? You'll be glad you did (page 69)!

You're about to learn that there are many different ways to accomplish goals. And that's good, because if you need to polish the copper in your kitchen and you don't have any lemons on hand but you do have a jug of vinegar, you'll be able to get the job done without running to the store to spend money needlessly (page 40). When there's more than one way to achieve the same result, *Cheaper, Better, Faster* will give you the choices.

And now to answer the question you will ask if you haven't already: No, I do not do everything recommended in *Cheaper, Better, Faster*. There's not a person on the face of the earth, myself included, who could do all of these things in a single lifetime, nor would I want to. Some of the tips are just not applicable to my life. And some won't apply to your life, either.

Think of *Cheaper, Better, Faster* as a grand smorgasbord loaded with every kind of delicacy you can possibly imagine—even some things you can't. As you pass by, look at everything, consider most things, and fill your plate with what suits your taste.

The best thing about *Cheaper, Better, Faster*, just like your favorite smorgasbord, is that you can come back again and again and again!

Mary Hunt
California
2013

1

Automobiles

Accident preparedness

Carry a camera, pad of paper, and pen in the glove box of your car. In case of an accident you'll have what you need to collect information and take on-the-spot photos even if you have left your cell phone with a camera in it at home. Be sure to draw a map and record all the details while they are still fresh in your mind.

Air-conditioning vs. open windows—4/40 rule

Not sure whether it's more cost-effective to use the air-conditioning or open the windows? Rule of thumb: If you're driving under 40 mph, open all four windows and turn off the air-conditioning. Over 40 mph, close the windows and run the air-conditioning.

Battery terminal—cleanup

Pour club soda or Windex on the battery terminals. It's a great way to quickly clean and neutralize the acid residue at the battery terminals. Remember to disconnect the battery before cleaning.

Battery terminal—protection

A car's starting problems are frequently related to corroded battery terminals. Clean the battery terminals occasionally with a paste of baking soda and water, and then reduce the corrosion problem by smearing them with a thin coating of petroleum jelly. Remember to disconnect the battery before cleaning.

Brakes—replacement

Have your brakes replaced before the rotors have to be turned. You'll save hundreds of dollars. Your mechanic should check for free and tell you how much of the pad is remaining. Don't push it past 5 percent.

Brakes—when stopped on a hill

When stopped on a hill, always use your parking or foot brake to hold the car still. Don't hold it by applying gas to the accelerator or, in the case of a standard transmission, by riding the clutch and applying gas. These bad habits accelerate wear of the engine, clutch, and transmission. Use your brakes. That's what they're for.

Bumper sticker removal

Remove a decal or bumper sticker by first softening the adhesive with a hair dryer. Use a medium-heat setting for a few seconds until the adhesive softens and the sticker starts to peel. Continue with the heat until the entire sticker peels off easily.

Buyer consideration—cost guide for any car

Find out what it will cost to own a particular vehicle at www.IntelliChoice.com. Part of Motor Trend Automotive Group, IntelliChoice evaluates depreciation, gas consumption, insurance costs, and frequency of repairs to derive the average five-year cost of operating each car.

Buyer consideration—current vs. new car operating costs

Keeping your old car instead of buying a new one can save you a lot of money over the years. Example: A four-year-old, four-door American sedan driven fifteen thousand miles per year on average will cost about half of what a new car will cost to operate over that same four-year period.

Buyer consideration—insurance

Check insurance rates before you make a decision to purchase a particular car. Call your agent with a couple of choices and get quotes.

Buyer consideration—older car with low mileage

Old cars with relatively low mileage are choice buys. Age pushes the value down, but the mileage is more representative of the vehicle's true age. A properly maintained car with fifty thousand miles on it is likely to have the same kick whether it is three years old or

eight. The eight-year-old car, however, will be much cheaper.

Buyer consideration—safest colors

In the market to purchase a car? Insurance actuarials say that if you're interested in safety, you should drive a greenish-yellow car to avoid being hit accidentally by another vehicle. The next safest colors are cream, yellow, and white—in that order. The least-safe colors are red and black. Light-colored, single-tone cars stand out from their surroundings, making them easier to see and avoid.

Buyer consideration—warranties transferable?

If the seller says the vehicle is still under the original manufacturer's warranty or any dealer service contract, double-check that these benefits can be transferred from the original owner. Take no one's word for it—read the contracts.

Buyer negotiation— contract scrutiny

Before signing a final auto purchase or lease agreement, check it with a magnifying glass. The folks who write up the final agreement often make mistakes. Occasionally the agreed-upon price gets listed incorrectly, or extras you crossed off get added back in, or a higher financing charge than the one you settled on finds its way back into the deal. Give the contract a brutal examination.

Buyer negotiation—dealer add-ons

Factory-installed options are good buys, but think twice about any option the dealer wants to add, such as a stereo or sunroof. Typically, specialty shops do better work and charge half the price.

Buyer negotiation—dealer option, rust-proofing

Rust-proofing as a dealer option is not advisable. Cars are rust-proofed at the factory, and unless you live in an area that goes heavy-duty on the wintertime salt, contemporary automobiles don't need extra protection. It isn't uncommon today to find new cars coming with five-, seven-, or even ten-year rust protection warranties. In many cases this option will invalidate any rust warranty that came with the car from the manufacturer.

Buyer negotiation—dealer option, upholstery protection

The dealer fabric protection offered as an option when purchasing or leasing an automobile amounts to a can of Scotchgard sprayed on the upholstery. Save money by skipping the option, picking up a can of Scotchgard, and doing it yourself.

Buyer negotiation—don't divulge bottom line

Don't tell a dealer you can afford, say, a $300 monthly payment. If you tell him, he'll gladly increase the interest rate or lengthen the terms until it exactly matches what you can afford. Either way, you lose.

Before you go car shopping, figure out what you can afford, but don't reveal it at the dealership. And negotiate for the lowest interest rate you can get too.

Buyer negotiation—get it in writing

If you want something fixed on the car you are buying, get it in writing the moment it is offered or agreed upon. Do not expect the dealer to pay for something you didn't get in writing.

Buyer negotiation—point by point

When shopping for a car, negotiate one point at a time: the price of the car, then the dealer add-ons you want eliminated, the trade-in value of a used car, then financing. If you try to cover all these points at once, you'll be so thoroughly confused you'll lose your leverage.

Buyer negotiation— willing to walk away

As a consumer, one of your greatest strengths when negotiating to buy a new car is your willingness to walk away

from it. Unless a salesperson believes you will walk away, you are not likely to get the best deal.

Buyer's Guide sticker

If you are considering buying a used car from a dealer, become familiar with the Buyer's Guide sticker posted on every used car offered for sale (for-sale-by-owner cars excluded). It was originated by the Federal Trade Commission (FTC) as a consumer protection device. Download the Consumer Buyer's Guide from the FTC website at www.FTC.gov.

Cleaning—aluminum mag wheels

If your car has aluminum mag wheels, check with the manufacturer to see if they are protected by a clear-coat finish. If yours are protected, as most are, do not use a brush to scrub them. This will scratch the clear coat and give the wheels a fuzzy look instead of the brilliance you paid for. Use only a mild, nonabrasive cleaning wax or polish.

Cleaning—bugs off windshield

To remove stubborn bug residue from a windshield, sprinkle the surface with baking soda and scrub gently with a wet sponge.

Cleaning—chrome

Briskly scrub rust spots on car bumpers with a piece of crumpled aluminum foil, shiny side out. (This tip also works well on the chrome shafts of golf clubs.)

Cleaning—floor mats

Some carpet floor mats will fit into your home washing machine and come out really clean after a wash in warm water with mild detergent. Spread them out flat to air-dry.

Cleaning—tar and tree sap

A little dab of butter, margarine, or even mayonnaise is great for removing unhardened sap or tree pitch from the surface of your car.

Cleaning—tires

A paste made of Bar Keepers Friend (a household cleaner available in most stores) and water works well to clean tires. Spread it on and allow to sit for about 10 minutes. Rinse. This works as well as special whitewall cleaner, but for a fraction of the cost.

Cleaning—vinyl dashboard and upholstery

Clean a car's vinyl upholstery with a damp cloth dipped in baking soda. Follow with a mild solution of dish-washing liquid and water. Rinse thoroughly.

Cleaning—wax marks

Car wax can be removed from automobile trim with ammonia that has been carefully applied with a rag or a cotton swab.

Cleaning—windshield wiper blades

Before you toss out those windshield wiper blades, clean

the rubber part with rubbing alcohol. You may be pleasantly surprised to find they were not worn out at all—just gunked up.

Clutch first

On standard or manual-shift cars, get into the habit of always pushing in the clutch before starting the engine, whether or not the car is in gear. Besides being an obvious safety practice, holding the clutch in while starting the engine lets it turn over just a bit more easily, lessening the power required from the battery and starter motor.

Condensation on windows

To take care of the condensation that builds up on the inside of car windows during the cold winter months, leave the air-conditioning on with the temperature in the heat position and windows will clear like magic. Or carry an ordinary chalkboard eraser in the car. Simply erase away the condensation.

Coolant, always

Always keep a mix of equal parts antifreeze and water in your car's cooling system, even if you live in a mild climate where it never freezes. Not only does antifreeze keep your cooling system functioning well, it also contains valuable rust inhibitors.

Crime—avoid being followed

A great way to avoid a possible carjacking is to be aware of what's going on around you. If you think someone is following you, make four right turns, which will in essence have you driving in a circle. If that suspicious car makes the same turns, immediately drive to the nearest police station, busy store, or service station to seek help.

Crime—cars thieves shun

Choose a car not coveted by criminals. A phone call to your local police department will reveal which cars are most likely to be stolen in your area.

Crime—parking habits make a difference

A car that's parked in the same place for the same amount of time each day and night lets thieves know where to look for it, and this gives them plenty of time to figure how much time they'd need to make off with it.

Crime—registration location

Never leave your car registration in the glove compartment. It gives a car thief automatic proof of ownership. Keep it with you.

Dealer repairs to avoid

Need a brake job, muffler repair, or front-end alignment? Head for shops specializing in these jobs. They offer lower prices than dealers, and polls show they deliver better customer satisfaction.

Deodorizer

To keep your car smelling fresh, put some of your favorite potpourri in a mesh bag and tuck it under the front seat. No more dangling pine trees from your rearview mirror.

Dipstick readability

Save the guesswork when checking your car's oil by making the dipstick easier to read. Drill tiny holes at the lines that read "full" and "add" so they'll never get obliterated.

Driving—automatic transmission shifting

Give your automatic transmission a little break by learning how to help it shift. Ease up slightly on the accelerator when you feel the transmission begin its shift. This increases engine vacuum and helps the transmission into a smooth, effortless shift.

Driving—don't downshift

If your car is a stick shift, don't downshift as a standard alternative to braking.

Downshifting uses more gas and wears out the clutch and transmission. Generally it's cheaper to replace worn brakes than a worn clutch.

Driving—don't use overdrive or fifth gear

Don't use overdrive or fifth gear until the car has warmed up sufficiently—approximately 10 minutes under normal driving and weather conditions. The rear axle and transmission fluids must be adequately warmed for these units to work properly and efficiently.

Driving—hands off the gearshift

Don't drive with your hand resting on the gear shift. It may feel good, but it adds unnecessary wear to the transmission selector forks.

Driving defensively—as if driving for five

Drive for five drivers: yourself, drivers in front, drivers at both sides, and the driver behind you. Be prepared at all times for at least four of them to do the unexpected.

Driving left-footed

If your car has an automatic transmission, you may be tempted to brake with your left foot. Bad habit. Left-footed braking leads to riding the brakes, which results in a slew of problems: poor gas mileage, reduced engine life, and worn brakes.

Driving shoes

Keep a pair of driving shoes in the car. Sharp heels and sport shoes wear holes in the carpet. Use a carpet sample or remnant under the pedals to prolong the life of your vehicle's carpet.

Driving too slowly

Don't poke along in city driving. The slower you go doesn't mean the slower the car will wear. Actually the opposite is true. Slow driving costs you miles per gallon and increases engine deposits. Keep your city speed in the economical 35 to

45 mph range when possible. Most cars reach their maximum mileage potential in this range, so this practice not only ensures top miles per gallon in the city but also promotes longer engine life.

Engine care—avoid super-short drives

You drive home and leave the car parked out front. Later you put it away for the night by starting the engine and putting it in the garage. Because 90 to 95 percent of engine wear occurs in the first 10 seconds after starting the engine and before the engine becomes fully lubricated, that start-up and short drive into the garage causes the equivalent of 500 miles of mechanical engine wear.

Engine care—no revving

Do not race your engine out of gear or in neutral. Revving an engine while the car is not moving can only do harm; it will never help. Many people like to rev the engine a few times just before putting it

to bed. The old theory held that the extra revs pumped extra oil through the cylinder walls and made the next start easier. Actually, the opposite is true. Those high rpms allow unburned fuel to dilute the oil, wash away protective cylinder coatings, and contribute to sludge buildup and oil contamination.

Engine care—park on pavement

Try to always park on pavement, even at home. Don't park in the alley when you can park on the paved street. You'd be surprised how much dirt and dust can be sucked into your car's engine compartment when it is parked in dusty areas. Abrasive wear caused by grit, dust, and dirt is one of the major causes of engine failure. Keep away from dirt and dust-producing areas, and you will enhance your car's longevity.

Engine care—short trips in cold weather

If at all possible, don't take your car on short trips of less than five miles on days when the temperature is below freezing. Really cold weather can affect the pressure, plugs, and oil, and short trips don't allow the engine to warm properly. If a bus is available, take it, or if you can accomplish your goal with the telephone or internet instead of going in person, do it.

Engine care—unplug electrical devices

Unnecessary use of electrical devices, such as headlights in the daytime (unless required for safety), or anything plugged into the cigarette lighter like a cell phone, hair dryer, curling iron, or electric razor will actually make an engine work harder by making it more difficult to turn the alternator.

Fan belt emergency

Pantyhose can come through as an emergency fan belt if your car's fan belt breaks. Cut away the panty portion and twirl both legs into a rope.

Then wrap the strong nylon rope around your car engine pulleys, tie your best knot, and cut off the loose end. Start your car and drive slowly for several miles to a gas station or phone or other sources of help.

Gadget caddy

A large handbag or other kind of handled tote with many zippered compartments makes a dandy storage system for the trunk of your car. Fill the pockets with battery cables, a flashlight, a first-aid kit, maps, window cleaner, paper towels, and a plastic window scraper.

Gas cap replacement

Have you ever left your gas cap at the service station? You won't be surprised to know that many others have too. The next time you're capless, ask the station attendants if you might look through their lost-and-found gas cap assortment. You're sure to find one that fits, and they'll be happy to have you take one off their hands.

Gas fill-up—make it Wednesday mornings

On average, Wednesday is the cheapest day to buy gas and the earlier in the day, the better. Many station owners wait to see their competitors' prices to make their own adjustments. While this is not always true, consistently buying gas on Wednesday mornings has been shown to minimize the price you'll pay over time. Every little bit helps.

Gas grade—go with what is recommended

Make sure you use the octane grade gasoline recommended in your car owner's manual. Using a more expensive higher-octane gas than recommended will deliver no benefit, and a lower-octane gas than recommended could damage the engine.

Gas mileage—better with an empty trunk

Don't carry more than you need. A light load results in much better gas mileage.

Clean out heavy items from the trunk, and leave only the spare tire and safety equipment. Don't make your car a mobile warehouse for stuff you can just as easily leave in the garage.

Gas mileage—better with turns on red

Save gasoline and contribute to the long life of your car's engine by taking advantage of "right turn on red" laws. After coming to a complete stop, if the way is clear, turn right on that red light and keep moving. Unnecessary idling time spent at red lights wastes your fuel and that of the cars behind you. Cut idle time and you cut carbon and sludge buildup.

Gas mileage—skip the roof and trunk racks

If you'd like to increase your gas mileage, avoid roof and trunk racks. These things affect aerodynamics and significantly reduce gas mileage.

Gas pumping—keep your hands clean

Keep a box of baby wipes in the car to clean your hands after pumping gas.

Gas savings—go with smallest car

If economy is your first priority, buy the smallest car you can live with. Weight is the biggest enemy of fuel economy.

Gas savings—park, walk, and save

When driving into a parking lot, take the first available space you see, and don't be afraid to walk the extra distance. Slow stop-and-go driving is the most gas consuming; so be willing to walk a little, and you'll save a lot.

Hubcap return—better your chances

With a permanent marking pen, write your name and phone number on the inside of your car's hubcaps. This way, if one goes flying you have a chance of having it returned.

Include the word "reward," and you will greatly increase the likelihood of a return. Even if it costs you 20 percent of the price of a replacement, you'll be 80 percent ahead.

Mechanics—opt for students

If your car has a ding, dent, or bent fender, check out the auto body department of a local vocational school or community college. You may be able to have your car repaired by the students—while under the watchful eye of the instructors. All you will be charged is the cost of parts. There is typically no labor charge under these circumstances.

Oil—bargains

Stockpile oil, oil filters, and air filters when they go on sale. Unopened bottles of oil have a long shelf life.

Oil—filter size

The most effective way to prolong the life of your car is to install the largest oil filter that will fit under the hood. Be sure to change the oil and filter often.

Oil—poor quality

Be very cautious if you are tempted to buy oil at a quick-service mart or food store. Many of these outlets sell only cheap brands of oil. If only SA- or SB-rated oil is available, know that it is practically worthless if you are planning to put it into a 1968 or newer car. Unless you have an oil burner, stay away from these light-service oils. Look for an oil that carries the designation API Service SG.

Oil—slippery

Consider using an additive that increases the slipperiness of the engine oil in your car. Workers at your local auto parts store will gladly make a recommendation. If you infrequently take long free-way trips, inquire about fuel additives that reduce carbon buildup as well.

Oil—top it off

Don't wait until your car's oil is a quart low before adding more. There is no law saying you can't add half a quart and put the other half away for later use. A full crankcase guarantees the engine will have the maximum amount of oil available to it at all times. Each time you add even a small amount of fresh oil, you are recharging the entire lubricating system with fresh additives. Forty percent of the engine is directly dependent upon the oil to cool it.

Overheating

At the first sign of your car overheating, shut off the air conditioner and open the windows to decrease the load on the engine and help it cool down. If the car is still over-heated, turn on the heater and blower to transfer heat from the engine to the interior. If you are stopped in traffic, shift into neutral and rev the en-gine a little to speed the water pump and fan. The increased circulation should help to cool things off.

Parts—dealer

As a rule, car dealers charge 30 to 70 percent more for auto parts than auto parts stores do. Make a habit of checking auto parts stores first before running to the dealer. And don't overlook the auto-wrecking yards. They're the best deal going when the part you need does not have to be new.

Parts—reconditioned

If possible, use reconditioned or secondhand parts for repairs, especially if you are nursing an old car and you don't expect to drive it longer than two more years.

Polishes to avoid

Avoid car polishes that contain abrasives and those that seal too well because they close the pores of the paint. If the polish can says the product has a mild abrasive cleaner or seals the finish, stay away from it.

Protection—backseat

A bedsheet (flat or fitted) makes a great cover for the backseat. Tuck it in well and the upholstery will be protected from pets and kids. When it gets dirty, just throw it in the laundry.

Protection—radio and CD

In cold weather it's wise to wait until the car's interior warms up before using the radio or CD player. These units should be warm, especially the CD player, before they are turned on. Be patient and allow the heater to warm the interior, and your expensive sound system will work better longer.

Protection—vinyl dashboard and upholstery

The greatest enemy of your car's vinyl dashboard and interior is the sun's heat and ultraviolet rays. Here's what you can do to slow down vinyl deterioration: First clean the vinyl upholstery and dashboard. Dry it well and apply sunscreen lotion with the highest UV factor you can find. Just rub it in as you would on your skin. When the sunscreen has had time to soak in, buff off any excess and apply a commercial vinyl protector, which will help seal it in.

Radiator—draining and replacement

Drain and replace your car's radiator fluid every other year. The anticorrosion elements of coolant are spent in about two years.

Radiator—sealing hole

Put a teaspoon of ground black pepper into your auto's radiator to seal a pin hole. Sounds a little wacky but it is nonetheless ingenious. It may take more than a teaspoon, but start with that. If you use too much pepper over time, however, you run the risk of clogging the heater core and losing your heat during cold weather. Consider this pepper trick a temporary measure to tide you over until you can afford a more permanent repair.

Rubber and plastic— make black like new

When black rubber or plastic trim on your automobile fades or gets ugly white spots, apply black paste shoe polish. It will look like new again.

Snow chains caddy

Start with an old pair of jeans. Cut off the legs like you're making short shorts. Then sew each leg shut, drop one chain into each "leg" compartment, and place the tools required for installation into the pockets. Attach handles for easy carrying.

Snow removal

Scrape snow from car windows with a plastic or rubber dustpan. It won't scratch the glass.

Static—dryer sheets to the rescue

Use fabric softener sheets to clean and remove static from your car's dashboard, upholstery, and carpeting. Hide the sheets under the seat and enjoy their subtle fragrance.

Sunglasses storage

Keep sunglasses handy when driving by storing them right on your car's sun visor. Attach the case to the visor by gluing adhesive-backed fasteners to each. Your shades will always be within easy reach.

Sunroof—more headroom

If you've found the perfect car except for one thing—your hair touches the ceiling—consider ordering it with a sunroof; or if it's a used car, you could have one installed. A sunroof typically will give you another inch or two.

Test-drive—after purchase of new car

When you finally take a new car home, give it a long and thorough test-drive. Take the car back to the dealer immediately if you detect a major problem. The courts have upheld demands for a refund

when the car was returned within the first few days.

Test-drive—before accepting new car

Insist on a test-drive of your new car before you accept delivery. Never take delivery at night, because you want to examine the car carefully in full daylight. Make sure there's been no damage in transit and that the car has not been repainted. Telltale signs of repainting are paint traces on the rubber striping or trim, mismatched colors, and ill-fitting panels.

Test-drive—inspect for hidden damage

Looking for a used car? Check for signs of a repaired accident—damage on the car. Vehicles that have been banged up and reconstructed will have telltale signs. Have someone drive behind the car to see if the back wheels align with the front, and look for water marks in the trunk. Check under the hood to make sure the fender seams haven't been sprayed over with paint. Most important, have the car checked by your mechanic.

Test-drive—nighttime assurance

Before making a final car-buying decision, test-drive the car at night. You want to make sure the headlights are powerful enough for your comfort and that everything else that's supposed to light up, does.

Test-drive—with rental car

If you are in the market for a new car, rent one or two of your choices for a weekend when the rental rates are at their lowest. Drive it under a variety of conditions and for long periods of time. A five-minute test-drive with a hovering dealer sitting in the seat next to you may not give you a true representation of the car's performance and comfort the way a few days on your own will.

Test-drive—without radio or CD

When you are test-driving a used car, turn the radio or CD

player off. The stereo system can mask other car sounds that a conscientious buyer should be listening for and creates a false sense of euphoria about the car. Listen to the stereo after you have completely evaluated other areas of operation.

Tire—change without getting dirty

Store a sweat suit, sneakers, a pair of old socks, surgical gloves, and/or a package of wet wipes in the trunk of the car next to the spare tire. This way, if there's a flat tire, throw the sweats on over your good clothes, change to sneakers, and even protect your hands with gloves if you'd like. Change the tire without having to worry about getting dirty. Another plus: If the car breaks down, the sneakers will feel better on your walk to the nearest service station.

Tire plugs

Always stash a tire-plugging kit with your car's spare tire. This is nothing more than a few small rubber plugs and a special tool for inserting them. It is quite simple to use following the directions on the kit. Often a damaged tire can be sealed and plugged right on the vehicle. Kit manufacturers recommend that you have the tire inspected by a professional afterward, but in most cases the plugs are permanent. Be sure to air the tire back up to recommended specs, and if you have removed the wheel, be sure to properly torque the lug nuts after you reinstall it.

Tire pressure

Check the pressure of your tires frequently. Underinflation increases rolling resistance, which increases tire wear and gas consumption by as much as 5 percent.

Tire rotation

Rotate your tires every 6,000 to 9,000 miles. The goal of rotation is to get the tires to wear uniformly. Check your car owner's manual for the recommended rotation

scheme. Some drivers get in the habit of rotating their tires every other oil change.

Tires—retreads okay

Consider buying retreads or blemished tires, particularly for an older car. You can save up to 50 percent of the cost of new tires, and the law requires that they be safe.

Tires—spotting wear

Uneven tire wear often is easier to spot with your fingers than with your eyes. Run your hands from side to side and up and down the tread. Uneven wear could indicate misalignment or loose chassis parts. Beware of pieces of steel belting or metal embedded in the tire that could cut your hand.

Touch-up paint

Liquid Paper (white correction fluid available at an office supply store) makes a great touch-up paint for white cars. It covers beautifully, dries to a hard finish, and holds up well through weather and washing. To apply, either use the built-in applicator or tear a match from a book of matches and use the cardboard end as a tiny paintbrush. If and when it wears away, simply reapply.

Traction—with cat litter

In winter weather carry a heavy bag of clay-based cat litter in your trunk so the extra weight will help keep the vehicle stable. If you are stuck in snow or ice, clear the area around your drive wheels, pour litter in front of the tires in the direction you want to go, and then drive away slowly. Clay is handy for gaining traction, but it is heavy. Once the possibility of snow is past, remove the litter from your trunk in the interest of optimum gas mileage.

Traction—with floor mats

If your car gets stuck in the snow, slip one or more of the floor mats under the stuck

tire(s) to provide the traction you need to get out.

Trailer hitch

Don't consider buying a used car that has a trailer hitch. Trailer towing indicates heavy service, and you'll be happier with a car that has been gently used, not possibly abused.

Vehicle Identification Number (VIN) matchup

Never buy a used car without seeing the ownership documents. Match the car's Vehicle Identification Number (VIN) on the driver's side of the dashboard with the VIN on the title and registration.

Windshield—snow and ice removal

You won't have to scrape snow and ice from your windshield if you place a large, plastic, cut-open trash bag over the dry windshield when your car is parked; secure the bottom edge under the windshield wipers and close the sides in the car doors.

Windshield—washer fluid

Mix together 3 cups rubbing alcohol and 1 tablespoon liquid detergent in a gallon-size jug. Fill with water, cover, and shake to mix well. Label it, cap tightly, and keep out of reach of children. Shake well, then pour the mixture into your car's windshield washer compartment. You can use this in your car year-round because the alcohol will prevent it from freezing in the winter.

Windshield wiper—blade renewal

To get a few more months' use out of windshield wiper blades, lightly sand the edge of the rubber blade with super-fine sandpaper. Be sure to carefully remove all traces of sand from the blades, reattach, and they'll work like new.

2

Cleaning

Air freshener—foliage "filters"

The world's best home air fresheners are green plants. Houseplants help filter the air of indoor pollutants such as formaldehyde and benzene. The best of these green air cleaners are spider plants, philodendron, and aloe vera. Work plants into your home's environment whenever you can. One plant for about every 100 square feet can remove up to 87 percent of toxic organic pollutants. And their gift to the home? They produce oxygen.

Aluminum cookware—cream of tartar

To remove stains and discoloration from aluminum cookware, fill the cookware with hot water and add 2 tablespoons of cream of tartar to each quart of water. Bring the solution to a boil, and simmer for 10 minutes. Wash as usual and dry.

Aluminum pots and pans—cream of tartar mixture

Mix together ¼ cup cream of tartar, ¼ cup baking soda, ¼ cup white vinegar, and 2 tablespoons liquid soap. Store the mixture in a container with a tight-fitting lid. Label and keep out of reach of children. To use, rub a small amount of the cleaner on the aluminum pan and scour with fine steel wool.

Ashes

Use a spray bottle filled with water to very lightly dampen ashes before you start to sweep.

Baking soda—all-purpose cleaner

Baking soda is a nonabrasive cleanser. Use it without worry on fine china, porcelain appliances, the inside of the refrigerator, stainless steel, aluminum, and cast iron. You can use it either in its powdered form or mix it with water to make a paste. Baking soda is a wonderful cleaner for everything from countertops to rolling pins to gold-trimmed dishes. And if you want to remove an offensive odor, think baking soda.

Baking soda—dispenser

Keep baking soda handy by pouring some into a dispenser with a sprinkle top. An old salt- or pepper shaker or Parmesan cheese dispenser that is refillable works well. Use it for microwave oven cleanup and to rid the counter of coffee stains.

Ballpoint pen ink on plastic

Really cheap hair spray removes ballpoint pen ink from plastic because it has a high amount of acetone.

Bathroom and kitchen cleaner—homemade

Dissolve 4 tablespoons baking soda in 1 quart of warm water for a basic bathroom cleaner. Use dry baking soda on a damp sponge for tough areas. Baking soda will clean and deodorize all kitchen and bathroom surfaces.

Bathtub—caulking

Use rubbing alcohol to clean silicone caulking around bathtubs.

Bathtub—clean with a mop

Mops offer an easy-on-the-back-and-knees alternative for cleaning the bathtub. Sprinkle tub with cleanser and swish away grime.

Bathtub—porcelain ring removal

To remove that really gross bathtub ring, apply a paste of hydrogen peroxide mixed with cream of tartar to stained porcelain surfaces. Scrub lightly, let dry, then rinse with warm water. Repeat if necessary.

Blender

To clean a blender, fill it less than halfway with hot, soapy water, replace the lid, and turn the machine on at the lowest speed for a minute or two. Rinse the blender thoroughly, then towel-dry it before using again.

Brass—lemon, baking soda

Rub the surface of brass with a slice of fresh lemon sprinkled with baking soda. Rinse well and wipe dry.

Brass—lemon, salt

Polish outdoor brass with lemon and salt. Cut a lemon in half, dip the cut side into salt, and use as an applicator. Do not use this on brass that has a permanent protective coating.

Candleholders

Clean wax drips from candle-holders by putting them on a cookie sheet lined with parchment paper or an old towel in a warm oven set to 200°F. The paper or towel will catch the wax as it drips.

Candles

Clean dusty, dingy candles by wiping them with rubbing alcohol.

Can opener blade

To clean that cruddy electric can opener blade, soak an old toothbrush in vinegar, hold it under the blade wheel, and turn on the can opener.

Carpet—blot it out

After you clean a spot on the carpet, don't rub it dry. Instead, place a clean, white towel on top of the spot and weight it down with a book or heavy jar. Leave it overnight and it will act as a blotter to transfer all traces of the stain and whatever you used to treat the stain to the towel.

Carpet—clean right before you leave town

Plan your departure time wisely so you can shampoo your carpets right before you're ready to walk out the door for a weekend trip or vacation. The carpet can dry without foot traffic for several days while you're gone.

Carpet—clean-spot protector

Use a small, clean, plastic basket in which berries are sold to cover a place on the carpet you've just spot-shampooed.

Upside down, the basket permits air to circulate, yet keeps family members and pets off the spot until it dries.

Carpet—deodorizer

Sprinkle liberal amounts of baking soda over a dry carpet; then wait 15 minutes before you start to vacuum.

Carpet—dry cleaning

Mix together 2 cups baking soda, ½ cup cornstarch, 4 or 5 crumbled bay leaves, and 1 tablespoon ground cloves. Store in a container with a tight-fitting lid. Label and keep out of reach of children. To use, shake a generous amount of cleaner over the area to be cleaned. Scrub mixture into the heavily stained area with a stiff brush. Leave overnight. Vacuum thoroughly in the morning.

Carpet—scrubber

The best tool for scrubbing a carpet spot is another piece of carpet.

Carpet—soaking wet

When pipes break and the carpet is soaked, put rubbing alcohol in the carpet steam cleaner to rinse away mildew and speed drying. Use approximately 8 ounces per tank.

Carpet—stain removal, rubbing alcohol

Rubbing alcohol is an easy and inexpensive spot remover for carpets. Lightly rub a drop or two into the stain, then blot the spot dry with a clean, white cloth.

Carpet—stain removal, Tide solution

Here's a highly effective and economical way to remove stains from carpeting: Mix together 1 part Tide powder, 2 parts white vinegar, and 2 parts warm water. Scrub the soiled area, then rinse with clear, warm water. From oil to mud to wine stains, they'll all disappear.

Cast iron seasoning

To season a new or newly scrubbed cast iron pan, coat it with mineral or vegetable oil and place it in a warm, 200°F oven for a few hours. The oil will slowly soak into the pan.

Ceilings

Textured ceilings collect fuzz and tiny dust bunnies. Don't try to wash that ceiling. Instead, grab two lint roller refills and cram one onto each end of a paint roller. Now roll the ceiling clean as you would any other linty situation. All the fuzz will stick to the lint rollers and you'll be so happy.

Ceramic tile

Wipe ceramic tile clean with a solution of automatic dishwasher detergent and water.

Chandelier

Hang an umbrella upside down from the chandelier to catch the drips while you're cleaning it. Pour 2 parts iso-propyl rubbing alcohol and 1 part warm water into a spray bottle. Spray chandelier liber-ally, and allow the fixture to drip-dry.

Chrome—baby oil

A quick and easy cleaner for chrome is baby oil sprinkled on a damp cloth.

Chrome—baking soda

Clean chrome fixtures with a damp cloth sprinkled with baking soda.

Chrome—nail polish remover

Nail polish remover gives chrome a nice sparkle. Be careful. It's strong stuff and could remove the color from anything it touches around the chrome.

Chrome—vinegar

To clean chrome, wipe with a soft cloth dipped in undiluted white or cider vinegar.

Cleaners with color coding

Add a tiny drop of food col-oring to a cleaning mix in a spray bottle to distinguish the contents from other sprays and keep a list of which color represents which cleaner. The food coloring will not affect the cleaner.

Cleaning tools—apron with pockets

Get an apron with lots of pockets to wear from room to room as you clean. Put the supplies you need for each room in the pockets so you have everything you need at your fingertips. Use one of the pockets to hold a soapy sponge in a plastic bag for touch-up work around light switches, doorjambs, and so on.

Cleaning tools—cleaning rags

To save yourself from rum-maging for cleaning rags every time you clean, use a rubber band to attach a cloth to each cleaning product that requires one. When you're finished, just tuck the rag back under the rubber band. Wash or replace cloths periodically.

Cleaning tools—colander for cleanup

Keep a colander in the sink and scrape food from dishes into it at dish-washing time. This is more efficient than your standing over the garbage pail, and liquids will go down the drain rather than into your pail.

Cleaning tools—dust cloths

Make your own dust cloths by dipping cheesecloth into a mixture of 2 cups water and ¼ cup lemon oil. Do not rinse, and allow to dry thoroughly before using. When the cloths are dirty, wash and repeat.

Cleaning tools—for skinny spaces

How do you clean that little bit of floor between the refrigerator and the wall? Tie a nylon-net scrubbing pad over the end of a yardstick

or broom handle, securing it tightly with string or twine. Use it first to pull out any debris and dust, then wet it with a detergent-water solution and scrub away.

Clothes iron—baking soda

You can clean the scorched starch from the bottom of an iron by making a paste of baking soda and a little water, rubbing it on the iron with a soft cloth, and wiping it off with a clean cloth.

Clothes iron—clogged steam ports

Clean the clogged steam ports in your iron with a bent-open paper clip, then fill the reservoir with a mixture of ⅓ cup white vinegar and 1 tablespoon baking soda that has been well blended. Allow to steam. Empty the reservoir by turning it upside down over the sink. Follow with plain water and allow to steam. You may have to allow three or four reservoirs of water to steam through to remove all traces of vinegar.

Clothes iron—salt, wax paper

To remove burned-on starch from your iron, sprinkle salt on a sheet of wax paper and slide the iron across it several times. Then rub the iron lightly with silver polish until the stain is removed.

Coffee and tea stains

Remove coffee and tea stains by scrubbing pots or cups with baking soda and a nylon-net scrubbing pad.

Computer—keyboard

As a cheaper alternative to canned air, a new paintbrush is great for dusting hard-to-get-at crevices in computer keyboards. Unplug the keyboard and vacuum it regularly, using the soft brush attachment. To dislodge particles of dirt and dust, turn the keyboard upside down and hit it several times with the flat of your hand. Periodically, clean the keys with a lint-free cloth dipped in rubbing alcohol.

Computer or TV monitor—cleaning

Spraying glass cleaner directly onto the monitor screen can cause damage. Instead spray a mild cleaner or rubbing alcohol onto a soft lint-free rag, then wipe the screen.

Computer or TV monitor—dusting

Save the dryer sheets from your laundry after they've softened a load of wash. They make great dusting and cleaning cloths for television and computer screens. Not only will they clean the screens, the antistatic properties will treat the screens to repel rather than attract dust.

Copper—vinegar, salt

For tarnished copper, fill a spray bottle with white vinegar and 3 tablespoons salt. Pop the open bottle into the microwave and heat on high for about 45 seconds or until quite warm but not too hot to handle. Screw on the spray pump, spray liberally, let sit briefly, then rinse with warm, soapy water, and wipe clean. Don't use on lacquered items.

Copper, brass—vinegar, flour

To clean copper and brass that does not have a factory-applied protective coating, dissolve 1 teaspoon salt in ½ cup white vinegar. Add enough flour to make a paste. Apply the paste and let sit for 15 minutes to 1 hour. Rinse with warm water and polish dry.

Copper, brass, bronze—toothpaste

Small brass, copper, or bronze objects can be cleaned and made to gleam with a little toothpaste. Be sure to remove all traces of toothpaste with a soft brush, soap, and water, because any that is left will dry as hard as cement.

Countertops—food stains

To remove food stains from countertops, cover the stains with a paste of baking soda and water. Let it sit a few minutes, then wipe with a cloth or sponge.

Countertops—laminate

Plastic laminate countertops like Formica that have become dull with age can be brightened by applying a coat of a good automobile wax; allow to dry slightly and buff off. This will also make the surface stain- and scratch-resistant.

Crayon—on chalkboard

An oil-base lubricating spray like WD-40 or a prewash treatment like Soilove should easily remove the crayon marks without damaging the chalkboard. Test first, then spray the stains and allow the spray to penetrate for a few minutes. Wipe off with a clean, dry cloth. Add a few drops of liquid dish-washing detergent to warm water, and with a clean sponge wipe down the board to remove all oily residue. Rinse well with warm water and dry with a clean cloth.

Crayon—on floors and walls

Get rid of crayon marks from a linoleum floor by rubbing lightly with a dab of silver polish. To remove your child's crayon marks from painted walls, dip a damp cloth into baking soda and rub the spots gently.

Crayon—on slate

To remove crayon marks on a slate fireplace hearth: Use an art-gum eraser available at an art supply or stationery store. Just knead the eraser until it's pliable, then press it against the crayon marks and "pull" them off. Continue kneading and pressing until all the marks are removed.

Crystal

To clean crystal vases, glasses, chandelier crystals, or any kind of bottle that's been clouded by a calcium coating, fill a large container with soapy water and add a good shot of white vinegar. Allow items to sit in the solution for 2 to 3 hours.

Curling iron

To clean the buildup of scorched hair spray and other products on a curling iron, scrub the cool iron with a soft cloth soaked with rubbing alcohol.

Cutting board—cleaning

Lemon juice cleans, deodorizes, and bleaches out stains on wooden cutting boards and wooden utensils.

Cutting board—seasoning

After scrubbing and disinfecting your wooden cutting board, season it by rubbing on a coat of mineral oil. Do not use vegetable oil because it may turn rancid.

Dishes: clean or dirty?

Never sure whether the dishes in the dishwasher are clean or dirty? Place an uncapped spice bottle upright in a front corner of the top rack. When dishes are clean, it will be full of water. Empty the bottle when you unload.

Dishwasher—as drain board

If you only occasionally hand wash dishes such as delicate

crystal, china, or a messy pot, don't waste money purchasing a drain board. Place just-washed items on the top rack of your empty dishwasher and they'll drain and air-dry.

Dishwasher—detergent only!

Don't be tempted to use soap meant for dishes or laundry when you run out of automatic dishwasher detergent or you'll wind up with a mountain of bubbles. If someone else makes the mistake, here's how to get rid of the mess: Open the dishwasher, slide out the bottom rack, and sprinkle salt on the suds, which will immediately reduce their volume. Pour 2 gallons of cold water into the bottom of the dishwasher and advance the cycle until you hear the machine begin to drain. Repeat until only a few suds remain. As a last step, run an entire cycle without any detergent.

Dishwasher—double duty

Use the dishwasher to clean brushes, dustpans, and even the dish drainer.

Dishwasher—flatware organization

Save time by presorting forks, knives, and spoons as you load them into your dishwasher's utensil compartment.

Dishwasher—rusty stains

If your dishwasher interior has rusty stains, try running a cycle with no dishes, and instead of automatic dishwasher detergent, fill the cups with Tang instant breakfast drink. The citric acid works miracles.

Dishwasher spotting—vinegar

To ensure your dishes come out sparkling clear with no soap or hard-water residue, pour a cup of white vinegar into the dishwasher during the final rinse.

Dishwasher spotting—vinegar, lemon juice

No matter the brand of automatic dishwasher detergent, glasses often come out of the dishwasher with spots. Solution: Mix equal parts water,

43

vinegar, and lemon juice in a spray bottle and spray the glasses before putting them in the washer.

Doorknobs and switch plates

Moisten a cloth with rubbing alcohol and wipe away the grime from doorknobs and switch plates.

Drains—hair removal

Remove hair from a drain with a bottle brush.

Drains—mesh bag debris catcher

Stuff a mesh produce bag into a drain to catch food particles, hair, and other debris. Be sure to wash it in hot water or in the dishwasher to get rid of bacteria.

Drains—odors and grease

To eliminate odors and keep grease from building up in your kitchen plumbing, regularly pour a strong saltwater solution down the drain.

Drapery sheers

If your sheer draperies are looking a little limp and tired, wash them and then dip them into a sink filled with warm water into which you've dissolved a cup of Epsom salt. Do not rinse. Hang to dry.

Dry-erase boards

To add luster and restore the surface of a dry-erase board, polish it with a dryer sheet.

Dust mop

To clean a dust mop indoors, pull an oversized plastic bag over the head of the mop, tie the top of the bag, and shake the mop vigorously so the dust falls into the bag.

Duster with reach—broom

Slip a pillowcase over a broom's bristles, tie it on with a twine tie or piece of string, spray lightly with furniture polish or water, and you'll be able to easily dust high spots and ceilings.

Duster with reach—fishing pole

Stick a fluffy feather duster into the hollow end of a cane fishing pole, sold at import stores for about $1. Now you have an extension handle that will allow you to remove cobwebs that form on your high-vaulted ceilings and ceiling fans.

Dusting—delicate items

New paintbrushes are terrific for dusting delicate items that need a light touch, such as a lamp shade or silk flowers.

Dusting—in tight places

Wear cotton gloves sprayed with furniture polish to dust hard-to-reach places.

Dusting—under beds

Wrap an old cotton T-shirt around the bristle end of a broom for cleaning under beds.

Dusting—with glycerin

Dampen vacuum brushes with a solution of several drops of glycerin to ½ cup water. It attracts dust and hair like a magnet. You can find glycerin in the drugstore.

Dustpan

Spray your dustpan with furniture polish and the dust will slip right off.

Dusty curtains

Don't dry-clean curtains that are simply dusty. Toss them into the dryer with a couple of dryer sheets on "air dry." This will fluff them up and loosen and release the dust.

Dusty curtains, pillows, slipcovers

Put dusty pillows, curtains, and slipcovers into the dryer. Set it on cool, and toss in a fabric softener sheet for fragrance.

Enamel cookware

If your enamel cookware has unsightly stains, fill it with a mixture of equal parts household bleach and water and allow to sit overnight. Then thoroughly rinse.

Eyeglasses

Mix ⅓ cup rubbing alcohol with 1 cup water. Put in spray bottle and use to clean eyeglass lenses. This mixture is safe to use on all ophthalmic eyeglass lenses, even those made from plastic material, as those materials are hardened and impervious to isopropyl (rubbing) alcohol.

Fan blades

There's nothing like static electricity to turn a fan blade into a dust magnet. But that's no match for a dryer sheet. Just take one of those gems and wipe down the blade to release dust—and pet hair and cobwebs too.

Faucets—lime deposits

Lime deposits around faucets can be softened for easy removal by covering the deposits with vinegar-soaked paper towels. Leave paper towels on for about 1 hour before cleaning. The vinegar leaves chrome clean and shiny.

Faucets—soap scum

Remove soap scum from a faucet with an old toothbrush dipped into a 50/50 ammonia and water solution.

Fiberglass—shower walls and tiles

For a brilliant shine and easy cleanups, give freshly cleaned tile and fiberglass shower walls a coat of car polish. Do not wax the shower floor or bathtub as it will become dangerously slick.

Fiberglass—showers and bathtubs

Clean fiberglass showers and tubs with baking soda sprinkled on a damp sponge. Scrub clean and wipe dry.

Floors—ceramic tile

Mop ceramic tile floors with a solution of 1 gallon hot water and 1 cup vinegar—no soap. The floor will shine and sparkle like new. No rinsing is required. While hot water might work to remove dirt, it will have a dulling effect because of the minerals left behind in the water. Vinegar cuts and removes those minerals, getting rid of that cloudy film.

Floors—hair spray removal

To remove hair spray from a no-wax floor, mix ¼ cup ammonia with a gallon of warm water. If you are not sure about the durability of the floor's finish, test this mixture on an inconspicuous part of the floor.

Floors—no-wax linoleum

To clean a no-wax linoleum floor quickly, mist with a foaming bathroom spray and let stand 5 minutes. Damp-mop the floor to remove the cleaner.

Floors—scratches on resilient flooring

Get rid of light scratches in resilient flooring by rubbing with a soft cloth moistened with a small amount of paste floor wax.

Floors—wax remover, homemade

Mix 3 parts rubbing alcohol to 1 part water for an excellent floor wax remover.

Framed art

When you wash the glass that covers framed art, spray the cleaner on your cloth, not the glass. Otherwise the liquid may work its way inside the glass, damaging the mat or the artwork itself.

Freezer

If your refrigerator isn't frost-free, use a hair dryer to quickly defrost it. Or rotate two pans of boiling water: one goes into the freezer compartment while the other goes back on the stove for reheating. When you've completed defrosting the freezer, spray a few coats of cooking spray on the top and sides of the freezer. The next time you defrost, the ice will fall right off.

Furniture polish, homemade

Mix 3 parts olive oil with 1 part lemon juice or vinegar in blender. Blend on high to emulsify, and apply with a clean, soft cloth.

Garbage disposal—ice cubes, citrus, baking soda

Mix 1 cup chopped lemon, orange, or grapefruit (rind and all); 1 cup baking soda; and 1½ cups water. Pour into an ice cube tray and freeze until solid. Remove cubes, place them in a resealable plastic bag if you don't intend to use them immediately, and label them. To use, turn on your disposal unit, dump in 6 to 10 cubes, and let the machine grind them up. Rinse with cold water.

Garbage disposal—ice cubes, vinegar

To clean the garbage disposal, dump in a tray of ice cubes made from white vinegar and water. Turn on the water and operate the disposal as usual. Or dump in a tray of regular ice cubes and a handful of lemon rinds and operate the disposal as usual.

George Foreman grill

You love your George Foreman grill. If only it was self-cleaning! Here's the next best thing: Throw a soaking wet folded paper towel on the grill after you unplug it, but while it's still hot. Close the lid. It will steam clean itself. When cooled, just wipe off the residue.

Glass—coffeepot

Coffee burned on the bottom of your glass coffeepot? Try this old restaurant trick: Fill it with a handful of ice cubes, add 2 teaspoons of salt, and swirl the pot around for a few minutes to remove the coffee stains.

Glass—decanter

Rub a glass decanter with a lemon or lemon juice to renew its shine. Dry with a lint-free cloth.

48

Glass—fireplace doors

To clean those dirty glass fireplace doors, mix some wood ashes with a little water. Apply this paste with a sponge in a circular motion and rinse off.

Glass—light globes

Clean the glass globes of your light fixtures in the dishwasher.

Glass—shower doors

Mineral oil will remove stubborn scum from the inside of glass shower doors. Give the tiles, faucets, and outside of the shower door a final once-over with glass cleaner to make them really shine.

Glass—thermos

To clean the inside of a glass thermos bottle, place a denture-cleaning tablet in it, fill with warm water, and allow it to sit overnight before rinsing thoroughly.

Glass cleaner, homemade

Add 2 tablespoons cornstarch and ½ cup white vinegar to 1 gallon of warm water.

Glass-top tables

Glass-top tables will repel lint if you wash them with a solution of 1 quart warm water and 1 capful liquid fabric softener.

Grater

An old toothbrush is perfect for quickly cleaning the holes in cheese and vegetable graters.

Grout—soak it

Use lengths of cotton stripping (the kind you'd use to protect your hairline during a dye job) that have been soaked in undiluted bleach. Push the wet cotton against the grout and leave it there. After half an hour, pull away the cotton. The same method works well to clean mildew that forms along the caulking between a wall and a bathtub.

Grout—toothbrush, denture cleaner

Scrub grout using an old toothbrush with denture-cleaning paste or cleanser.

Grout—toothbrush, dishwasher detergent

Make a paste of automatic dishwasher detergent and water. Apply to grout using an old toothbrush. When it's dry, rub it off with a terry washcloth.

Grout—whiten with baking soda, hydrogen peroxide

Mix a paste of baking soda and hydrogen peroxide. Using an old toothbrush, apply the paste to the grout and give a little scrub. Leave on for a few minutes; rinse. For stained grout between floor tiles, try rubbing the area lightly with folded sandpaper.

Grout—whiten with bleach

Whiten grout between tiles with bleach dabbed on a cotton swab.

Gum

Raw egg whites will remove chewing gum from anything, including hair, without leaving a trace.

Gum—on upholstery

To remove bubble gum from upholstery, make a loop of duct tape around your fingers with the sticky side out. Press on the gum and jerk your finger up quickly. Repeat until all the gum is pulled away.

Heel marks

To remove black scuff marks from any hard-surface floor, rub them with a paste of baking soda and water and a plastic pot scrubber like a Scotch-brite pad. Use as little water as possible to ensure best results.

Ivory

To clean anything ivory, like piano keys or carved objects, wipe with a solution of 1 tablespoon hydrogen peroxide and 1 cup water. No need to rinse.

Jeweler's professional cleaner

Here's the fine-jewelry cleaner professional stores use: Mix equal amounts of household ammonia and water. Drop jewelry into a small container of this cleaner. Allow to sit for a few minutes and brush with an old toothbrush. Rinse well in clear water. It's cheap and it works. Caution: Never use this solution on opals, pearls, or other soft stones.

Jewelry

Dissolve a denture-cleaning tablet in a cup of water. Add diamond rings, earrings, and other jewelry. Let them sit an hour. Do not use this with opals, pearls, or other soft stones.

Keeping up—one bite at a time

Set aside 15 minutes each weekday to clean one area of your house. By the weekend, you won't have much more cleaning to do.

Keeping up—photo instructions

To remind everyone in your family what has to be done to call a room in the house "clean," take pictures of each room and put them in a flip photo album. On the reverse side of the photos, list the chores to be done in each room. If someone asks if a room is clean enough, you can just tell them to check the list.

Keeping up—tidy up for the evening

After dinner, set a timer for 5 minutes and have everyone in the house pick up and put away the day's accumulated clutter.

Keeping up—touch-ups between cleanings

Cut some old rags into small squares and stuff them into a jar. Add water and a bit of pine-scented cleaner. Keep these handy for between-cleaning bathroom touch-ups. When finished, simply wash the rags and use them again.

Keeping up—use gloves

Wear white canvas work gloves sprayed with polish to speed up cleaning. Wash and reuse each week.

Kitchen disinfectant

We know how important it is to disinfect cutting boards and countertops. Instead of buying expensive kitchen disinfectants for this job, make your own: Combine 1 teaspoon liquid chlorine bleach per quart of water. Flood your food-cutting surface with the solution, let stand several minutes, then rinse.

Knives and scissors

To remove rust from knives or scissors, soak them in a mild solution of water and ammonia (½ cup household ammonia to 1 quart water) for 10 minutes. Scrub off rust with a steel-wool pad. Rinse and dry.

Lime buildup

Apply a paste of cream of tartar and vinegar to faucets to remove lime sediment easily.

Liquid detergent—cut harshness

To make liquid dish detergent easy on the hands, add 3 table-spoons of white vinegar to a full bottle and shake well. As a bonus the vinegar will help make your dishes shine.

Liquid hand soap, homemade

Save all those little slivers from your bar soaps. Grate them on a cheese grater, mix with water (the amount depends on how much soap you have, but generally speaking you want about 1 part grated soap to 3 parts water), and melt in microwave or on the stove. Beat with a rotary beater until smooth. If you don't want to bother collecting little slivers of soap, but like the idea of making your own liquid soap, follow these instructions grating a new bar of soap to about 3 cups of water.

Liquid hand soap for kids, homemade

If your small children are really into washing their hands and go fairly nuts with the soap dispenser, make up a special batch of liquid hand soap just for them: Mix 10 parts generic shampoo to 1 part water.

Louvered doors

To clean, dampen a disposable foam paintbrush and wipe between the slats.

Metal furniture

To clean aluminum, steel, or wrought-iron furniture, wash with a mild liquid detergent and water, then rinse and dry thoroughly. Once a season, apply a coat of automobile wax. If a scratch occurs on wrought iron or steel, apply matching exterior paint with a small artist brush.

Microwave

Steam clean the interior of your microwave with this method: Stir 2 tablespoons baking soda into a cup of water. Set in the microwave and allow to boil for at least 5 minutes. Remove the cup and wipe the inside of the microwave with a sponge.

Mildew—caulking

Get rid of mildew in caulking between the walls and tub by saturating paper towels with diluted chlorine bleach. Allow wet towels to sit for a few hours or until all traces of mildew have vanished.

Mildew—in corners

To remove mildew from the corner of the tub or other hard-to-scrub places, place a cotton ball saturated with bleach on the mildew for an hour or two. Rinse with warm water and repeat if necessary.

Mildew—refrigerator

To prevent mildew from forming in the refrigerator, wipe the inside with white vinegar. The vinegar acid effectively kills mildew fungi.

Mildew—shower curtain bleach soak

If mildew and soap scum are only at the bottom of the shower curtain, fill the tub with enough water to cover the spots, add a little bleach, and let soak. Rinse the curtain and the tub well to remove the bleach.

Mildew—shower curtain in washing machine

To clean mildew and soap scum from a shower curtain, place the curtain in the washing machine along with two or three white towels. Fill with warm water and then add detergent and ½ cup baking soda. Add 1 cup white vinegar to the rinse water to prevent mold from forming. Hang on the shower rod to dry.

Mildew—shower stall

Here's a way to get rid of mildew buildup in your shower stall without using harsh, household bleach. Fill an empty spray bottle with vinegar and a cup of salt. Shake to encourage the salt to dissolve more quickly. Spray the stall, allow the solution to sit for at least a half hour, and then rinse thoroughly. Tougher jobs may require a second application.

Mildew—tile

To remove mildew from tile, wet surface with water and then spray with a solution of 1 cup liquid chlorine bleach mixed with 1 quart water. Let the solution remain on the tile about 15 minutes, then rinse. Caution: Never mix chlorine bleach with other cleaning products that might contain ammonia. A potentially fatal gas may result.

Mildew—tile grout

Borax and baking soda mixed together make an effective nonabrasive cleanser for removing mold and mildew from tile grout.

Mini-blinds—cleaning on driveway

Clean metal or vinyl mini-blinds the fast and easy way: Simply lay the mini-blinds in your driveway and spray them with an all-purpose liquid or foaming bathroom cleaner. Rinse with the garden hose, then hang the blinds on a clothesline to dry.

Mini-blinds—quick clean

Use a dampened fabric softener sheet to quick-clean mini-blinds and reduce the static cling that attracts dust.

Mini-blinds—superclean

Put on a rubber glove and an old sock over it. Douse the sock in straight rubbing alcohol and clean away while blinds are in place.

Mirrors—hair spray removal

To remove hair spray spots from the mirror, dampen a soft cotton cloth with rubbing alcohol and, using a circular motion, wipe them away.

Mirrors—use cold tea

Clean mirrors with cold tea. They'll really shine.

Mops

Has floor wax made your favorite mop stiff and foul-smelling? Soak it for a half hour in a gallon of water mixed with ½ cup of no-suds ammonia. It will look brand-new. To prevent repeat performances, clean the wax mop thoroughly with an ammonia-water mixture after each use. Never clean a wax mop with soap or detergent, and use it only for the purpose of applying liquid floor wax.

Odor—food containers

To remove odors from food containers, fill them with water and several tablespoons of baking soda. Let them sit overnight, then wash and rinse.

Odor—garbage cans

To inhibit the growth of odor-producing molds and bacteria, sprinkle ½ cup borax in the bottom of the garbage can.

Odor—smoke in upholstery

To get rid of the unpleasant smell of smoke on chairs and sofas, sprinkle baking soda on the fabric and allow it to sit there for a few hours—then vacuum.

Odor—thermos

Here's an easy solution for a sour-smelling thermos. Fill the container with 1 quart of water and 4 tablespoons baking soda, and let it sit overnight. In the morning, wash as usual. Do this every week or so as preventive maintenance.

Odor—use a match

You can buy all kinds of room deodorizers and pretty-smelling things for the bathroom that do nothing more than cover up bathroom odors. Or you can simply light a match and blow it out immediately to completely eliminate the odor.

Oven

Sprinkle water and then a layer of baking soda on oven surfaces. Rub gently with very fine steel wool for tough spots.

Oven racks

To clean grease buildup from oven racks, bathe them. Put enough hot water in the bathtub to cover the racks, add ¼ cup automatic dishwasher detergent and ¼ cup white vinegar. Stir to dissolve the detergent. Wait for an hour or so, then rinse and dry the racks. Drain the tub immediately, or you'll end up with a major-league bathtub ring.

Oven spills

Pour salt on oven spills when they occur and while they are too hot to clean up. The salt will make the cleanup easier once the spills have cooled, and it will prevent the spill from smoking or flaring up.

Paper towel substitute

As a substitute for paper towels, coffee filters will shine glass, mirrors, and chrome perfectly without lint or streaky marks.

Permanent marker stains

Tough stains from permanent markers are easily removed from most surfaces with rubbing alcohol.

Pet hair on carpet—spray

To remove unsightly dog and cat hair from your carpet, spray a mixture of 1 part liquid fabric softener to 3 parts water on your rug, wait a minute or two, and then vacuum. No more animal hair.

Pet hair on rug—squeegee

To remove pet hair from a rug, try a window squeegee. Just pull the rubber edge toward you and let physics do the rest.

Static electricity will cause the hair to cling to the rubber strip.

Phones

Use a clean, soft cloth dipped in a bit of rubbing alcohol to remove grease and grime from your phone. Use an ordinary cotton swab dipped in alcohol to clean around the buttons.

Picture frames

To clean a carved picture frame, reach in all the nooks and crannies by using an empty plastic squeeze bottle. Just squeeze a few times and you'll blow the dust away with a puff of air.

Range drip pans

Before cooking on the range top, give the stove's burner drip pans a light misting with cooking spray. Any spills will clean up fast with soapy water.

Range hood filter

Many metal mesh filters found in range hoods can be removed

and washed in the dishwasher on the normal, hot-water wash cycle. Wash them as a separate load to provide for plenty of water action.

Refrigerator

When vacuuming the kitchen floor or nearby, take a couple of minutes to remove crumbs and other dried debris from refrigerator shelves and food bins while narrow vacuum attachments are handy. Check the freezer area, too, where crumbs have a way of collecting.

Rubber gloves that stick

Rubber gloves difficult to put on? Sprinkle a little baby powder or some baking soda in them first.

Rust—porcelain

To remove rust rings or stains from porcelain fixtures, make a paste of cream of tartar and hydrogen peroxide. Apply a small amount to the stain and gently scrub with an old toothbrush. Repeat as necessary. Rinse thoroughly.

Rust—pots and pans

Remove rust from pots and pans with white vinegar. For quick action, heat the vinegar before applying. Or remove rust from household items by soaking them in a cola soft drink.

RV holding tank

If you have a recreational vehicle with a holding tank, flush ½ cup to 1 cup of baking soda down the toilet once a week while the RV is in use. Baking soda helps maintain proper pH and alkalinity, controlling sulfide odors, according to the folks at Arm & Hammer.

Scouring pads—no rust

Cut scouring pads such as Brillo or SOS in half or quarters. Now you can use a new, smaller pad every time, throw it away, and avoid a rusty, yucky mess.

Scouring powder—avoiding waste

Scouring cleanser is often wasted because holes in the containers are too numerous or too large and the cleanser comes out too fast. To avoid this, cover half the holes with tape.

Scouring powder, homemade

For a basic scouring cleanser, mix together 1 cup baking soda, 1 cup borax, and ¾ cup salt.

Shellac

Clean paintbrushes of shellac and shellac-base products with rubbing alcohol.

Shower and bathtub

Use a garden watering can to pour clean rinse water on tub or shower walls. The water will go where you'd like it to go because you'll have more control than if you were using the showerhead.

Shower curtain watermarks

Having trouble getting those filmy water spots off your shower curtain? Fill your washing machine with warm water, liquid detergent as you would for any load, and 1 capful of liquid fabric softener at the beginning of the wash cycle. Add fabric softener again in the rinse cycle. Your shower curtain will come out sparkling with not a water spot in sight.

Shower doors—soap scum

Apply a dab of ordinary cooking oil to a damp sponge and use it to remove soap scum from your shower doors. Rinse the doors well. Cooking oil will also prevent soap scum buildup.

Shower doors—tracks

To clean the shower door tracks, fill them with white vinegar and allow them to soak a few hours. Scrub them with an old toothbrush. Flush the tracks with hot water to rinse away the gunk.

Showerhead clog

A showerhead really mired in sediment that can't be completely removed with vinegar needs a heavy-duty treatment. Dissolve a denture-cleaning tablet in a plastic bag full of water. Tie the bag over the showerhead so it is immersed in the liquid. Secure the bag with a rubber band or twist tie. After several hours remove the bag and turn on the shower to clear all traces of sediment.

Silk flowers

Want to freshen up silk flowers? Pour ½ cup of raw white rice into a paper bag. Add your silk flowers. Close the bag and shake for a couple of minutes. Carefully remove the flowers, making sure the rice stays in the bag. Your flowers will come out dust-free and looking like new.

Silver polishing

Polishing silver while wearing rubber gloves promotes tarnish. Instead, choose plastic or cotton gloves.

Silver tarnish

Place a piece of aluminum foil, shiny side up, on the bottom of a glass bowl or pan. Fill the container with boiling water and a few teaspoons of baking soda. Drop silver pieces into this bath, making sure they touch the foil, and the tarnish will disappear.

Silverware

To remove stubborn stains from your good silverware, rub the utensils with a clean cloth that has been dipped in wet salt.

Sink stains

To remove mineral deposits caused by a dripping faucet, place a slice of lemon on the area and leave it there overnight. The next day, remove the lemon and wipe the area clean.

Sink-stopper leaks

To stop water from leaking out of the kitchen sink while you're doing dishes, put a piece of plastic wrap between the drain and the drain stopper. This is also a handy trick to remember if you're soaking something overnight.

Sponges—freshen and disinfect

Easily freshen and disinfect your sponges by putting them in the dishwasher along with all the dirty dishes. Clip them to the top shelf to keep them from falling to the bottom and getting scorched on the heating element.

Sponges—sudsy scrubbers

Cut a slit in the side of a sponge and place soap slivers inside to make a sudsy scrubber.

Stainless steel sinks

(1) Rub stainless steel sinks with olive oil on a soft cloth to remove unsightly streaks;
(2) Remove streaks or heat stains from stainless steel by rubbing with club soda;
(3) Pour some baking soda on a sponge to scour a stainless steel sink; it is nonabrasive;
(4) Remove hard-water spots from a stainless steel sink with a sponge dipped in a mixture of 3 teaspoons of laundry detergent and 1 cup of warm water.

Steel wool pads—no rust

After using an SOS or similar brand scouring pad, just set it back in the box with the unused pads. It won't rust. This way it will last until it is used up and not thrown away too soon because it is rusted out.

Sticker and label removal—decals

To remove stubborn decals or residual adhesive, soak a rag in mineral spirits or laundry stain pretreatment and lay it over the area. After 10 minutes or so, scrape away decal or adhesive with a plastic windshield scraper or an old credit card. Wash as usual.

Sticker and label removal—plastic and mirrors

Sticky labels on glass or plastic containers or mirrors come off easily with rubbing alcohol or cooking oil. If neither is handy, use your laundry prewash treatment, or, as a last resort, nail polish remover may work. But be careful; nail polish remover might remove more than the offending label.

Sticker and label removal—wood

If your kids decide to decorate your fine-wood furniture with stick-on labels, remove them with lemon oil (the labels, not the kids). Using a paper towel or cloth, dab oil on the labels and allow it to soak in for only a few minutes. The oil will penetrate into the glue and act as a solvent to soften it. Rub the labels off with a nylon-net scrubbing pad, being sure to rub in the direction of the wood grain.

Tar or sap from shoes

Petroleum jelly easily removes tar and sap from the soles of shoes.

Teakettle

To remove hard-water and lime buildup in a teakettle, pour in 2 cups of vinegar and bring to a boil. Let simmer for about 10 minutes, then rinse well.

Tea stains in china cups

To remove stains from china teacups, pour an equal amount of salt and white vinegar in the cups and let stand. Rub off stains with a soft cloth and rinse with clear water.

Toilet—baking soda

Using a plunger, plunge the water in the toilet until the bowl is nearly empty. Sprinkle baking soda onto the sides of the toilet bowl, then drizzle with vinegar and scour with a toilet brush. This both cleans and deodorizes. Flush to rinse and refill bowl.

Toilet—denture cleaner

If your toilet bowl has stubborn stains, drop one or two denture-cleaning tablets into the bowl and allow them to sit overnight. Brush and flush.

Toilet—sandpaper

If you have stains in your toilet that will not budge with any other method, here's the severe, last-ditch, toilet-stain-removal secret. Pick up some wet/dry sandpaper with a grit of between 400 and 600 at the hardware or automotive supply store. This is very fine sandpaper that, when used with water, will not scratch the porcelain but should remove the offending stain. Remove as much water as possible from the bowl, and go to work on the stains.

Toothbrush holder

To remove gunk from the toothbrush holder, roll up

a paper towel, wet it with cleanser, then slide it right through the holes.

Trash can

Sprinkle baking soda in the bottom of the trash receptacle before putting in the plastic bag.

Upholstery

In a pinch, use shaving cream as an upholstery cleaner to spot-clean small areas. It's very effective.

Vacuum bag reuse

In a pinch, you can reuse a vacuum cleaner bag. Take a full bag outdoors, cut the bottom seam, and empty contents in the trash. Carefully, reroll and staple closed, then cover the area with strong tape to restrict any dust from escaping and clogging your machine.

Vases—icky buildup

To remove mineral and hard-water deposits from vases,

scrub them with a wet cloth that has been dipped into salt. Follow with warm water and soap.

Vases—narrow and hard to clean

Narrow-necked, hard-to-clean vases and other glassware will sparkle when you clean them with denture-cleaning tablets. Put one or two tablets into the container and fill with water. Wait a few hours and then rinse.

Wallpaper

First, blot the wallpaper with talcum powder to absorb the stain. Then wash the wallpaper with warm, soapy water. Add white vinegar to the water to clean grease stains.

Wastebaskets

Use a plastic wastebasket as a bucket for mopping the floor, and you'll get two jobs done at once.

Wicker furniture

Dust wicker furniture with a stiff, clean paintbrush.

Window frames

Use silver polish cream to shine aluminum window frames.

Window screens

First, run a dry sponge over the screen to remove any loose dust. Then, with the screen propped at a slight angle against a tree or wall, pour a solution of sudsy ammonia and water (1 cup to 1 gallon) across the top. When it starts to dribble down, rub with a scrub brush, using an up-and-down motion. When you finish, turn the screen over and repeat on the other side. Use the garden hose to rinse it, and place it in the sun to dry.

Windowsills

Clean spotted windowsills with a cloth damp with rubbing alcohol.

Window washing—on cloudy days

Never wash windows on a bright, sunny day. Choose an overcast day instead. The windows will dry more slowly and have fewer streaks.

Window washing—with alternate strokes

Use vertical strokes when washing outside and horizontal strokes when washing inside. This way you'll know which side the streaks are on.

Window washing—with newspaper

Rather than use paper towels to clean mirrors and windows, use newspaper. It cleans much better than paper towels with less streaking, and the ink never comes off on the glass. (It may come off on your hands, but they can be washed.)

Wood—scratches

Use brown shoe polish for covering scratches on wood cabinets, shelves, furniture, trim, or anything wood. It blends in well even if it is a darker shade. Apply and wipe off with a dry rag.

Wood—white ring treatment

Rub with a mixture of mayonnaise and white toothpaste. Wipe the area dry, then treat the entire surface with furniture polish.

Wood cabinets—cleaning

Dirty wooden cabinets can be cleaned with a mixture of 10 parts water and 1 part ammonia or Murphy's Oil Soap, either of which will strip old polish or wax and accumulated dirt. Then spray or rub with wax.

Wood cabinets—restoring

To improve the look of wooden surfaces that have become dark or cloudy with age, make your own fantastic furniture restorative by combining 1 part each boiled linseed oil, turpentine, and vinegar. Shake well. Apply with a soft cloth and wipe completely dry. With a second clean cloth, wipe again. Incidentally, don't boil linseed oil. Buy it already boiled at a hardware or paint store and use as is. Caution: Work in a well-ventilated room and wear rubber gloves. *Never* store rags that have been soaked in linseed oil or turpentine.

Wood paneling

Clean wood paneling with 1 ounce of olive oil mixed with 2 ounces of white vinegar and 1 quart of warm water. Emulsify in a blender. Wipe paneling with a soft cloth dampened in the solution, then follow with a dry cloth to remove yellowing from the surface.

Woodwork—cleaning

Apply a thin layer of paste wax to doorjambs, windowsills, and other woodwork that collects fingerprints and smudges. Cleaning will become a breeze.

Woodwork—stains

To clean painted woodwork stained by grease and smoke, dissolve old-fashioned, dry laundry starch in water according to package directions. Paint it on, and when dry, rub with a soft brush and clean cloth. This removes the stains without harming the finish.

3

Clothing and Accessories

Bargains—consignment stores

Consignment shops are everywhere these days and are a wonderful source for previously owned clothing. These shops are many cuts above a thrift store and offer wonderful merchandise for a fraction of the original retail price. Look for specialty consignment stores just for kids. And don't be just a buyer but also a seller. Typically you will share 50/50 with the store's owner when your items sell. Call ahead to learn of the store's policies regarding the condition of acceptable garments and other guidelines.

Bargains—debit merchandise

Make friends with the managers of your favorite stores, and you might be able to tap into a gold mine. Ask if their "debits," or used merchandise, are for sale. These are the items that have been returned for one reason or another but can't be put back on the floor or returned to the manufacturer. Typically these items are sold for pennies on the dollar.

Bargains—unclaimed dry cleaner or repair shop goods

Ask your dry cleaner or neighborhood repair shops to let
you know when they have
unclaimed goods for sale. This
is a great way to find terrific
clothing bargains.

Boots—stretch them

If you have boots that are too
snug, try this: Place a strong
plastic bag (test first to make
sure it is watertight) in each
boot, and put enough water in
the bags to fill the foot areas.
Tie the bags closed, and place
the boots into the freezer. As
the water freezes it will ex-
pand and stretch the boots at
the same time. This technique
works well for shoes too.

Boots—stuff them

Instead of using expensive
boot stuffers to keep your
boots from flopping over, use
one of those long, dense-foam
pool toys called "noodles"
that kids play with when they
are in the swimming pool.
They're cheap, help your

boots retain their shape, and
are cleaner than rolled-up
newspapers.

Buttons—on jeans

If the metal button on your
jeans comes apart and falls off,
it is impossible to sew it back
on. Instead, use some super
glue to affix the knob and
back stud through the fabric.
Let it set for a few days, and
then wash and dry. Your jeans
should be perfectly wearable
again.

Buttons—on new clothes

Buttons on new clothes often
fall off after just one wearing
and washing. Before you wear
a new item, cover the thread
on each button with clear nail
polish or a drop of superglue.
Just be careful not to get any
on the fabric.

Buttons—rescue

A button hanging by a few
threads can be rescued by
wrapping a narrow strip of
clear tape around the threads

on the back of the garment to hold them until they can be reinforced.

Buttons—sewing in some slack

Place a toothpick between the button and fabric as you sew. When the button is secured, remove the toothpick. This gives the button a little slack and will make it easier to operate.

Buttons—sewing in spares

Sew extra buttons into the seams of jackets and pants. If you need a spare, you'll always know where it is.

Buttons—sewing in to stay

When attaching a four-hole button, stitch through two holes, then knot the thread before you sew through the other two holes. If the thread breaks on one side, the button won't come off.

Buttons—sewing with floss

Dental floss makes a sturdy thread for securing buttons on heavy fabric. You'll never lose a button from your winter coat again.

Buttons—sewing with nail polish

Before sewing, place clear fingernail polish on the center of a button, on the side toward the fabric. Once the button has been securely attached to the garment, place another dab on the top center. This will help keep that button from going anywhere for a long, long time.

Closets—a place for slacks

Install towel racks on the backs of closet doors for hanging slacks.

Closets—dust protectors

Convert extra pillowcases (king-size are extra long) into garment bags to protect the clothes hanging in your closet, especially those that are out of season. Just cut a hole into the end of the pillowcase and insert the hangers.

69

Closets—increase the space

Hang a length of chain from a strong hanger. Each link can hold one hanger, which takes up much less space and effectively doubles or triples your closet space.

Dry cleaning—don't leave in car

When taking clothes to the dry cleaner, be careful not to leave them in the car or its trunk for any length of time, especially if they're stained. This is particularly important in hot weather when the heat in the car may bake in the stain, making it difficult, if not impossible, to remove.

Dye your darks for longer wear

Use Rit Dye to revitalize navy and black cotton T-shirts and turtlenecks—even stretch pants—when they start to fade. You'll be able to get a few more seasons out of items you might have considered too far gone.

Earring back temporary replacement

If you lose the back piece of a pierced earring, cut the eraser off a pencil and insert it on the post for a temporary fix.

Gloves—double up

To keep your hands warm and dry while playing or working in wet, cold weather, wear thin latex gloves under your gardening gloves or woolen mittens.

Hanger marks—removal

If you have pointed hanger marks in the shoulders of a knit top, put on the top and relax the hanger bumps with your handheld blow dryer. It's amazing how quickly the hanger bumps disappear.

Hangers—don't store clothes on wood

Don't store clothing on wooden hangers. Over time, the acid in the wood can react with the fabric. Pad wooden

hangers with unbleached muslin or cotton.

Hangers—slipping pants

Put a piece of adhesive-backed
weather stripping on the bar
of a hanger to keep slacks
from slipping off.

Hangers—slipping straps

Fasten unused shoulder pads
to the ends of hangers to cushion fragile clothing and keep
thin straps from slipping off.

Hemlines—remove with vinegar

When you lengthen a garment
and want to get rid of the
original hemline, dampen a
washcloth with white vinegar,
place it on the crease line,
and just iron the crease away.
The vinegar odor will dissi-
pate quickly. This works well
on new clothing. With older
clothing, results will vary, but
for best results, let down the
old hem and clean the garment
according to the care label before ironing.

Hemlines—remove with vinegar and foil

To remove the permanent
press line from a hem that has
been let down, dampen the
crease with white vinegar and
press with a piece of aluminum foil between the material
and a clothes iron.

Hemming

When hemming a skirt or
pants, knot the thread every 3
or 4 inches. A small break in
the thread won't mean an entire rehemming job.

Hosiery—avoid snags

Fine hosiery, pantyhose, and
tights will be easier to put on
and less prone to snags and
tears if you slip on a pair of
latex or vinyl gloves before
starting the process.

Hosiery—increase longevity

According to the Morton Salt
Company, your pantyhose and
other hosiery will last longer
and snag and run less if you

perform this little longevity trick before you wear them the first time: Mix 2 cups salt with 1 gallon water, and immerse pantyhose in the solution. Soak for 3 hours. Rinse in cold water, and drip-dry. Apparently one of the properties of ordinary table salt is that it toughens fibers. That's true for pantyhose—and broom bristles!

Hosiery—manage holes

To keep small holes in pantyhose or other hosiery from turning into nasty runs, rub a glue stick over the hole. It's less sticky and works better than nail polish.

Hosiery—wear pantyhose times two

Instead of throwing away a pair of pantyhose with a run in one leg, match it with another pair in the same shade that has a run in one leg. Simply cut off the "injured" legs about 6 inches below the crotch. Wear both pairs of one-legged pantyhose at the

same time. Yes, you'll be wearing two panty tops, but that will simply create the equivalent of industrial-strength, control-top pantyhose, for which most of us would pay a premium. To make use of this technique more often, always buy the same brand, style, and color of pantyhose to avoid the embarrassment of LDCS (legs of different colors syndrome).

Jeans—make them soft

To soften new jeans, place them in a sink filled with cold water and 1 cup of liquid fabric softener. Let the jeans soak overnight, then wash as usual.

Jewelry—bracelet assist

Here's an easy way to put on a bracelet without assistance. Place the bracelet across the top of your wrist and secure one end to the inside of your wrist with clear tape. Now that the bracelet isn't sliding around, it should be easy to secure the other end and close the clasp.

Jewelry—tarnish-free silver

To keep silver jewelry tarnish-free and shiny, slip the pieces into a small resealable plastic bag. Before sealing the bag, squeeze out as much air as possible.

Jewelry chains—prevent knots

Prevent chains from tangling and knotting in your jewelry box this way: Cut a drinking straw to half the length of the chain, slip the chain through it, then fasten the catch.

Jewelry chains—remove knots

Lay the chain on a flat surface and, with a straight pin in each hand, gently work out the knot. If the knot is really tight, apply a single drop of baby oil or cooking oil to the offending area and repeat the procedure.

Kids—big tees for kids

Buy a three-pack of all-cotton, white T-shirts to use as pajamas or beach cover-ups for small children. Select a size large enough so the bottom edge is just below those cute little knees.

Kids—jeans knee patches

When your kids' jeans require a knee patch, simply remove a back pocket, open the inside leg seam with a seam ripper, and sew the pocket over the hole. Close the seam. Since the pocket has been washed as many times as the jeans, the material always matches perfectly.

Kids—patches on new pants

When kids' pants are new, apply iron-on patches to the inside knees.

Kids—remake boy clothes for girls

Revamp little boys' clothes for your little girl by sewing lace around the hems, necklines, and sleeves. Use fabric paint to draw little hearts and flowers around the necks of solid-colored shirts and onesies.

Kids—shoelaces that stay put

When first lacing up kids' new shoes, tie knots in the laces after the first two sets of holes have been threaded to prevent the laces from coming completely unthreaded through active play.

Kids—sleepers and tube socks

Instead of throwing out children's sleepers that are either too small or have worn-through feet, cut off the part just below the elastic at the ankle. Next, get an adult-size tube sock and cut off all but about 3 inches of the leg part (more or less depending on your child's size). Turn the sleeper and the tube socks inside out and sew a sock to each leg of the sleeper at the elastic (right sides together). Turn right-side out.

Kids—sweat shorts

Save children's sweatpants, even if they have holes in the knees. When summer rolls around, cut them off and hem them by machine to make comfortable, cheap shorts for the kids.

Kids—telling right from left shoes

Put a sticker inside your children's right shoes or sneakers. They will begin to learn right from left and also get their shoes on the correct feet all by themselves.

Kids—trade clothes

An alternative to making your children always wear their siblings' hand-me-downs, trade with neighbors or friends who have children of the same sizes. The kids get a new look, and the price is right.

Kids—tube socks save time and money

Buy tube socks for your kids rather than the traditional type of sock. Tube socks last longer since the heel is not always wearing in the same spot. Get in the habit of always buying the same brand, same style, all-white tube socks, and you won't have to spend half your life matching socks into pairs.

Kids—upgrades optional

When buying kids' clothes and shoes, set a budget figure, and if the child wants to upgrade to a trendier brand or style, require her or him to pay the difference.

Label scratching solution

If back-of-the-neck labels cause irritation, don't cut them out. That just produces a scratchy raw edge or a lump, and removes important care information you'll need in the future. Instead cover them with iron-on bonding tape.

Odor—cigarette smoke

To remove cigarette odors from a blouse, skirt, or pair of pants, place a fabric-softener sheet on the hanger with the garment and cover with a plastic bag. The cigarette odor will be gone by morning.

Odor—mothballs

Remove mothball odor from clothing by placing garments in the dryer with a couple of fabric softener sheets. Run on the "air only" setting for fifteen minutes.

Odor—preventing in shoes, boots

To keep shoes and boots from developing an unpleasant odor, make your own odor eaters. Pour a few teaspoons baking soda onto a small piece of cotton fabric. Tie the ends of the fabric together and secure them with a rubber band to make a sachet. Set one sachet in each shoe overnight. The sachets can be used again and again.

Odor—removing in shoes, boots

Stuff some newspaper into your shoes and boots to remove unpleasant foot odor. The paper absorbs odors.

Odor—smoke in clothes

To remove smoky odors from clothes, fill the bathtub with

the hottest water available. Add 1 cup white vinegar. Hang garments above the steaming water and close the bathroom door.

Padded cases for many uses

Surprisingly some eyeglass cases fit a cell phone or digital camera better than they do spectacles. Even more amusing, some padded cases created for cell phones or digital cameras are much better suited for eyeglasses. Just another way to use "this" for "that."

Repairs—collar and cuff turn

Save money on men's dress shirts. If the collar or cuffs wear out first, take the shirt to a dry cleaner or tailor (or learn to do it yourself) and have them turned over. It will cost about $5 to $10, which of course is much less than the cost of a new shirt.

Repairs—frayed collars

Use an old electric razor to "shave" the collars of men's cotton oxford dress shirts when they begin to pill. Men's neck whiskers chew up collars, and the "shaving" actually helps to slow the wearing process. They come out looking like new.

Repairs—handbags, backpacks, luggage

Don't throw out that handbag, backpack, or piece of luggage because of a broken strap, tear, or busted zipper. Have these items repaired at your local shoe repair shop. You'll be amazed at the low cost and high-quality service you'll receive on the repair of all kinds of things—even belts, gloves, bags, and so on.

Repairs—shoes

Repair, resole, and reheel shoes. You can easily double or triple the life of a good pair of shoes with simple repairs. Even expensive sneakers and athletic shoes can be resoled and repaired at some shops using new techniques and products. Check with your local shoe repairer or sporting goods store to see if they offer these services.

Rest your clothes

Your clothes will last longer if you allow them to "rest" between wearings. Clothing should hang for at least 24 hours between wearings to allow the fabric to return to its original shape.

Shoes—and driving

Ironically, the enemy of many good shoes is not walking but driving. While working the gas and foot pedals, the back of the shoe repeatedly scrapes dirty, abrasive carpet. Wear sneakers when driving, then slip into your good shoes upon arrival.

Shoes—heel shields

Protect high heels from wear and tear by having your shoe repair shop cover them with heel shields, a thin protective plastic wrap that goes around the heel. If the shields get scuffed, they are easy to remove and replace.

Shoes—leave them at the office

Leave your good business shoes at the office. Change into an older pair for the trip up and down steps and out to the parking lot.

Shoes—polish

Out of shoe polish? Spray dull, dirty-looking shoes with furniture polish, then buff lightly with a soft cloth. Self-polishing floor wax works particularly well on patent-leather shoes.

Shoes—rotation

You've heard of rotating your car's tires to make them last longer, but how about rotating your footwear? Research shows that your feet produce about ½ pint of water every day. If you wear a particular pair of shoes no more than once every 3 days, three pairs will hold up as long as four pairs worn more frequently.

Shoes need 48 hours to rest, dry out, and resume their normal shape.

Shoes—shining

Save and use your fabric softener sheets to shine shoes to a high gloss.

Shoes—slip 'n' slide

When the soles of new shoes are too slippery, rough them up with a piece of sandpaper.

Shoes—stretching leather

To stretch leather shoes that are a bit snug, pour rubbing alcohol into a fine-mist spray bottle. Spray inside the shoes, and then wear them immediately; the alcohol evaporates quickly. This technique works beautifully, but only on leather shoes.

Shoes—suede

Rub very fine sandpaper on suede shoes to remove stubborn scuff marks.

Shoes—trees

Shoes should be stored with cedar shoe trees in them. Cedar absorbs moisture that damages the leather.

Shoes—white sneaker protective coating

Before wearing a new pair and after each wash, spray white canvas sneakers with a fabric protector like Scotchgard. They'll be sparkling white till the day they wear out.

Shoes—white sneaker quick restore

To keep white canvas shoes looking new, apply white shoe polish after they are washed and while they are still wet. Allow to air-dry. You won't believe the results.

Shopping—dry-clean only?

Think twice—or three times—before buying something that says "dry-clean only." This kind of expensive maintenance will double or even triple the cost of a garment over the years.

Shopping—girls in boys' department

To cut down on clothing costs for girls and young women, shop for T-shirts, shorts, jackets, and other accessories in the boys' and men's departments.

Shopping—high-maintenance materials

Think twice about leather, suede, and silk. They are lovely but very expensive to maintain.

Shopping—outlets

Try on more than one size when shopping at outlets. Think about it: All of these items landed in this store for some reason. Maybe they were mislabeled.

Shopping—remnants for making clothes

Keep a list of yardage and notions needed for your favorite clothing patterns in your purse. When you're out shopping, stop by the yardages store or sewing department and check out the remnant table. If you find fabric you like, check your list to see if it works for any patterns you have. This is an easy way to add a cute skirt or blouse to your wardrobe for hardly any cost, and keeps you from buying fabric or notions that won't work with the patterns you like.

Shopping—shoe selection

When trying on shoes in the store, walk around in them on a hard surface. Standing on a carpet is deceiving. It makes the shoes feel more comfortable than they would be on hard floors or other surfaces.

Shopping—women in men's T-shirts

Ladies, buy men's white T-shirts to wear under jackets. They're cheap, easy to dye or trim, machine washable, and quite fashionable.

Ski pants

Take an old pair of jeans or canvas overalls and turn them

into cheap and comfortable ski pants. Simply spray them with good waterproof fabric protector available at fabric, sporting goods, and hardware stores.

Socks—all alone

Uses for widowed socks:
(1) Slip one over your hand to use as a waxing, dusting, or shoe-polish mitt; (2) put one over the top of the bathroom powdered cleanser can when not in use to avoid spills; (3) when you travel, slide one over each shoe to keep the clothes in your suitcase clean.

Stains—perspiration

"Dry-clean only" garments that are stained with perspiration should be taken to the cleaner as soon as possible. The longer the salts from perspiration remain in the fabric, the greater the chance of permanent damage.

Stains—winter coats

Try spraying stains on your winter coat with oven cleaner

and allow to dry overnight. This is a tried-and-true trick used in some used clothing stores to get coats ready for sale.

Storage—belts on a hanger

For a great belt holder, install a row of big cup hooks along the bottom of a wooden hanger.

Storage—shoes in socks

Store your off-season shoes inside socks to keep them scuff- and dust-free.

Storage—winter outerwear

To pack away your winter scarves and hats, store them inside a handbag or purse that you don't plan on using during the spring and summer. The winter accessories will help the purse keep its shape.

Static cling—use fabric spray

Mix 1 part liquid fabric softener and 20 parts water in a spray bottle set to spray a fine mist. Use as you would commercial aerosol antistatic spray by spraying on clinging petticoats, pantyhose, socks, and dresses.

Static cling—use hand lotion

Annoyed by static cling? Massage a small amount of hand lotion into your hands. Then lightly rub your palms over your pantyhose, tights, or undergarments.

Swaps—clothing

Arrange a clothing swap with friends. Ask everyone to bring at least five items in good condition that no longer meet their needs. One person's disaster could be your delight.

Swaps—neckties

If the man of the house wears ties often and easily tires of his favorites, find another such person to participate in a tie swap. Twice a year the swappers should go through their ties and get rid of the ones that have become boring or were unwanted gifts. Make sure the items are freshly cleaned, and then do a tie-for-tie swap. Donate anything left to a local charity.

Swimsuits

To prolong the life of swimsuits that are exposed to harsh chlorine, buy a bottle of chlorine remover, sold in pet supply stores for removing chlorine from the water in fish tanks. Add a few drops of the liquid to a pail of cold water, pop the suits in when swimming is over, and rinse with cold water.

Tailoring

Someone skilled at alterations can take in, let out, take up, let down, and redesign any classic or well-made garment.

Wool

To clean and soften new, washable winter woolens, add ½ cup of hair conditioner or creme rinse to 1 gallon of lukewarm water and soak.

Rinse the woolens thoroughly with tepid water.

Wrinkle-free

Throw wrinkled clothes into the dryer along with a wet towel. Turn it on for a few minutes and all the wrinkles will steam themselves away while you're getting ready.

Zippers—jams

Paint those fraying threads that constantly get caught in a zipper with clear nail polish.

Zippers—tab replacement

If the tab on your zipper is lost or broken, replace it with a safety pin or paper clip. Paint or wind fine yarn around it in a color that complements the garment.

Zippers—trouble

You can do several things to get that stubborn, sluggish, sticking metal zipper back into tip-top shape: Run the lead of an ordinary pencil along the metal teeth to lubricate them. Or with a cotton swab, apply a bit of lubricating spray such as WD-40 to the teeth. Be careful to wipe away any excess so it won't soil the garment. Another solution: Rub the edge of a bar of soap or an old candle up and down the teeth and along both sides of the zipper.

4

Food and Cooking

Asparagus—tenderness pouch

For perfectly tender asparagus, fold aluminum foil into a rectangular shape to form a cooking pouch and bake the asparagus inside it. The asparagus will steam within the pouch.

Baby food—homemade

Puree some of the family's regular food (not highly spiced items) in the blender. Pour into ice trays, freeze, then pop "food cubes" into large freezer bags to store. Keep the cubes frozen until needed,

and simply heat them in the microwave.

Bacon—no-stick slices

Before opening a new package of bacon, roll it up like a jelly roll, then unroll. Slices won't stick to each other.

Baking—adjust oven for glass bakeware

Glass bakeware conducts and retains heat better than metal, so oven temperatures should be reduced by 25 degrees whenever glass containers are used.

Baking—biscuit squares from dough scraps

To use up the scraps left after cutting out rounds, roll the dough into a square and cut square biscuits with a knife or large pizza wheel.

Baking—bread, dough rising

Create the perfect environment for bread to rise. Bring 2 cups of water to boil in a lidded 2-quart pot. Remove the pot from the heat, invert the lid on the top of the pot, and lay a pot holder on the inverted lid. Put the bread dough into a mixing bowl, balance the bowl on the inverted lid, and cover with a dish towel. The water releases its heat gradually and keeps the dough at an ideal proofing temperature.

Baking—bread, dough rising chamber

To create a great environment for bread to rise, use the clothes dryer. On the high setting, tumble a clean bath towel for 2 to 3 minutes. Turn off, and place the towel in the bottom of the dryer and the bowl of bread dough on top of the towel. Shut the dryer door to allow dough to rise. Put up a sign or a piece of tape across the door, or use some other signal in case someone decides it's a perfect time to do a little laundry.

Baking—brownie cutting

Remove brownies from the pan first and then cut them with a pizza cutter. It zips right through. No muss. No fuss. And it makes it easier to cut them straight. This works well with most bar cookies too.

Baking—brownies, extra fudgy

For extra-fudgy brownies, add 1 tablespoon corn syrup to the batter, either a box mix or from scratch. Bake as usual. Also, don't assume it always pays to bake from scratch. Brownies, for example, are often cheaper to make from a mix.

Baking—cake cooling

To cool a cake just out of the oven, place the pan on a wet towel. The cake is less likely to stick to the pan, and after it cools it will come out of the pan easily.

Baking—cake layer anchors

To keep the cake layers from slipping while you ice the sides of a cake, push three long strands of dry spaghetti through all of the cake layers. Frost the sides and top, and then pull out the spaghetti once the icing sets.

Baking—cake plate drips and smears

To prevent frosting drippings and smears on the cake plate, slip several strips of waxed paper just slightly under the edge of the cake all the way around it. Once the frosting is set, gently remove the

paper to reveal the clean plate.

Baking—cookie cutters, no sticking

A thin coat of cooking spray will prevent dough from sticking to cookie cutters. This also works with your children's play dough.

Baking—cookie sheets

If the cookie sheet you are baking cookies on is half or less than half full of cookies, it may absorb too much heat. Place an inverted baking pan on the empty half.

Baking—cookie dough, storage

An 8-ounce juice can is just right for storing homemade cookie dough. Cover the open end with foil or plastic wrap and either refrigerate for a few days or freeze for later. When you're ready to bake a batch, push the can at the bottom and squeeze out the dough. Cut it into slices and bake, following the recipe directions.

Baking—cookies, avoid burning

If you have trouble with cookies burning in your oven, bake them with a second cookie sheet under the first one.

Baking—cookies, peanut butter

When making the traditional fork marks on peanut butter cookies, first dip the tines in cinnamon, allspice, or ginger, then press down. This is effective, and tasty.

Baking—don't peek in oven

Don't open the oven when something is baking. Each peek can reduce oven temperature by as much as 25 degrees, will affect the baking quality, and can change the baking time. Watch the clock instead.

Baking—don't use whipped butter

Whipped butter contains more than 30 percent air, so it should never be used in baked goods.

Baking—freeze your rolling pin

Chill the rolling pin in the freezer so the dough won't stick to it. This prevents more flour from being added to the dough.

Baking—fruit for pies

Always taste the fruit before making a fruit pie filling. If the fruit isn't sweet enough, slice it very thinly so there'll be more surfaces to absorb the sugar.

Baking—glaze and butter brushing

A new paintbrush is perfect for brushing glaze on bread and pastry dough before cooking or melted butter on corn or dinner rolls.

Baking—location in oven

Bake pies, tarts, and quiches in the lower third of the oven. The bottom crust will be crisp, and the edges or top crust won't overbrown.

Baking—maple frosting

For a quick, easy, and delicious frosting, add maple syrup to confectioners' sugar and stir until rich and thick. Spread on cakes, cookies, and buns.

Baking—multiples in the oven

When baking more than one item at a time, make sure there's plenty of room between the pans, walls, and racks of the oven for air to circulate.

Baking—no cupcake batter spills

A spill-proof way to pour cupcake batter into muffin tins or pancake batter onto a griddle is to transfer it to a clean milk carton, using a funnel. The carton's spout lets you pour with precision and provides an excellent container for storage in the refrigerator.

Baking—quick-bread muffins instead of loaves

When it's too hot to crank up the oven for an hour, bake your favorite quick bread as muffins rather than loaves. Baking time is only 15 to 20 minutes, and the muffins are great take-alongs for summertime picnics and potlucks.

Baking—quick bread, measure ingredients carefully

Too much baking powder or baking soda gives quick bread a crumbly, dry texture and a bitter aftertaste. It can also make the batter overrise, causing the bread to fall.

Baking—toasted oats

To give your homemade cakes, cookies, and breads a crunchy texture and nutty flavor, place uncooked oats on a cookie sheet in your oven and toast until they're golden brown. Mix the toasted oats into the dough or batter.

Baking—use nonfat dry milk

Use nonfat dry milk in baking. It's cheaper than whole milk and will help you stretch your budget. Try stretching your fresh milk by mixing 50/50 with reconstituted dry milk (mixed with water according to package instructions). Make sure it is very cold and your family is not likely to detect your cost-cutting ways.

Baking—with blueberries

When making muffins, pancakes, or quick breads that call for blueberries, freeze the berries first. The frozen blueberries will keep their shape, and they won't break up in the batter.

Bread—burned toast

Scrape the really dark part off with a cheese grater, and no one will have to know.

Bread—hot dinner rolls

To keep dinner rolls hot at the table, heat a ceramic tile in the oven while the rolls are baking. Put the warm tile in a breadbasket, cover it with a napkin, and lay the rolls on top. Cover the rolls with a napkin, too,

and they'll stay warm for the entire meal.

Bread—making crumbs

Don't discard bread, rolls, bagels—even garlic bread— that have become hard. Store them in a plastic bag in the freezer, and when you need bread crumbs, simply grate a piece of your stash with a cheese grater. You'll have uniform, perfect bread crumbs.

Bread—mini hamburger buns

Use a biscuit cutter to cut the centers out of bread ends and you have a perfect-size hamburger bun for a young child. Use the scraps for bread crumbs.

Bread—soften

To freshen bread or rolls that have become a little bit hard, sprinkle the inside of a brown paper bag with water, add the bread or rolls, fold the top over tightly, and place in a 400 degree oven for 3 to 5 minutes to heat.

Broth—clear

Pour broth through a coffee filter to produce clear broth.

Broth—fat free

To get rid of the fat from canned beef and chicken broth, store the cans in the refrigerator upside down so the fat congeals on the "bottom" of the can, which will be at the top as they stand in the refrigerator. To use, turn the can upright and use a can-punch-type opener to pierce a hole. Pour the broth, and the fat will stay behind.

Broth—seasoning meats and veggies in the microwave

To season meats and veggies when cooking in the micro-wave, add chicken broth or beef broth, not salt. Cooking in broth enhances flavor, while sprinkling with salt can cause food to cook unevenly, discolor, and dry out.

Browning while broiling

Broiled meat, fish, or poultry will brown more evenly if brought to room temperature before cooking.

Butter—creaming with sugar

To cream butter and sugar quickly, first rinse the bowl with boiling water.

Butter—grated

When a recipe calls for dotting the surface of a pie filling with butter, rub a cold stick of butter across the coarse side of a grater and sprinkle the grated butter on the filling.

Butter—substitute

When baking, you can cut down or omit the butter or margarine by substituting applesauce. A good rule of thumb: no more than 1 tablespoon of applesauce per 1 cup of flour.

Butter spread—homemade

To make your own butter spread, combine 1 pound softened margarine with 1 cup buttermilk, ½ cup vegetable oil, and 1 teaspoon butter flavoring. Mix well and store in the refrigerator in a container with a tightly fitting lid. Tastes just like butter and stays soft.

Buying—cereal

Buy plain cereals, and then add your own extras like raisins, sliced almonds, honey, and dried fruit. You'll save a lot of money. You'll also know exactly what and how much has been added.

Buying—dairy

The date on dairy products is the date retailers must pull unsold products from the shelf. Properly stored, the product will be good for at least 7 days past the printed date. Unsalted butter has a shorter shelf life than salted. Whichever kind you buy, extra sticks are best stored in the freezer. Milk, cream, cottage cheese, and similar products should be stored in their original containers.

Buying—fish

For best quality, buy from supermarkets that display fish on ice in refrigerator cases. A fresh-caught fish has almost no odor; it will not smell "fishy." An ammonia-like smell develops when fish has been stored several days—don't buy! The eyes should look clear, not cloudy; the scales should be bright pink, not gray. The flesh should be unblemished, edges intact, not torn; when pressed with a finger, the flesh should give slightly but bounce back.

Buying—meat

Never purchase more meat than you can properly refrigerate and reasonably use within the following periods of time: Ground beef and beef cut into small pieces, such as stew meat, should be used within 2 days of purchase. Steak should be used within 4 days of purchase, and roasts should be used within 1 week. If you can't use the meat that quickly, be sure to freeze it as soon as possible.

Buying—nuts

Buy walnuts, almonds, pecans, and other nuts after the holidays at sale prices. Shell, then store the nuts in individual plastic bags in the freezer. The nuts won't stick together, so it's easy to remove the amount you need for each recipe.

Casseroles—for camping

Before you go camping, prepare casseroles and freeze them in waxed milk cartons. Simply open the top of the empty carton completely to allow ample room to fill the container, then refold to close. They will fit perfectly into the cooler and stay cold longer.

Casseroles—no spills on the go

To prevent spills when transporting a casserole dish, stretch one rubber band from each handle to the knob on top of the cover. The lid stays secure, making the dish easy to carry.

Cauliflower—keeping white

To keep cauliflower white while cooking, add a little milk to the water.

Celery—keep crisp

To keep celery crisp, stand it up in a pitcher or jar of cold saltwater, and refrigerate.

Celery—restore crunch

Tired of throwing out celery that's lost its crunch? Cut off the bottom stem and separate the stalks. Fill a pan that is deep enough to cover the celery with cold water, and stir in ¾ cup granulated sugar. Let the celery soak 4 to 5 hours. Drain well and refrigerate.

Cheese—equivalents

A 1-ounce piece of cheese equals ¼ cup shredded cheese; 2 ounces equal ½ cup, and so on.

Cheese—grater care

Spray the cheese grater with cooking spray to speed up

grating and to avoid cheese buildup.

Cheese—Parmesan cheese

To quickly shave or shred fresh Parmesan cheese, use a vegetable peeler or a zester.

Cheese—soft cream cheese

Make your own soft cream cheese. Combine one room-temperature, 8-ounce package of regular cream cheese with 2 tablespoons milk, or one 3-ounce package of regular cream cheese and 1½ teaspoons milk. Store in the refrigerator.

Chip clips—substitute

Instead of purchasing plastic "chip clips," keep a supply of sturdy clothespins on hand. Clothespins work great for keeping bags of chips, cookies, rice, flour, and coffee closed tightly.

Chocolate—melting

Before melting chocolate, spray the container with cooking spray, and the melted chocolate will slip right out.

Cleanup made easy—broiler

Make cleanup easy by spraying the clean broiler pan with nonstick vegetable spray before beginning to cook.

Cleanup made easy—graters, blades, and beaters

For easy cleanup, coat the grater, the knife blade of a food processor, and the beaters of an electric mixer with cooking spray before using.

Cleanup made easy—measuring cup, molasses or honey

Dust your measuring cup with flour before measuring molasses or honey for your next cookie recipe. The molasses or honey will pour from the cup easily, and cleanup will be a snap.

Cleanup made easy—oatmeal pot

Love hot cereal but hate the mess? Coat the pot with

cooking spray first. Cleanup will be a breeze.

Coconut—preparation

Pierce the eyes of a coconut with an ice pick and drain the liquid. Wrap the coconut in plastic wrap and microwave on high for 5 minutes or until fragrant and very hot. Let it stand 15 minutes. Wrap the coconut in a kitchen towel and split it with a hammer or mallet. Pry out the meat with a sturdy knife.

Coffee—bitterness

Put a pinch of salt into dry coffee grounds to remove any bitterness.

Coffee—café mocha

Company's coming, and you're nearly out of coffee. Make this café mocha, and you can serve six people with just 2 cups of coffee. Add ⅓ cup cocoa and 3 cups warmed milk to 2 cups of coffee. Sweeten to taste, or add about ¼ cup sugar.

Coffee—cappuccino

To make four cappuccinos, place 2 cups of milk in a glass measuring cup. Microwave on high until hot, about 2 minutes and 20 seconds. Place hot milk and 1 tablespoon of sugar in a blender. Cover with a vented lid and blend until frothy, about 1 minute. To serve, divide 2 cups strong coffee among four coffee cups. Top each with frothy milk. Sprinkle with cinnamon or grated chocolate (optional).

Coffee—European light

To make European-style "light" coffee, purchase coffee beans—half decaf and half regular—and have them poured into the same container. To use, set the grinder at the finest setting, which produces European-style ground coffee. Use a much smaller amount of grounds than you are accustomed to because of the fine grind. Store ground coffee and coffee beans in the freezer to keep them fresher longer.

Coffee—filters

Unbleached tan coffee filters last longer and are stronger than the bleached white type. They can be rinsed out and reused several times before discarding.

Coffee—for later

Don't leave the coffeepot warming for hours on end. Instead, transfer the brewed coffee to a thermos and turn that energy-sucker off.

Coffee—gourmet

Break up a cinnamon stick or sprinkle ground cinnamon into coffee grounds before brewing. Or add a drop of vanilla to the coffee once it's brewed.

Coffee—made ahead

Instead of making a half pot of coffee each morning, brew a whole pot every other day. Drink half and store half in a Mason jar that has a screw-on lid. When you pour hot coffee into the glass jar and tighten the lid, you will find the jar actually seals as it would in the canning process. Store in the refrigerator. The next day the coffee tastes great, and you can microwave a cup whenever you want.

Cook topside whenever possible

Your oven uses a lot more energy than the stove burners.

Cooking surface

When cooking, keep as much of the surface-unit heat as possible from escaping. Use pots and pans with flat bottoms, and always use a pan that is the same size or larger than the burner.

Corn—kernel removal

Use a new, clean metal shoehorn to scrape kernels off an ear of corn. It's the perfect shape for the job.

Corn—silk removal

Keep it cool. Don't pack fresh corn on the cob in a hot trunk after you leave the store. Be sure to put it in the refrigerator immediately when you get home. To get the silk off the corn quickly, put on a pair of rubber gloves and rub the cob. The silk will come off easily. When boiling corn, add sugar to the water instead of salt. Salt will toughen the corn.

Cornstarch—substitute

Substitute 2 tablespoons of flour for every tablespoon of cornstarch.

Cracker crumbs—substitute

Substitute 1 cup fine, dry bread crumbs for ¼ cup fine cracker crumbs.

Croutons—easy bake

Cut 4 slices of bread (stale is fine) into ¼-inch cubes. Toss the cubes with 2 tablespoons Parmesan cheese, 1 teaspoon Italian seasoning, ¼ teaspoon garlic salt, and 2 tablespoons canola oil. Bake at 300°F for about 20 minutes, or sauté in hot olive oil.

Crumbs—make with rolling pin

A rolling pin makes crumbs without the mess. Place dried-out bread in a large, sealed plastic bag and roll away.

Cutting—dental floss

In the kitchen, dental floss can do the job of a sharp, serrated knife—and with better results. Stretched taut between your hands, a length of floss can split a cake into layers without a turntable and with a minimum of crumbs. It will also slice a log of soft fresh cheese into rounds that stay intact, instead of crumbling into bits. Cut creamy cheesecake with dental floss. Stretch a length of floss over the top of the cake and, holding it taut, bring it down top to bottom through the cake to cut it into halves. Repeat until you have the desired number of pieces.

Dessert—mousse

For a quick, cheap, and low-fat chocolate mousse, mix cocoa powder into Cool Whip. Add as little or as much cocoa powder as your palate dictates. Stir well and serve. You can also use this to frost cakes.

Dessert—thawing

Thaw bread, desserts, and baked goods at room temperature in their original wrapping to avoid moisture loss.

Dip—green peppers for bowls

Use green peppers with the tops cut off and seeds removed as dip dishes. You'll have fewer items to wash later.

Double boiler or steamer

Here's a way to save a little money on your electricity or gas bill: Cook with a double boiler or steamer. For example, boil pasta in the boiler's bottom pot and steam vegetables in the top section.

Drinking straws—sanitary

Flexible drinking straws always seem to come in a cellophane bag or box that opens at the top. This represents a sanitation problem if every member of the family reaches in to get a straw. It's impossible not to touch the top of all the straws. Here's the solution: Empty the entire box of drinking straws into a gallon-size food storage bag, placing the straws horizontally in the bag. Now when you reach in to get one, you are not touching the drinking end but rather grabbing one from the middle.

Drinks—Crystal Light, homemade

Make your own product like Crystal Light with these ingredients: 1 cup lemon or lime juice, 5 cups cold water, and five packets sweetener (Sweet'N Low or Equal). Mix in pitcher, serve over ice, and enjoy!

Drinks—for school lunches

Pop-up, screw-on plastic tops that come on syrup bottles and sport-water bottles fit perfectly onto 1-pint plastic soda bottles. For a cheap alternative to individually packaged drinks, fill these small plastic bottles with water, milk, or 100 percent fruit juice for school lunch boxes.

Drinks—orange drink, homemade

Ingredients: 2 cups orange juice, ½ cup powdered coffee creamer, ½ teaspoon vanilla, 2 tablespoons sugar, 5 large ice cubes. Place ingredients in a blender, and add ice cubes one at a time. Blend until frothy. Yield: 1 or 2 servings.

Drinks—orange juice, squeezing

Before squeezing oranges for fresh juice, heat two oranges in a microwave on high for 45 seconds to 1 minute until slightly soft and just warm to the touch. Squeezing will be easier, and you'll get twice the juice because the fibers will have broken down a bit.

Drinks—punch cubes

Freeze whatever drink you are serving in an ice cube tray ahead of time. If serving tea, make tea cubes; if punch, punch cubes. Drinks will stay

chilled and won't get all watered down.

Drinks—soda quick chill

Chill a warm can of soda fast. Swirl the can in ice water for 5 minutes.

Drinks—tea

Give tea a zingy twist by adding an orange peel to the teapot a few minutes before serving.

Dry staples—protect from bugs

To protect dry staples such as flour, meal, grits, pastas, and rice from contamination, pop in a couple of bay leaves. This won't affect the taste, but it will prevent pesky bugs from ruining these products.

Duck—no stuffing

Unlike turkeys, chicken, and game hens, you don't want to stuff a duck. The bread in the stuffing absorbs so much fat that the stuffing becomes inedible.

Egg—quick salad

For quick egg salad, break 1 large egg into a custard cup. Puncture the yolk with a knife. Cover with plastic wrap; vent. Microwave on medium (50 percent power) for 2 minutes. Chop and use in your favorite egg-salad recipe.

Egg test—cooked or uncooked?

When you hard-cook eggs that you plan to save for a few days, put a tea bag in the water. The shells will turn slightly beige, and you'll be able to distinguish them from uncooked eggs.

Egg test—fresh?

Place an egg in cool, salted water to determine its freshness. If it sinks, it's fresh. If it floats, throw it out.

Egg whites—beating tricks

Separate whites from yolks as soon as you remove eggs from the refrigerator. Cold yolks are firmer and less likely to break. Do not pierce yolks.

One speck will keep whites from beating properly. To get the greatest volume, bring egg whites to room temperature before beating. Use a small, deep bowl so beaters are immersed and mixture is thoroughly aerated.

Egg whites—clean equipment

Whenever you are working with egg whites, it is important that your beating equipment be impeccably clean and free from oil or grease, which will prevent the eggs from creating the greatest volume possible. A copper or stainless steel bowl is ideal.

Egg whites—separate with a funnel

Separate egg whites from the yolk by breaking eggs, one at a time, into a narrow-necked funnel. The whites will pass through, leaving the yolk in the funnel.

Egg whites—through your fingers

Crack the eggshell and pour its contents into your clean hand held over a small bowl. Allow the white to drip between your fingers into the bowl.

Egg whites—use acidic mix

When beating egg whites, add ⅛ teaspoon acid (cream of tartar, lemon juice, or vinegar) per white just as they begin to become frothy during beating. This stabilizes egg whites and allows them to reach their full volume and stiffness. This is not necessary if using a copper bowl, as the natural acid on the surface achieves the same result.

Eggs—easy peel

Eggs can be shelled easily if you bring them to a boil in a covered pan, then turn the heat to low and simmer for 15 minutes. Pour off the hot water, shake the eggs in the pan until they're well cracked, then add cold water. The shells will come right off.

Eggs—from refrigerator to room temp

If a recipe calls for room-temperature eggs and yours are straight from the refrigerator, immerse them in very warm water for a few minutes.

Eggs—half of three

To halve a recipe calling for three eggs, use two eggs and decrease the recipe's liquid by 2 to 3 tablespoons.

Eggs—omelet fluff

Add a pinch of cornstarch to beaten eggs to make a much fluffier omelet.

Eggs—poaching

Put a few drops of white vinegar in the water to help poached eggs hold their shape.

Eggs—reducing cholesterol

When making scrambled eggs, use the yolks from only half of the eggs to cut cholesterol by 50 percent without affecting taste.

Eggs—storage

Always store eggs large end up. This keeps them fresher

and helps keep the yolk centered. Never store eggs near pungent foods like onions because they easily absorb odors right through their shells.

Eggs—substitute

Out of eggs? Use 2 tablespoons of mayonnaise for each egg required in your baking recipe.

Equivalents—one pound

The following amounts are equal to 1 pound: 2 cups butter; 2⅓ cups white granulated sugar; 2 cups packed brown sugar; 3¾ cups confectioners' sugar; 3½ cups all-purpose flour; 4 cups cake flour; 3¾ cups whole wheat flour; 4 cups cocoa; 3 cups loosely packed raisins; 2¾ cups sliced apples; 2 cups fresh pitted cherries; 5 cups sliced, fresh mushrooms; 3 cups sliced white potatoes; 4½ cups coarsely sliced cabbage.

Fish—better smelling hands

Before handling fish, rinse your hands in cold water and they won't smell so fishy later.

Fish—cooking time

General rule: Fish should be cooked 10 minutes per inch of thickness. Measure the thickest part of the fillet or steak; turn over the fish at the halfway point. Example: Cook a 1-inch-thick fish 5 minutes per side. The fish is done when the flesh is opaque. If a fish steak is unusually thick, check the center with a knife.

Fish—deboning

Tweezers are perfect for removing fine bones from cooked fish.

Flour—puff

Keep a powder puff in your flour container and use it for dusting cake pans before you pour in the batter.

Flour—shaker

Put flour in an old saltshaker and leave it in the freezer.

When you need to flour a
pan or dust a pastry board,
the shaker will save you from
wrestling with a big bag and
spilling flour everywhere.

Flour—sifter

A kitchen strainer works just
as well as a flour sifter. Lightly
press flour or powdered sugar
through with the back of a
wooden spoon or gently shake
the strainer back and forth
until the product has worked
its way through.

Foil liners in pans

It sounds so simple, but it's
not always that easy. Here's a
way to make lining any pan
with foil a cinch. Turn the pan
to be lined over and lay a piece
of foil over it, molding it to the
exact shape of the pan. Now
turn the pan right-side up and
set the perfectly molded foil
into it. Perfect fit every time.

Food—expiration dates

Mark a rotation date on any
food container that does not

already have an expiration
date on the package. Store the
food in airtight, pest-resistant
containers in a cool, dark
place. Most canned foods
can safely be stored for at
least 18 months. Low-acid
canned foods like meat products, fruits, or vegetables will
normally last at least 2 years.
Use dry products, like boxed
cereal, crackers, cookies, dried
milk, or dried fruit within 6
months.

Food—inventory

Place a chalkboard on the refrigerator. List what snacks or
leftovers are available inside.
This will prevent family members from eating things you're
planning to have for dinner.
And it will keep them from
opening the refrigerator to
search for snacks that may or
may not be there while all the
cold air leaks out.

Food—list on display

If your supermarket receipt
clearly lists every item you
purchased by name, post it

on the refrigerator door. It lets everyone know what you bought so they can decide quickly what they want.

Freezer—labeling

Label and date new items for the freezer, and place them in the back. Doing this brings the older items to the front so they can be used first.

Freezer—list

Keep a current freezer inventory list posted to the outside of the freezer door. The longer you leave the door open while you look to see what's in there, the more cold air escapes and the harder the freezer has to work.

Freezer—storage

Heavy-duty freezer bags can be reused, but if you've written on them, it can get confusing. Instead, write the contents and also instructions for heating on a separate piece of paper that you can slip inside the bag. You can see through

with no problem, and the bag stays blank for its future jobs.

Freezing—cakes

Freeze frosted cakes uncovered until hard, then lightly wrap with plastic wrap and aluminum foil. Store unfrosted cakes and cheesecakes in plastic wrap, and freeze. Thaw all cakes with the wrapping in place to minimize condensation.

Freezing—chicken

Freeze skinless, boneless chicken breasts uncovered in a single layer, then wrap them individually and stack in resealable plastic bags. Thaw in the refrigerator, or if you're in a hurry, submerge them in the airtight bag in a bowl of cold water.

Freezing—eggs

If you have more eggs than you can use in the near future, crack them open and place them individually in an ice cube tray. Once they're frozen, remove them and store in a resealable plastic freezer bag in the freezer. Frozen eggs should always be thawed in the refrigerator and used in recipes in which they will be thoroughly cooked.

Freezing—fish in milk cartons

Freeze cleaned fish by packing them loosely in clean milk cartons and filling the cartons with water. When you defrost, save the water to use as fertilizer for your houseplants.

Freezing—fish with high fat content

Fish with a relatively high fat content, like salmon and trout, freeze best. Thaw, without unwrapping, at room temperature in a bowl of cold water or in the refrigerator. Before you freeze a fish, it should be cleaned, gutted, rinsed, and dried.

Freezing—ground meat

Freeze 1 pound of ground meat in a 1-gallon resealable plastic freezer bag. Flatten

the meat inside the bag and you'll have a package that takes up very little space when you stand it on end in your freezer. When you want to use the meat, simply whack the package on the side of your counter to break it up; it will thaw very quickly once broken into pieces.

Freezing—heavy cream

Heavy cream can be frozen if you intend to use it for cooking, but it won't whip once it has thawed.

Freezing—herbs

Place fresh herbs in tightly sealed plastic bags and freeze. Their color will fade slightly, but their flavor will remain true. Another method is to mince the herbs, place them into ice cube trays, and add water to freeze them in cubes.

Freezing—lemon juice

If you have an overabundance of lemons, you can squeeze the juice into ice cube trays, freeze, and then keep cubes in a plastic bag for future use.

Freezing—liquids

Allow at least ½ inch of space for expansion when freezing liquids.

Freezing—onions

To freeze onions, chop them and then spread the pieces out in one layer on a cookie sheet. Immediately place the cookie sheet in the freezer. When the onions are frozen, transfer them to a resealable plastic bag or container and seal.

Freezing—snack foods

Keep marshmallows, potato chips, pretzels, and crackers in the freezer. They are best if frozen in their original unopened containers.

Freezing—soups

Freeze soup or casseroles in a loaf pan. When they are hard, remove, wrap, label, and return them to the freezer. You'll have use of your pan again immediately, and the product will easily stack in the freezer.

Freezing—soups not to freeze

Don't freeze soups containing milk, cream, or coconut milk, which can separate or curdle.

Freezing—vegetables

Blanch vegetables before freezing. They contain enzymes that, if the action is not stopped, will cause vegetables to become coarse and flavorless. To blanch, drop fresh vegetables into boiling water, followed by a complete immersion into ice water. Work with small batches. Blanching time depends on the type of vegetable. For example, boiling time for green beans is 2½ minutes while asparagus should boil for 3 minutes. Find a handy blanching times chart at http://www.ochef.com/617.htm.

Freezing—whipped cream in dollops

Whipped cream can be frozen in dollops on a flat sheet. Once the dollops are hard, store them in resealable plastic freezer bags.

Freezing—whipped cream in milk carton

Fill a milk carton with whipped cream and freeze. When you need some, cut the required amount off the top with a carving knife, carton and all. Recap the carton with plastic wrap or aluminum foil, secure with tape or a rubber band, and return to the freezer.

Fresher—asparagus

Asparagus will stay fresher longer if you set the spears upright in a container in the refrigerator with the cut ends sitting in an inch of water.

Fresher—bananas, plastic bag

If you store bananas in a closed plastic bag, they will keep at least 2 weeks on your counter.

Fresher—bananas, tree

A banana tree is a great invention that prevents bananas from bruising so they will last longer. Purchase a big cup hook and screw it into the underside of an upper cabinet. Your bananas can hang properly and be up and out of the way.

Fresher—berries

Berries keep for several days in the refrigerator if stored unwashed in a colander or in their original container with airflow. Wash right before eating.

Fresher—cookie dough

Most cookie dough can be refrigerated for at least a week, and frozen for up to a year if it has been wrapped in airtight resealable plastic freezer bags or in aluminum foil.

Cheaper, Better, Faster

Fresher—cookies

Put a slice of bread in the cookie jar to absorb the moisture that causes cookies to become stale.

Fresher—cucumbers

To extend the life of a cucumber once it has been cut, wrap it in a paper towel. The cucumber will not get soggy for up to 2 weeks.

Fresher—eggs

Eggs will stay fresh all month in the refrigerator if you keep them on the shelf in their original cartons instead of putting them in the egg holder on the refrigerator door. The temperature variations from opening and closing the door cause eggs to spoil more quickly.

Fresher—lettuce

Remove the core from the lettuce head with a nonmetal utensil, fill the cavity with cold water, and drain well. Wrap the head in a clean damp towel and refrigerate. As long as you keep the towel damp, your lettuce will stay fresh and crisp.

Fresher—milk

To keep milk fresh longer, add a pinch of salt when you open it. This will greatly increase its useful shelf life and does not affect the taste in any way.

Fresher—nuts

Keep nuts in the freezer to retard spoilage. Nuts left in the pantry can become rancid.

Fresher—onions, potatoes

Cut off a leg of an old, clean pair of pantyhose, drop onions or potatoes into it, and hang it in a cool, dark place. The hose lets air circulate, which helps keep the onions or potatoes fresh longer.

Fresher—popcorn kernels

Keep popcorn kernels in the freezer. They will stay fresh much longer, and freezing will encourage every kernel to pop.

106

Fresher—raisins

Raisins stay fresh longer when stored in an airtight container in the refrigerator. If they become hard, pour very hot water over them. Drain immediately, then spread them on a paper towel to dry.

Fresher—salt

Add a few rice kernels to a saltshaker in humid weather to keep the salt fresh.

Frosting—spreader

Use a 6-inch scraper or putty knife, which you can buy in hardware stores or home improvement stores, as a spreader for icing the side and top of a layer cake. It's smaller than a spatula and much easier to hold straight. Position the scraper perpendicular to the side of the cake that you've placed on a lazy Susan; hold it gently, and rotate the cake's turntable. The scraper also will maintain an even amount of frosting on the cake sides.

Frosting—to go

To keep plastic wrap from sticking to cupcakes (and other frosted treats), spray the plastic wrap with some cooking spray. The cupcakes will arrive at their destination with the frosting intact.

Fruit—citrus peeling

When grating or cutting citrus peel, use fruit straight from the refrigerator. The fruit will be firmer and easier to handle.

Fruit—repel fruit flies

Garnish fruit bowls with fresh basil, which repels fruit flies.

Fruit—slices without browning

Fill a spray bottle with lemon-lime soft drink to spray on apple and banana slices to prevent them from turning brown.

Fruit juice—extend with water

Stretch concentrated fruit juice. Add more water than

instructions recommend. You will be pleasantly surprised when you detect little difference, if any. Start by adding half a can of water extra. Work up to one full can of water beyond the amount recommended.

Fruit juice—leftovers

Use the leftover juice from canned fruits to sweeten your iced tea or lemonade. This gives both the tea and the lemonade an excellent tropical flavor, and you won't waste that juice.

Fruit juice—lemon juice with no seeds

For seedless lemon juice, wrap half a lemon in a piece of cheesecloth before squeezing.

Frying—draining

When deep-frying, use only one paper towel with a thick section of newspaper under, and place food on it to drain.

Frying—grease removal

Use a turkey baster to remove grease from the frying pan as you're browning ground beef.

Frying—splatters

When frying foods, invert a metal colander over the frying pan to prevent hard-to-clean oil splatters.

Frying—sticking

Heat the frying pan before adding oil or butter. It's guaranteed to keep food from sticking.

Funnel—substitute

Make an emergency funnel out of aluminum foil, or cut the corner from a plastic bag.

Garlic—quick roasted

Trim the top of one whole head of garlic. Place in a 1-cup measuring cup with 3 tablespoons chicken broth. Cover with plastic wrap; vent. Microwave on high for about

10 minutes, until tender. Let stand 5 minutes. This is good spread on toasted French bread.

Garlic—substitute

Use ⅛ teaspoon of garlic powder in place of a clove of garlic.

Gravy—brown coloring

To make gravy brown, stir in 1 teaspoon of brewed coffee. It doesn't affect the taste, just the appearance.

Gravy—keeping it hot

Serve gravy in a small thermos-type coffee decanter. It holds a lot, is easy to handle, and keeps the gravy piping hot.

Gravy—salvage after freezing

To salvage gravy and other fat-based sauces that have separated as a result of freezing, whisk or process them briefly

in a blender or food processor to emulsify.

Gravy—spatula stir

Always stir thick brown or turkey gravy with a spatula instead of a wooden spoon. The spatula's broad, flat edge thoroughly sweeps the bottom of the pan so the gravy won't stick or scorch.

Grease fires—use pan lid

Smother a grease or oil fire in the kitchen by sliding a pan lid over the flames. Never carry the pan outside.

Grease fires—use salt

To douse flames from grease fires, keep a box of salt near your stove.

Greasing—use butter wrappers

Save your leftover butter and margarine wrappers in a plastic bag in your refrigerator. They'll come in handy the next time you need to grease a pan.

Grilling—brushing meat, poultry, fish

Use a bundle of thyme sprigs to brush olive oil on meat, poultry, or fish as it grills.

Grilling—change platters

Don't place the grilled food back on the same platter it was on before cooking. Wash the platter after it has held raw meat, or use a separate plate for serving grilled food.

Grilling—fish

Prepared mayonnaise generously smeared on fish fillets and fish steaks will prevent them from sticking when they are grilled. Most of the mayonnaise will cook off, leaving the fish moist and tasty. Leave the skin on fish fillets to be grilled, and they'll retain their shape better. If desired, remove the skin after cooking.

Grilling—flank steak

For an uncomplicated, great-tasting grilled entree, soak flank steak in soy sauce for 3 to 4 hours. Cook on a very hot grill for 7 to 8 minutes on the first side, and 6 to 7 minutes on the other. Slice thinly on the bias and against the grain.

Herbs—as garnishments

Wrap bunches of fresh rosemary, thyme, or basil from your garden with raffia and use to garnish platters of food.

Herbs—avoid steam

When adding herbs to a dish you're preparing, hold the jar away from the saucepan while adding. Steam from the pan will get into the jar and be absorbed by the herbs.

Herbs—basil leaves

Clean and pat dry fresh basil leaves, then layer with coarse (kosher) salt in a widemouthed glass jar until ready for use.

Herbs—fresh vs. dried

It takes three times as many fresh herbs to give the same flavoring as one measure of dried herbs.

Herbs—make butter

If you have an overabundance of fresh herbs, try storing them by making herb butters, which can be frozen and used during winter months on homemade bread, melted over vegetables, or swirled in a simple sauce to provide a great burst of summer flavor. To make herb butters, chop a cup or more of fresh herbs and combine with a stick of softened butter; blend until smooth. Add a few drops of lemon juice. Place in an airtight container and freeze.

Herbs—need to be bruised

When you add an herb to something you're cooking, you should "bruise" the herb first to release the oils that give it the flavor. If it's a dried herb, crumble it into the pot.

If fresh, first tear or mash with the back of a spoon.

Herbs—store for freshness

Place stems of fresh herbs such as basil and parsley in a small container of water, cover with a plastic bag, and refrigerate to store and keep fresh before using.

Herbs and spices—not above stove

Even though it seems convenient, don't store herbs and spices right above the stove. Heat is bad for them, as is direct sunlight. The best storage place for dried herbs and spices is in a cool, dark cupboard.

Honey—substitute

One cup of honey can be replaced with 1¼ cups sugar and an additional ¼ cup of whatever liquid is used in the recipe.

Ice—crushed

Freeze water in clean milk cartons. Several strong whacks

111

with a hammer to the four sides and bottom of the carton will produce great crushed ice for homemade ice cream and your other crushed-ice needs.

Ice cream—at the campground

Ingredients: 1 cup heavy cream, 1 cup milk, 1 egg beaten, ½ cup sugar, 1 teaspoon vanilla. Mix well and place in a clean, 1-pound coffee can. Cover and tape shut. Place in a 3-pound coffee can with 1 part rock salt and 4 parts crushed ice. Cover. Roll back and forth on a picnic table for 10 minutes. Open both cans and stir ice cream. Reclose the small can and tape it shut. Return it to the large coffee can with the salt and ice, close tightly, and roll 5 minutes more. Caution: Be sure to use an egg that is not cracked, and wash the shell before cracking it open.

Ice cream—carton peel

When no microwave is available to soften hard ice cream,

peel away the carton and cut the ice cream into slices.

Ice cream—in prepared portions

If large quantities of ice cream disappear too quickly in your house, divide it into individual portions ahead of time. Put single servings into empty yogurt containers and freeze. Or line a baking pan with graham crackers, then a layer of softened ice cream, followed by a top layer of graham crackers. Freeze, cut into individual squares, wrap, and refreeze.

Ice cream—not on the freezer door

Store ice cream in the freezer compartment, not on the freezer door. This keeps ice cream fresher because it isn't exposed to temperature variations from opening and closing the door.

Ice cream—softener

To soften a quart of rock-hard ice cream, microwave it at 30 percent power for about 30 seconds. Hardened high-fat ice cream will soften more quickly than low-fat ice cream because of the fat.

Ice cream cones— freezing until later

Prepare ice cream cones as soon as you get home from the market, when the ice cream is soft and easy to scoop. Wrap them in plastic and freeze them for special treats.

Ice cream cones— marshmallow plug

Stop messy leaks from ice cream cones by dropping a marshmallow into the bottom of the cone before filling with ice cream.

Iron—from iron pots

Cook in cast iron pots. Doing this boosts the iron content of food. Soup simmering for a few hours in an iron pot has almost 30 times more iron than soup cooked in another type of pot.

Jelly or jam bottle

Transfer jelly or jam to an empty squeeze bottle like a mustard or ketchup bottle. Snip the end of the tip to make a slightly larger hole. No more messy jelly or jam jars.

Ketchup flow

Ketchup flows out of a new bottle more easily if you push a soda straw to the bottom of it. This allows air to get in and break the vacuum.

Lemon juice—get more from the lemon

Get more juice out of a lemon. Roll it around on the countertop with the palm of your hand to break up the fibers inside, or put it in the microwave for 30 seconds to a minute before cutting.

Lemon juice—quick seasoning

Store lemon juice in a shaker for quick seasoning. Keep it in the refrigerator.

Lettuce—wilted

To restore wilted lettuce, quickly dip the lettuce in hot water, then rinse in ice water to which you've added some salt. Shake, then refrigerate for an hour.

Lunch supplies

For the lunch crowd, store all sandwich and lunch fixings in the same refrigerator drawer. Keep some plastic and brown bags there too.

Marinade—repurposed as dipping sauce

Once meat has been removed from a marinade, the marinade can be used for a dipping sauce or saved for future use—provided you first boil it for a full 5 minutes to destroy any bacteria left by the raw meat or poultry. Since boiling can change the texture and flavor of some marinades, it may not work a second time as a marinade, but you can expect to enjoy a lovely dipping sauce.

Marinating—acids

Marinate meat in resealable plastic bags, glass, plastic, or ceramic containers. Most marinades contain acids, which can react with metal and affect the flavor.

Marinating—fast and easy

For fast and easy marinating, all you need is a resealable plastic bag and a straw. Mix the marinade in the bag, add the food, and seal the bag, leaving one corner open. Insert about a ½ inch of the straw into the bag, then gently inhale on the straw. As you create a vacuum, the marinade will draw up around the food. When the marinade nears the top, quickly pull out the straw and seal the bag. You'll need less marinade, use less space in your refrigerator, and have less to clean up.

Meat—for stir-fry

It's easier to slice meat thinly for quick-cooking dishes such as stir-fries if you first freeze the meat for 30 to 60 minutes.

Meat—handling without sticking

Rinse your hands in cold water before mixing or shaping ground meat. Meat won't stick to them.

Meat—salt after cooking

Salt your steaks after cooking, because salt draws the juices out.

Meat—seasoning check

To check seasonings when mixing raw ground meat for meat loaf, meatballs, or burgers, cook a tiny amount of the meat mixture in the microwave. Taste and adjust seasonings if necessary.

Meat—steak doneness test

To check a steak for doneness, press on it. Rare will be soft, medium will give slightly, and well done will be firm.

Meat loaf

Bake meat loaf in muffin tins instead of a loaf pan or in a large free-form shape. It will cook faster, be easier to serve, and the cleanup will be a breeze.

Messy jobs

Before starting a messy kitchen job such as peeling potatoes or grating cheese, cover the counter or sink with a ripped-open brown grocery bag. When you're finished, just roll up the mess and dispose of it in one step to the garbage can.

Microwaving—popcorn

Before putting a bag of microwave popcorn into the oven, knead it until the lumps are broken. Now all the kernels should pop.

Microwaving—water

Before adding anything (such as instant coffee, a tea bag, or cereal) to water you have just heated in the microwave, stir the water to prevent it from boiling over.

Milk—buttermilk, homemade

Add 1 tablespoon of lemon juice to enough milk to equal 1 cup. Let stand 5 minutes before using.

Milk—sweetened condensed

Combine 2 cups instant, non-fat dry milk, 1½ cups sugar, ⅔ cup boiling water, and 6 tablespoons butter, melted and slightly cooled. Mix dry ingredients and slowly add to boiling water. Stir in melted butter. Whip in blender or by hand until smooth. Store in refrigerator for 1 week or freeze for up to 6 months. Yield: 20 ounces.

Mincing

When mincing garlic, shallots, or onions, sprinkle a pinch of salt over them. This will keep the pieces from sticking to the knife and cutting board.

Mint

Freeze washed mint leaves or edible flowers in ice cubes to be used for special occasions. They look pretty and add a subtle hint of flavor.

Mustard—prepared and dry

One tablespoon prepared mustard is equal to 1 teaspoon of dry mustard.

Nuts—toasting

To toast nuts, cover the bottom of your microwave with waxed paper. Spread with ¼ cup chopped nuts. Microwave uncovered on high for 5 minutes until lightly browned.

Oil—glass bottles

Since oils can become rancid more quickly when exposed to light, use designer water bottles made of colored glass to store oils.

Oil—spray with cooking oil

Put cooking oil in a clean plastic spray bottle. This is much cheaper than buying oil in a spray can, and you can use the exact type of oil you want.

Odor—cabbage

When cooking cabbage, place a half-filled cup of vinegar on the stove near the cabbage, and it will absorb offensive odors.

Odor—onions on hands

Remove onion odor from your hands by rubbing a stainless steel spoon between them while they're under running water. Or rub hands with the end of a celery stalk to remove the odor.

Odor—shrimp

Add a few drops of sesame oil to the water when boiling shrimp to eliminate the odor.

Onions—even browning

While sautéing onions, sprinkle with a bit of sugar if you notice they are browning unevenly. They should begin to cook evenly thereafter.

Onions—no crying, cold water

Peel onions under cold running water, then freeze them for 5 minutes before chopping or slicing. This will keep you from crying while working with them.

Onions—no crying, vinegar

Before chopping onions, sprinkle a little vinegar on the cutting board. It will keep your eyes from tearing.

Onions—sautéing

Chop enough onions to fill two skillets, then sauté them in margarine until they're translucent and slightly browned. After letting them cool, wrap portions in plastic wrap and freeze them in a large resealable plastic bag. When you need them, just add directly to the dish you're making or thaw in the microwave prior to adding.

Onions—substitute

Out of onions for gravy or stock? A few teaspoons of dried-onion soup mix make a tasty substitute.

Onions—too soft

Boiled onions that have become too soft can be firmed up again by dipping them briefly in ice water.

Organizers

Plastic berry baskets make terrific holders for powdered soups, drink mixes, and envelopes of seasonings that seem to collect around the pantry.

Oven—when to preheat

Preheat your oven only if the recipe tells you to. Casseroles and roasts don't suffer from starting out in a cold oven, but breads, cakes, and pies do.

Pantry shelving

Create more pantry shelving by laying a narrow board across two tall soup cans.

Pasta—and Parmesan

Drain pasta noodles after cooking, then add a little grated Parmesan cheese. The cheese creates a bumpy texture for the sauce to cling to. Add the noodles to sauce in the saucepan, then toss until the pasta is coated.

Pasta—boiling with vegetables

When cooking pasta, add cut-up vegetables such as broccoli, cauliflower, green beans, or carrots to the boiling water. They can cook together even if they will not be served in the same dish.

Pasta—draining, coat the colander

Coat your colander with cooking spray before using it to drain pasta. This will keep the pasta from sticking.

Pasta—draining, skip the colander

To skip the step of transferring pasta from the pot to the colander to rinse, cook pasta in a pot with a removable inner basket, or use a metal colander or large strainer inside a pot of boiling water. Lift out and drain.

Pasta—fresh

Fresh pasta can be wrapped airtight in a plastic bag and refrigerated for up to 5 days or double wrapped and frozen for up to 4 months.

Pasta—shapes

Match the pasta shape to the sauce you will be serving. Serve long, thin pasta such as spaghetti or vermicelli with smooth sauces that will cling to the long strands. Serve long, flat pasta such as fettuccini and linguini with rich sauces based on butter, cheese, or cream. Serve short pasta such as fussili or rigatoni with chunky vegetable, meat, or cream sauces (good choice for baked pasta dishes). Serve fun-shaped pasta such as bow ties or shells with cream, seafood, or tomato sauce.

Pasta—stretch prepackaged dishes

To receive more value from prepackaged pasta dishes such as Kraft Macaroni and Cheese or Hamburger Helper, add up to a cup of extra macaroni or pasta to extend the dish without losing flavor. To save on calories and fat, use skim milk and half the recommended amount of butter.

Pasta—unsticking

If cooked pasta sticks together, spritz it gently with hot running water for just a few seconds. Drain.

Pastry blender—for chopping and slicing

Use a pastry blender to chop hard-cooked eggs or canned tomatoes and to slice sticks of cold butter into parts.

Pie—cover for meringue or custard

Before refrigerating leftover meringue or custard pies, cover with plastic wrap treated with vegetable oil or cooking spray so it won't stick to the pie's surface.

Pie—pumpkin

When making a pumpkin pie, mix the filling in a 1-quart or larger liquid measuring cup or a large pitcher instead of a mixing bowl. To add the filling, pull the oven rack partway out, place the pie plate on the rack, and pour the filling into the crust. Gently push the rack back in place, then bake the pie. No spills, no fuss!

Piecrust—extra flaky

Substitute ice-cold sour cream or whipping cream for water for an extra-flaky piecrust.

Piecrust—firm up

Place your unfilled piecrust in the freezer for 10 minutes before baking to reduce shrinkage and to hold fluted edges in place.

Piecrust—hands off!

Body heat will melt the fat and toughen piecrust, so touch the dough with your hands as little as possible.

Piecrust—prevent overbrowning edges

To prevent piecrust edges from overbrowning, cut the bottom

and sides from a disposable aluminum foil pie pan, leaving the rim intact. When the crust is golden brown and the filling isn't quite done, place the foil ring on top to slow the browning process. It can be used again and again.

Piecrust—use cold ingredients

Piecrust ingredients, even the flour, should be cold to produce the best results.

Pizza crust—not so soggy

If you need a pan with sides to hold your pizza, prebake the crust on a pizza stone or in a perforated pan, and then transfer it to a deep dish before filling. The crust will be sealed and less likely to become soggy.

Portions—single-size

Here's how to freeze single-size portions if you don't have lots of small containers or you have limited freezer space: Spoon a single serving of food, such as chili or stew, into a large container; freeze it briefly until hard; cover with two pieces of waxed paper; then add another serving. Repeat layers with remaining food. When ready to use, just grab the edges of the waxed paper, lift out what you need, and return the rest to the freezer.

Potato—brightener

A teaspoon or two of lemon juice in the cooking water will keep potatoes white after cooking.

Potato—peeler uses

Uses for a potato peeler: (1) Grate cheese, and save time on cleanup; (2) shave off small pieces of butter or margarine from a frozen or hard stick with a potato peeler; (3) pit cherries.

Potato—salad

For more flavorful potato salads, add a vinaigrette dressing while drained potatoes are still hot so they'll absorb some of the dressing.

Potatoes—buttermilk or skim milk with seasoning

Make mashed potatoes with buttermilk or skim milk and butter-flavored seasoning instead of using butter and whole milk.

Potatoes—mashed, ahead of time

Mashed potatoes can be made ahead of time. Make a batch, then spoon the prepared whipped potatoes into a buttered casserole dish. Dot with pats of butter and cover with plastic wrap and refrigerate. To warm before serving, bake in a 350°F oven for about 25 minutes, or until a knife inserted in the center comes out hot. Or cook in the microwave until hot.

Potatoes—mashed, with mayo

Add a good-quality mayonnaise along with the butter, salt, and pepper to your mashed potatoes. Prepare as you would for whipped potatoes.

Potatoes—saltwater soak before baking

Soak potatoes in saltwater for 20 minutes before baking so they will bake more rapidly.

Potatoes—scooping tool

Use a curved grapefruit knife to scoop out baked-potato halves when making twice-baked potatoes or when preparing a halved eggplant for stuffing.

Potatoes—washed in the dishwasher

When you have to wash a lot of potatoes, just put them in your dishwasher—but don't add soap! Set it on a short wash cycle. The clean potatoes can go right into the oven or pot.

Potluck surprise

Get a group of friends or relatives and pick a day or week of the month when everyone's cupboards are lean. Everyone brings an item to share for dinner together. Saves money on going out and you can have fun with all the surprises on the menu.

Poultry—baked chicken coating

Ingredients: 1 cup bread crumbs, 2 teaspoons celery salt, 1 teaspoon garlic powder, ½ teaspoon salt, ½ cup flour, 2 teaspoons poultry seasoning, 1 teaspoon paprika, ½ teaspoon pepper, 5 teaspoons onion powder, and ½ teaspoon cayenne pepper. Mix all ingredients, and store in a tightly closed container. Will keep for up to 4 months in the pantry. To use, dip chicken pieces in mixture of ½ cup milk and one beaten egg. Pour 1 cup coating mix into a resealable plastic bag, add chicken one piece at a time, and shake. Bake at 375°F for 1 hour or until juices run clear.

Poultry—basting with margarine or butter

For crisper skin on your turkey, prebaste it with margarine or butter. Avoid a mess by using a plastic sandwich bag as a mitt.

Poultry—basting with cheesecloth and butter

Turkey or chicken will almost baste itself if you cover it with a double layer of cheesecloth that's been soaked with butter. When the cheesecloth is removed at the end of the roasting time, the bird will be moist and golden brown. For a crisp, brown skin, remove the cheesecloth 30 minutes before the bird is done.

Poultry—chicken yield

How many chickens in a cup? A 3- to 4-pound broiler-fryer will yield about 3 to 4 cups of cooked chicken, after deboning. A ¾-pound skinned, deboned chicken breast will yield about 2 cups of cooked chicken.

Poultry—cutting with scissors

It is easier to cut cooked or raw poultry with scissors than with a knife, and it doesn't

shred the meat as much as a knife does.

Poultry—fried chicken crunchy coating

Crushed cereals like cornflakes, Rice Chex, Wheat Chex, or Corn Chex can be used as a coating for fried chicken instead of flour or as part of the flour mixture.

Poultry—fried chicken in cornstarch

For super crispy fried chicken, use half flour and half cornstarch instead of flour only. Season as usual and add ½ teaspoon baking powder.

Poultry—game hen stuffing

When stuffing a game hen, count on about 1 cup dressing per bird.

Poultry—mayo rubdown

Rubbing mayonnaise all over the skin produces a crisp, deep golden-brown roasted chicken or turkey. Note: Low-fat or nonfat mayonnaise will not produce satisfactory results.

Poultry—roasting chicken without the skin

To keep skinless chicken moist and ensure even browning during roasting, spray pieces with cooking spray, then season.

Poultry—skinning

To remove skin from uncooked poultry, grasp it with a paper towel and pull.

Poultry—turkey and fresh herbs

For a delicious and festive roast turkey, insert sprigs of fresh herbs in a single layer between the skin and breast meat, arranging them in a decorative pattern. Then roast the turkey as usual. The herbs will flavor the meat and show through the skin in an attractive design.

Poultry—turkey broth to moisten

To keep turkey moist and tender after it has been sliced,

drizzle turkey broth mixed with apple juice or cider over the meat.

Poultry—turkey soak

Cooked poultry, especially turkey, can dry out very quickly. To save your guests the ordeal of a dry meal, slice the turkey and arrange on a heat-proof platter. Prepare a sauce of half butter and half chicken broth. Pour it on the sliced bird, and let it stand in a 250°F oven for 10 minutes to soak up the juices.

Poultry—turkey sling

Before roasting your turkey, place a 3-inch strip of folded cheesecloth crosswise on the rack in the roasting pan. (Wash the cheesecloth first, to remove sizing.) Place the turkey on the cheesecloth in the pan, pulling the ends of the cloth up between the wings and the body. Roast as usual. To remove the turkey from the pan, lift it with the cloth, steadying the bird with a big spoon if necessary.

Poultry—turkey trussing

Out of string to truss the turkey? Dental floss works well. Use unflavored because minty-fresh and turkey don't go together very well.

Range top reflectors

Make sure the reflector pans beneath your stove's burners are bright and clean. Shiny reflector pans help focus heat rays on the bottoms of pots.

Recipes—clothes hanger holder

To keep recipe cards clean, clip them to a clothes hanger, the kind you use for skirts, and hang it from a cupboard doorknob.

Recipes—in photo albums

Keep recipes clean and easy to use by storing them in small photo albums. They stay open and lie flat, and the pages can be wiped off easily. They're especially great for recipes printed on thin paper from magazines and newspapers.

Recipes—on coated cards

A recipe written in ink on a card won't smear if you rub a piece of white paraffin (a candle will do) over the card to coat the surface.

Refrigerator access

A lazy Susan on a refrigerator shelf ensures easy access to items often forgotten in the back.

Rice—whitener

A teaspoon or two of lemon juice in the cooking water will make cooked rice whiter.

Rice—storage

Store white rice in an airtight container in a cool, dark place for up to 1 year; store brown rice for up to 6 months. In warm climates, or for longer storage, refrigerate or freeze rice.

Rice—using broth

When cooking rice, you can substitute chicken broth or

beef broth for part of the cooking water.

Ripening—faster

Tomatoes, avocados, peaches, and nectarines ripen faster when enclosed in a brown paper bag and kept at room temperature in a dark place for 2 to 3 days.

Roast—faster with the bone

A roast with the bone in will cook faster than a boneless roast. The bone carries the heat to the inside of the roast, so it cooks more quickly.

Roast—no sticking

To keep a rib roast or pot roast from sticking to the pot, place celery sticks on the bottom. This works like a rack to keep the meat up and out of the fat and the celery flavors the roast at the same time.

Salad—make ahead of time

Here's how to prepare a green salad ahead of time without the greens getting soggy. Place dressing in the bottom of the bowl. Add cucumbers and other ingredients that marinate well. Then add greens. Cover with a damp towel and refrigerate. Toss just before serving.

Salad greens—outside spinner

Wash salad greens thoroughly and load them into a clean, cotton pillowcase. Step outdoors. Grasp the end of the case in one hand, then spin the case in a windmill motion next to your body. In about 30 seconds—just before your arm gets tired—the greens will be dry and the pillowcase damp. Bonus: You got some exercise and your neighbors got some great entertainment. If you are not making a salad right away, just fold the damp pillowcase loosely, greens and all, and store in the refrigerator.

Salad greens—washing machine spinner

Wash fresh greens thoroughly and load them into a clean lingerie laundry bag or pillowcase. Close the bag securely and throw it in the empty washing machine. Run the spin cycle for 2 to 3 minutes. The case will be damp; the greens will be dry.

Sautéing—with less fat

For less fat in a meal, sauté meat and vegetables in fruit juice or Worcestershire sauce instead of oil.

Skewers—natural and safe

If you have an abundant supply of strong, woody rosemary sprigs, pull off the leaves and use the stems as skewers for tiny potatoes. Just make a hole in the potatoes with a real skewer first, thread the potatoes onto the rosemary stems, then grill. Never use twigs or sticks from bushes or trees for skewers. Many plants are toxic, and you could inadvertently poison your guests.

Soup—cover or not?

The general rule is that soup should be cooked in a covered pot to help retain nutrients and flavor. However, when a very thin soup needs to reduce, the pot should be only partially covered to allow for evaporation of the water and to intensify the flavors.

Soup—getting rid of fat in cans

Store cans of condensed soup upside down in the refrigerator for a while. The excess fat will rise and then stick in the bottom of the can when it is turned upright and opened. It's an easy way to get some of the fat out.

Soups and stew grease

To degrease cooled meat soups and stews, put a sheet of waxed paper or plastic wrap directly on top of the liquid before refrigerating. Before reheating, peel off the waxed paper and the fat will come with it.

Special occasion ingredients

Keep all the items you buy for special occasions, such as a

dinner party or holiday baking, in a grocery bag that you store in the refrigerator or the basement so you can just grab the bag when you're ready to start cooking.

Spices—in baby food jars

Attach tops of empty baby food jars to the underside of shelves. Fill the bottles with spices or small objects and screw them into their tops.

Spices—in drawers

Fill a drawer near your food preparation area with spices. This is an excellent way to use drawer space. Label the jar tops for easy identification.

Spices—in the summer

If the summer heat and high humidity sap your powdered spices and seasonings, store the closed bottles in the door of the freezer compartment or your refrigerator. They'll be handy and fresh when you need to use them.

Splatters—bowl in sink

When mixing batter, cookie dough, or pudding mix, place the bowl in the sink before mixing. No more messes on the wall or window.

Splatters—paper plate guard

To prevent splatters from an electric mixer, cut a hole in the middle of a paper plate and put the beaters through it while mixing.

Squash—scooping out

To remove cooked squash from its shell, use an ice cream scoop. No mess, no fuss!

Stew—salt substitute

If your soup or stew seems flat, don't automatically go for the salt. Add a little red wine vinegar or lemon juice instead.

Stew—tenderize meat, with wine corks

Here's a great way to tenderize stew meat: Add at least three wine corks to the pot. Corks release enzymes and reduce the cooking time by as much as half. Be sure to remove corks before serving!

Stew—tenderize meat, with black tea

Tea can be used as a meat tenderizer, particularly for stew meat. In a Dutch oven, sear chunks of stew meat in fat or oil until very well browned. Add 2 cups strong black tea, bring to a boil, then cover and simmer for 30 minutes. Add stock and continue to cook stew as usual with additional ingredients.

Stew—with pumpkin pieces

After carving jack-o'-lanterns, add the cut-out pumpkin pieces, with the outside shell removed, to beef and vegetable stews for a terrific fall flavor.

Sticky stuff—candied and dried fruit

It's much easier to chop candied or dried fruit if you freeze it first for 1 hour. And dip the knife into hot water before cutting.

Sticky stuff—dates and marshmallows

Before halving dates or marshmallows with your kitchen shears, coat them with cooking spray to help keep them goo-free.

Stock—freeze scraps to make later

Keep a container in the freezer specifically for the collection of fresh scraps, juices, and bones that might otherwise land in the garbage. When the supply becomes sufficient, make stock. If you don't need the stock immediately, freeze it.

Stock—substitute

One cup of beef or chicken stock can be replaced with 1 cup boiling water plus 1 bouillon cube or 1 envelope of instant broth granules.

Sugar—brown sugar, homemade

If you use brown sugar so infrequently that it turns rock-hard between uses, stop buying the stuff and make your own as needed. Measure out granulated sugar in the amount of brown sugar required. Stir in enough molasses to make either light or dark brown sugar. Color is the key.

Sugar—brown sugar, soften

Lumpy, old brown sugar can be made usable again by running it over a cheese grater, which softens the sugar.

Sugar—brown sugar, without lumps

Freezing brown and powdered sugars will prevent lumps.

Swizzle sticks—for chocolate drinks

Use a peppermint stick to stir hot chocolate and make a minty chocolate drink.

Swizzle sticks—for fruit kabobs

Thread raspberries or strawberries on a straw or swizzle stick to dress up summer drinks quickly.

Syrup—catching drips

Before placing an opened bottle of pancake syrup or honey on your pantry or kitchen cabinet shelf, place a cupcake baking cup under the bottle to catch the drips. This will keep surfaces clean.

Syrup—corn, homemade

Mix together 1 cup sugar and ¼ cup water.

Syrup—for pancakes

Mix ½ tablespoons cornstarch into 1 cup cold fruit juice. Heat to boiling, stirring constantly. Or stir a cup of corn syrup and 4 tablespoons of your favorite jam or preserves in a saucepan over low heat.

Tomatoes—from the can

When fresh tomatoes are high priced or poor quality, use canned tomatoes for salads. Drain well, and save the liquid to dilute condensed soup.

Tomatoes—puree

Purchase a huge can of tomato puree from your local grocery warehouse club. Divide it into small amounts by filling small resealable plastic bags and placing them in the freezer until needed. After one portion is thawed, add water to make it the consistency of tomato sauce, then add salt and spices for flavor. Tomato puree contains no additives or preservatives.

Tomatoes—slicing for sandwiches

Slice tomatoes from top (bud end) to bottom. They'll lose less juice, and sandwiches won't get so wet and soggy.

Vegetables—blanching green vegetables

Here's how to cook green vegetables to retain their color and crispness: Plunge them into boiling water for 2 to 3 minutes, then immediately turn them into a bowl of ice water. Let them stand in the water only until cool, then drain. The veggies can be reheated quickly by returning them to boiling water right before serving.

Vegetables—cooking with lemon rind

Brighten the flavor of frozen or canned peas, carrots, green beans, broccoli, or cauliflower by dropping a piece of lemon rind into the cooking water.

Vegetables—cooking with sugar

Add ½ to 1 teaspoon sugar to cooked vegetables such as carrots, corn, or peas. This reduces the starchy flavors and highlights natural sweetness.

Vegetables—keeping green

To keep green beans, fresh spinach, asparagus, and peas green, add a pinch of baking soda to the cooking water.

Vegetables—limp to crisp

If vegetables such as raw carrots and potatoes go limp, they'll regain much of their crisp texture if soaked in ice water for at least 1 hour.

Vegetables—root veggies, boiling

To cook root vegetables (such as potatoes, carrots, beets, and turnips), place them in cold water and bring the water to a boil. Add non-root vegetables (such as corn, peas, beans) to water that's already boiling.

Vegetables—root veggies, with leaves

If you buy root vegetables like beets and carrots with their leaves attached, remove them as soon as you get home. These greens leach the moisture from the vegetables.

Vinegar—strain

Strain fruit-flavored or herb vinegars through cheesecloth to remove the sediment.

Stretch the cheesecloth over the bottle top, then secure with a rubber band before pouring.

Vinegar—substitute

Use 2 teaspoons lemon juice for every teaspoon of vinegar needed.

Whipping cream— everything must be cold

Cream will whip more quickly and have greater volume if you first chill the cream, bowl, and beaters in the refrigerator. Chill the cream too.

Whipping cream— forget the blender

Don't try to beat cream or egg whites in a blender. It won't work because the action is different. Fold in flavorings after the cream is whipped.

132

5

Gifts

Basket—blueberry theme

Fill a blue basket with a variety of blueberry products such as jam, muffin and pancake mix, syrup, blueberry-scented candle, bath salts, room freshener, and blue notepaper. Or make strawberry, lavender, peppermint, or other flavored variations.

Basket—for someone who seems to have everything

Don't know what to give someone—especially a senior citizen—who seems to have everything they need and then some?

Put together a basket filled with consumable goodies such as teas, coffees, cookies and biscuits, chocolates, and special baked and canned delicacies. Think about enclosing some snack foods unavailable at most local grocery stores. These are especially appreciated.

Basket—for the breakfast lover

Fill a basket with homemade jelly, pancake mix, muffin mix, biscuit cutter, honey, cinnamon sugar, mugs, gourmet coffee, crepe pan, favorite recipes, and tea.

Basket—for the kitchen gourmet

Fill a basket with fresh herbs tied in a bundle, fresh spices, unique kitchen tools, recipe cards, and jars of gourmet mustards and salsas.

Basket—for the letter writer

Fill a basket with an assortment of greeting cards, stamped postcards, stationery, postage stamps, pens, pencils, return address labels, and a small calendar with clever notations of significant dates.

Basket—for the mother of preschoolers

Fill a basket with activities (books and games) for the kids, coping manuals, babysitting coupons for a night or weekend away from it all, bubble bath liquid, and romantic novels.

Basket—for a picnic lover

Fill a basket with a tablecloth, napkins, plastic plates, utensils, wineglasses, corkscrew, candleholders, candles, salt-and pepper shakers, plastic bags, and bug spray.

Basket—for a pizza lover

Fill a basket with checkered napkins, a pizza stone, pizza recipes, special flour, spices, a jar of pizza sauce, cheese, and a pizza cutter.

Bistro tray—from a cookie sheet

To turn a plain cookie sheet into a fancy bistro tray, glue on canceled foreign stamps and/or domestic commemorative stamps. Add some unique food labels or vintage recipe cards, if you can find them. Cover the entire tray, then apply several coats of polyurethane varnish.

Books—new and used

Books make great gifts. But don't limit yourself to shopping in the big bookstore chains. Secondhand bookstores are less expensive and often have out-of-print titles that can't be found in the big chains. Also, these stores may sell old prints or maps that you could frame for your family members or friends.

Boxes—as part of the gift

Cover gift boxes with appliqués, needlework, quilts, or embroidery with the recipient's name. These kinds of containers are especially appreciated because they become part of the gift itself. Wrap the box and the lid separately, and the gift box becomes an heirloom to be cherished for years to come.

Breakfast in bed

Purchase or find a wicker bed tray or other container to fill with fixings for breakfast in bed—muffin mix, jams or jellies, coffee beans, and a copy of a newspaper like the *New York Times*.

Calendar—with family photos

To make a calendar with special meaning for a family member, start with a fun wall calendar from your local bank or another business. Select twelve family photos, preferably ones commemorating such special occasions as birthdays, a christening, or wedding. Make a color photocopy of each photo, the same size as the illustrations on the calendar. Paste the photos on the month in which the pictured occasion took place.

Calendar—with kids' artwork

For all parents who collect hundreds of artwork papers every school year and hate to throw them out, here's an excellent gift suggestion: Select twelve of the most precious pieces of your child's artwork. You can either create your own calendars by making color photocopies and putting together calendars, or scanning the artwork and using websites like www.Snapfish.com or www.shutterfly.com. This really makes a practical gift that is even more special because of its sentiment. Grandparents, godparents, aunts, and uncles are always delighted; the child is ecstatic with the gift, and the cost is minimal. Finish off the calendar by attaching the child's photograph and autograph.

Cards sent to hospitals

You never know for sure when someone will be going home from the hospital. So if you send get-well cards to friends and family members who are hospitalized, instead of placing your return address in the upper left-hand corner, write the patient's home address there. Then if the card must be returned to sender from the hospital, the patient will still get it.

Chauffer or errand service

Set aside 2 hours a week to serve as chauffeur, escort, or errand runner for a special person who doesn't drive or doesn't have time to get to the library, grocery store, pharmacy, dry cleaner, post office.

Christmas—Angel Tree program

Participate in an Angel Tree program at a local mall or church. Many charitable organizations decorate a tree with slips of paper, each listing the name, age, sex, and wish list of an underprivileged child. You select a name, purchase the gift, and bring it back to the tree to be distributed in time for Christmas.

Christmas—cards as gifts

Make your holiday card the gift. Include a family picture, poem, story, original song, or painting—anything of lasting significance.

Christmas—cookie-of-the-month club

Start your own Cookie-of-the-Month club (or Quarter for the less ambitious). Bake one dozen cookies to include in the holiday gift, along with a card announcing that your recipient will receive a dozen each month all year long. This can be one of those gifts that's easy to give but more difficult when it comes to following through, so give cautiously.

Christmas—easy bath salts for kids to make

Kids can make bath salts as presents for a favorite teacher, a grandparent, or friend. Mix 3 cups Epsom salts, 1 tablespoon glycerin (from the drugstore), a few drops of food coloring, and a bit of cologne for scent. Put the salts in a sealed container, such as a small jar with a screw top, and paint a holiday message on the lid.

Christmas—gift tags from Christmas cards

Use Christmas cards from previous years to make gift tags. One side has the design; the other side is blank. The same idea works nicely for children's birthday gift tags, using greeting cards recycled from previous occasions.

Christmas—inexpensive wrapping paper

Instead of buying expensive holiday wrapping paper, purchase a large roll of white butcher paper and a bolt of red plaid ribbon from a florist supply store.

Christmas—multiple gifts from one candy recipe batch

A single recipe can be divided into several gifts. Simply arrange pieces of fudge or toffee on pretty Christmas plates (paper is fine), and wrap them in plastic wrap topped off with a pretty ribbon or embellishment.

Christmas—Santa Sacks

Make a Santa Sack for each of your children, or all members of the family for that matter. Sew together two large panels of Christmas fabric (approximately 1 yard each) on three sides, add a drawstring to the top, and then attach a name tag. Drop in the gifts from Santa, and place the sack under the tree. You can explain that the elves are much too tired for wrapping after making all those toys. These Santa Sacks can be reused every year, which will create a new family tradition.

137

Claim check—for large or late items

If the gift is too cumbersome to wrap, didn't show up in time, or didn't quite get finished, wrap a smaller box containing some kind of clue about the gift to come, plus a claim check for redeeming it.

Coupons—IOU gifts

IOU gifts are often the most valuable and appreciated of all. Make up a coupon that is redeemable for something you do well, and tuck it inside a meaningful card. Examples: shuttle service to and from an airport, babysitting the kids so Mom and Dad can have a day of fun, a day of general repair. Give what you do best, and you will have given the best gift of all.

Coupons—IOU gifts and more suggestions

Here are some IOU gift suggestions . . . but the possibilities are endless!

- Two hours of silver polishing

- Six 1-hour computer lessons (great for a teen to give to a parent or grandparent)
- The making and delivery of a dessert the next time you have company (24-hour notice, please)
- One pair of mittens—you pick the yarn
- One complete car wash, wax, and thorough cleaning inside and out
- Total care and appropriate spoiling of your children for a whole weekend so you can get away
- One I'll-Teach-for-a-Day coupon to a homeschool mom, with a lesson centered around your special talent or expertise

Coupons—organized as gifts

Don't know what to do with all the coupons you can't use? Clip neatly and categorize them with gifts in mind. For instance, for the next baby shower, make up a clever holder full of coupons for diapers, baby food, and other items for the expectant mom.

Provide a great coupon assort-ment for the newly married couple to assist them in stock-ing their pantry. Have a friend or relative with a pet? Enclose some good coupons for pet food or supplies in their next birthday card. Always make sure the coupons haven't expired.

Decorating gifts—candy topper

Tie a couple of pieces of a child's favorite candy (wrapped in colored plastic wrap) to the outside of a gift.

Decorating gifts—sponge painting

Snip sponges into fun shapes, then dab in poster paint and press in a decorative pat-tern on the insides of those brown paper grocery bags, which you've cut open to use as wrapping paper. This also works well for decorating cards and invitations.

Donate—old eyeglasses

Your old eyeglasses will put the world in focus for a person living in a developing country. Don't throw away someone's chance for a clearer tomorrow. Contact a local club to find a drop-off point. Or you can ship eyeglasses to Lions Clubs International Headquarters, 300 West 22nd Street, Oak Brook, IL 60523. Read more about the need for eyeglasses at www.LionsClubs.org.

Donate—to food banks

When a local merchant has a two-for-one special on canned or other nonperishable foods you intend to purchase, keep one of the items for yourself and give the free one to a food bank or charitable orga-nization. Passing this kind of savings to someone else in need is an effective way you can give back even if you are on a limited income.

Flowers—forcing narcissus paperwhites bulbs

Force bulbs so you can give a beautiful blooming plant of narcissus paperwhites. Fill a shallow container with rocks or decorative pebbles and add water until it reaches just below the surface. Set the bulbs on the rocks, adding more to hold the bulbs upright. Set the container next to a window away from direct heat. As the leaves appear, rotate the container so the bulbs will grow evenly. The flowers will bloom in 4 to 6 weeks and will last 2 weeks at room temperature. (The bulbs can't be repotted.)

Flowers—order directly and locally

Before you call a local florist or a national floral-delivery company to arrange for an out-of-area delivery, think about this: These services end up involving all kinds of middlemen, which means extra fees and surcharges for phone calls and delivery. They usually have minimums of about $40, and you're never sure what your recipient will get because you don't speak with the person who will actually create the arrangement. You can skip past all of these extra people by making one call to a florist in the neighborhood where your recipient lives. You'll get three times the bouquet and service for the money by dealing directly.

Food—presented in special containers

Present your edibles in special containers: an interesting bottle, a nostalgic candy box, a pretty jar.

Food—repackaged in unique containers

Even if you don't cook or bake, you can still give wonderful, inexpensive gifts of food. Buy quantities of nuts, fancy cookies, fresh coffee blends, candies, and dried fruits. Repackage these into small, unique containers you've been collecting all year.

Food—snacks in inexpensive containers

Snack foods can be presented in a small tin or Chinese takeout container. If you don't tell, no one will have to know just how easy and inexpensive these delicious gifts really are.

Food—sweets from your kitchen

- **Cinnamon crunch.** Ingredients: ⅓ cup granulated white sugar, 1¼ teaspoon cinnamon, ¼ cup (4 tablespoons) butter or margarine, 4 cups Corn Chex, Rice Chex, or Crispix cereal or 3 cups bran or Wheat Chex. Mix sugar and cinnamon, and set aside. Melt butter or margarine in large skillet. Add cereal and mix well. Heat over medium heat, stirring until coated (5 to 6 minutes). Sprinkle half of the sugar mixture over the cereal, and continue stirring until well coated. Sprinkle with remaining sugar mixture and heat several more minutes. Spread on a layer of paper towels to cool. Yield: 3 to 4 cups. This recipe multiplies well if you have a large enough skillet.
- **Holiday fudge.** Combine in a large mixing bowl and set aside: 1 6-ounce package semisweet chocolate morsels, 1 cup chopped walnuts, 1 teaspoon vanilla, ½ cup (1 stick) butter or margarine. Combine in a saucepan: 12 large marshmallows, 2 cups granulated sugar, 1 6-ounce can evaporated milk. Bring ingredients in saucepan to a boil, stirring constantly. Boil exactly 6 minutes (time this carefully) and remove from stove. Immediately pour this hot mixture over ingredients in the bowl. Stir to combine, and then beat by hand for exactly 20 minutes. (I cheat and use my electric mixer at the lowest setting.) Pour into a lightly buttered 8-inch square glass dish. Sprinkle a few ground nuts on top and refrigerate to harden. Cut into squares.
- **Homemade English toffee.** Ingredients: 2 cups sliced almonds, 2 cups milk chocolate morsels, 1 cup butter chilled and cut into bits, 1½ cups light brown sugar, firmly

packed. Preheat oven to 325°F. Spread almonds on baking sheet and toast in preheated oven, stirring occasionally until lightly browned, about 5 minutes. Allow to cool (and I mean very cool—even cold so the nuts don't melt the chocolate). Chop the chocolate morsels by hand or in a food processor, pulsing on and off until they are coarse. Transfer to a medium-size mixing bowl. In the same processor bowl, coarsely chop the toasted almonds. Add to chocolate morsels. Toss to combine. Spread half of mixture evenly over bottom of a well-greased 13- by 9-inch baking pan. In a heavy medium saucepan, bring butter and brown sugar to a boil, stirring constantly over medium heat. Cook 5 to 7 minutes, or until syrup is light golden-brown and just reaches the hard-crack stage (300°F on a candy thermometer). At that point, a bit of syrup when dropped into a bowl of ice water should separate into hard, brittle threads. Pour hot syrup evenly over nut mixture. Top with remaining nut mixture, smoothing and pressing down gently with a spatula. Refrigerate until toffee is set and chocolate is firm, about 1½ hours. Cut into squares or break into irregularly shaped pieces. Store in a tightly covered container in the refrigerator for up to 2 weeks. Yield: 20 large pieces.

Food—with your own label

Personalize your food gift with your own label: Millie's Chutney or Minerva's Cookies sounds very special.

Food—with your own label and more

Personalize food gifts with your own decorated label, for example, "Marilyn's Chutney" or "Cathy's Cookies." Attach your recipe and other instructions to the gift with ribbon, raffia, or tasseled cord. Add a spoon or spreader for chutneys or flavored butters.

Gadgets and widgets— from hardware and home improvement stores

Check out hardware and home-improvement stores for all kinds of gadgets and widgets. For the home chef try an 18-inch length of $1\frac{7}{8}$-inch wooden dowel for a professional-style rolling pin, a large unglazed terra-cotta tile for a pizza and baking stone, and a new $1\frac{1}{2}$-inch paintbrush for a pastry brush. A collection of screws, cup hooks, small tools, and so on all packed in a small toolbox is perfect for the homeowner. Stroll the aisles and you'll get all kinds of great ideas, including unusual wrapping materials such as wire and painter's tape. Let your mind wander. You'll be quite a hit.

Gift for a college student— product refunds

When you have everything you need to qualify for a product

refund or rebate, fill out the coupon with the name and address of your favorite college student. The refund check will arrive in the student's mailbox, made payable to him or her. Who doesn't love a little surprise now and again?

Gift for a college student or single—laundry time

Make or purchase an oversize laundry bag with the recipient's name on the front. Fill with detergent, fabric softener, bleach, and a roll of quarters. Add a couple of magazines for the laundry-room wait. Great for a college student or single.

Gift for a garden or plant lover—watering can

Make a beautiful watering can for a plant or garden lover on your gift list. Either buy a new watering can or give an old one a face-lift. You'll need some self-adhesive-backed shelf paper or covering and a pair of scissors. Cut the covering into a strip to wrap around the handle, another for the spout, then larger pieces for the can itself. Peel away the backing and carefully wrap the can completely. The end result: a watering can that's pretty enough to be used as a vase.

Gift for the homebound—birdbath

Brighten the life of a person who's confined to home. Set a low, shallow pedestal birdbath near a window. Plant a ring of flowers around the base, and change it seasonally. In winter, a wreath of holly with red berries would be like a living Christmas card. Give the new bird-watcher a wild-bird guide, notebook, and pen for recording sightings.

Gift for the homebound—DVDs

When a friend or family member is recuperating from an extensive illness, more flowers and balloons may not truly reflect your concern. Instead, rent several DVDs to cheer the patient. Just don't forget to return them in a day or two.

Gift for a hostess—herb bouquet or special herb salad dressing

A bunch of herbs tied together with a ribbon makes a welcome gift for any hostess. Or fill a slender bottle with cider vinegar and your favorite herbs. In a few weeks you'll have a flavored vinegar to enhance anyone's salad dressings or marinades.

Gift for a kid—beginner stamp collector kits

The United States Postal Service offers beginner stamp-collector kits for children. They are very inexpensive and geared for the young philatelist. Visit your local post office or go to www.USPS.com and click on "Shop" for more information.

Gift for a kid—take your pick!

- Give books, books on tape, and download-able books, which are always welcome gifts for kids of all ages. Ask a librarian or an elementary school teacher for recommendations.

- Give a unique book-of-the-month. Either write and design the book yourself or buy an inexpensive one that reflects the appropriate holiday or season or child's interest.

- Cover a shoe box with pretty wrapping paper inside and out for a young girl who loves to play dress-up. Fill it with inexpensive makeup and costume jewelry.

- Find an old suitcase and fill it with secondhand dress-up clothes such as shawls, dresses, hats of all kinds, veils, pocketbooks, and high heels.

- Make a homemade balance beam with proper supports for an aspiring gymnast. Make sure you start with sturdy material and sand and finish the surface so it is very smooth.

- Give a small child an appliance box with doors and windows cut out and decorated to look like a house, castle, office, or school. This idea is in accordance with the rule that says the bigger and more expensive the toy, the more likely the child will want to play with the box it came in.

- Start a child on a life of savings with a piggy bank and starter money.

- Make a simplified map of the town in which the child lives. Highlight the location of significant landmarks: child's school, place of worship, parents' workplaces, the zoo, and library.

- Buy or make a bird feeder with a supply of birdseed.

- Piggyback on a proven hit with coupons. Kids love to create little books with "coupons" in them for their siblings, good for things like one night's dish washing or a kiss and hug. Parents can give reverse coupons to their kids also—good for exemptions from making their beds, setting the table, and so on.

- Purchase a ticket to a favorite sporting event

or for a ride on a real train (accompanied by an adult, of course).

- Give an embroidery piece, thread, needles, and hoop, and a certificate for lessons from the giver.
- Buy a magazine subscription.
- Make a one-of-a-kind puzzle. Mount an enlarged photo of yourself or some family occasion onto a piece of foam board (available at stationery or art supply store). Cover the photo with a piece of tracing paper and lightly draw a jigsaw pattern, making as many or few pieces as would be appropriate for the age of the recipient. Using a utility knife, carefully cut through the tissue paper, photo, and board along the puzzle lines. Separate the pieces and place in a gift box.
- Make a preschooler puzzle. Lay a strip of masking tape on a table, sticky side up. Press about 10 Popsicle sticks (or wooden tongue depressors) side by side, evenly across the tape. Draw a picture and write the child's name on the sticks. Then remove the tape and shuffle the sticks to make a great puzzle.

- Surprise a budding artist with an artist's box, starting with a clear storage box (12 quarts is a good size). Write the child's name on it and fill it with plain white paper, construction paper, crayons, colored pencils, glue, tape, a ruler, plastic stencils, and a pencil sharpener.
- If parents approve, help a child adopt a kitten or puppy from the local animal shelter. Include the necessary equipment, such as a food dish, litter box and litter, toy, and a collar.
- Begin a collection of Christmas tree ornaments for a child. Then add to it every year.

Gift for a mom—a dinner each month

Offer a piping hot and ready-to-eat casserole to an

overworked mom once a month. Ask her to specify her busiest evening.

Gift for a new mom—beauty makeover and babysitting

Make an appointment for a beauty makeover for a new mother (haircut, facial, and manicure) at a local beauty college. Volunteer to take care of the baby.

Gift for a new neighbor— welcome map

When newcomers arrive in your neighborhood, welcome them with a useful gift: a neighborhood map. Include such hot spots as the dry cleaner, schools, churches, grocery stores, and so on. It's helpful to see the location of places in relation to the others.

Gift for a parent— overnight child care

Offer to keep children overnight once a month or once a quarter to give parents a break. Arrange to pick them up midafternoon so their parents can prepare for the evening together.

Gift for a senior—take your pick!

- Give date-a-month coupons to elderly parents. A man setting aside time to spend with his mother or an adult daughter taking her dad out once a month is a lovely gesture. Some months your evening together might include a movie, other times just dinner and time to talk and listen.

- Donate your services as chauffeur to an otherwise homebound senior or offer to do their food or gift shopping.

- Take Grandma or Grandpa on a "movie date" at their house. Rent a movie or take one out of the library. Take along drinks and popcorn. Great gift for a teen to give.

- Give a book on CD to a senior citizen whose eyes are failing. Wrap with a small headset and CD player. Lend them your CDs and drive them to the library for more.

- Present a pretty box with a variety of different-occasion greeting cards, a pen, and a roll of stamps for someone who is housebound.

- Make a photo album for grandparents, filled with pictures of baby's typical day—morning bath, breakfast, taking a walk, playing, greeting Daddy, being rocked to sleep. Update photos throughout the year as baby grows and the days are more eventful. A movie with baby as the star is also a terrific gift.

Gift for a teacher—photo and story

Help your child create a "teacher feature" for a Christmas or end-of-the-year gift. Paste a drawing or a photo of the teacher on a large sheet of paper, then have the child write a lively newspaper-type action story about the teacher, complete with photo caption.

Gift for a teenager—take your pick!

- Create Night-on-the-Town certificates for fast food, a movie, and ice cream or coffee.

- Make an appointment for a beauty makeover at a local beauty college. Prices are typically inexpensive and all work done by students is highly supervised. Stick with temporary work such as a hairstyle, manicure, pedicure, and facial and stay away from a haircut, perm, and hair color.

- Give a calligraphy pen and instruction book.

- Put together an address book with names, phone numbers, addresses, birthdays, and anniversary dates of family and friends.

- Get parental permission first, then give a pretty drawstring pouch to the soon-to-be-teen filled with lip gloss, clear nail polish, bubble bath liquid, dusting powder, and light scent.

Gift for a woman— emergency workplace kit

Give a working woman's emergency kit: a small Swiss Army knife, a good lint roller (a pet-hair remover from a pet store is the best bargain), an assortment of safety pins, needles, thread, Kiwi Shine Wipes (instant shoe shines), double-stick tape to fix hems in a hurry, small scissors, a glue stick (better than clear nail polish for arresting a hosiery run), antistatic spray, several pencil erasers (the tiny eraser end from a pencil makes a dandy temporary replacement for the back piece of a pierced earring). Put everything in a small, compact container such as a pretty box or fabric bag.

Gift for the whole family— take your pick!

- Subscription to the family's hometown newspaper
- Two decks of cards and a book of card games
- The hottest new board game on the market
- A 1,000-piece jigsaw puzzle
- Croquet set
- Badminton set
- Gift certificate to a local pizza parlor
- Subscription to a magazine that reflects the family's interests—travel or skiing—or to *National Geographic*, *Smithsonian*, *Air and Space*.
- Food dehydrator
- Ice cream maker
- Binoculars
- Charitable donation made in the name of the family
- DVD movie
- Computer game
- Bird feeder and supply of birdseed

Gift for you and your spouse—"everything" gift

Buy an "everything" present for the two of you that covers the year's worth of gifts (birthday, anniversary, Christmas, and so on). Not only does this free your time, but you're not purchasing items you neither need nor want just to be buying a gift. And the fringe benefit? The money you'll then have available at

Christmastime and throughout the year can be used to help those less fortunate, pay down debt, or save for retirement, just to name a few opportunities.

Gift list—save with business card records

Avoid returning unwanted gifts (or pretending you like them) from your spouse or immediate family members by keeping an ongoing record of the things you would like, along with the specific details. Through the year as you see items of particular interest, pick up the store's business card and write the details on the back of it: red cardigan sweater, brass buttons, wool blend, size 8, $49.98. These cards serve as a practical gift list to make gift giving a positive experience for both the giver and receiver.

Gift stash—for hurried and free gifting

Create a gift box in a closet or cupboard into which you can put any free samples you receive, door prizes you win, and gifts you don't like but somebody else might. Always be on the lookout for things to add to your box. When you need a present in a hurry or don't have the cash to buy one, go directly to the gift box, and chances are you'll find just the right thing.

Heirlooms

Perhaps you have something that a friend or relative has long admired and enjoyed. If you're tired of dusting it, give it as a gift for a special occasion. Be careful though. Not everyone is sure to cherish your possessions the way you think they should, so be confident you have a perfect match before you wrap up that Ming vase or special possession.

Mug—drink mixes and a book

Fill a nice or comical mug with flavored coffee, tea, or hot chocolate mix. Wrap it along with a suitable book.

Mug—with candy

A simple mug or teacup and saucer (either antique or new) can be a wonderful gift when filled with special candies. Wrap in a piece of clear cellophane gift paper gathered at the top and tied with a lavish bow.

Pet care

Offer to care for a pet during a vacation.

Photos—framed copies

Before spending a lot of money for enlargements and reprints of color photographs, consider making color photocopies at your local stationery or quick-print shop. For example, an 8- by 10-inch color copy enlargement costs less than the price of a color-print enlargement. The paper is not as sturdy, but once a photocopy is framed or mounted, it is very difficult to detect any difference. Framed photos make great gifts.

Photos—vintage

Everyone has a box or two of old family photographs. For a special vintage touch, choose a black-and-white photo that has a special meaning for the recipient. You can frame it in its original form or have a photocopy enlargement made at the quick-print shop. An inexpensive black or silver frame will turn this treasure into an heirloom.

Recipe—book

Foolproof recipes are always welcome gifts. Make a pretty little notebook and copy (by hand or photocopy) twenty of your favorite recipes. Add a personal note, if you like.

Recipe—favorite family dessert

Write down a favorite family dessert recipe and place it along with all the required ingredients in an appropriate new baking or serving dish. Wrap everything and top with a big bow.

Shipping and packaging—addressing

Enclose a piece of paper inside the box on which you've written the address of the recipient and yours as the return. Use a waterproof marker if you write the recipient's name directly on the box. And the US Postal Service says address labels should be legible from 30 inches away. That's about an arm's length.

Shipping and packaging—antistatic for Styrofoam "peanuts"

If you use Styrofoam "peanuts" as a packing cushion, first spritz them with an antistatic spray.

Shipping and packaging—diapers for baby gift padding

If you need to send a fragile gift for the new baby who lives far away, pack the breakable object in a box of disposable diapers. The soft padding will keep the gift well protected, the packing material will be as usable as the gift, and you won't have to worry about finding a suitable box.

Shipping and packaging—mark it fragile

Mark "Fragile" in three different places on packages that contain breakables: above the address, below the postage, and on the reverse side.

Shipping and packaging—padded envelopes

Make your own padded envelopes. Start with several layers of paper grocery bags and cut to the size you need. Sew three sides of the bag on your sewing machine using a zigzag or decorative stitch. Once stitched, trim close to the stitching. Address, fill, and then sew the fourth side closed and trim to match. You can make great-looking parcels in just minutes that will please your recipient, and you'll save a lot of money.

Shipping and packaging—paper tubes

Cut empty wrapping-paper tubes to line a box you are mailing. They cushion the contents, but add little weight.

Shipping and packaging— plastic bags

Surround dishes, glassware, and other fragile items that you're sending as gifts with plastic air pillows by filling resealable plastic bags with air and sealing.

Shipping and packaging—recyclables

When you need to pad a package, recycle wherever possible. Instead of bubble wrap and Styrofoam, use newspaper. If someone you know has a paper shredder, ask for a bagful of shreddings. Or use stale air-popped (not buttered) popcorn and include a note instructing the recipient to leave the popcorn out for the birds or other wildlife.

Shopping to save—at art supply and stationery stores

Search art supply stores for stationery items (mine sells lovely writing papers by the sheet, ounce, or pound—and matching envelopes), imported brushes ideal for makeup, fine writing instruments at reasonable prices, photo albums, and all kinds of wonderful portfolios. Chalk, crayons, pads of modeling clay, and packets of construction paper make terrific gifts for kids who will always be attracted to the simple things.

Shopping to save—at office supply stores

Search office supply stores for memo books, calendars, pens, and pencils. An appreciated gift for anyone would be a nice box with a lid (or any other kind of unique container, even a wastebasket) full of those items you need around the house but can never seem to locate: colored paper clips, staples, clear tape, labels, write-on-anything pen (Sharpie is the best), coin wrappers, index cards, and yellow sticky notes, or any combination thereof. Great idea: yellow pads or any kind of writing paper and a personalized rubber stamp. Rubber stamps are fairly cheap and can be ordered from an office supply store.

153

Shopping to save—in unique places

Unique places for shopping for gifts include military surplus outlets, marine supply stores, garden centers, health food stores, damaged-freight outlets, restaurant supply stores, antique stores, and museum and gallery gift shops.

Shopping to save—on make-your-own stationery supplies

You can avoid spending if you get into the habit of making your own cards, stationery, postcards, gift bags, and so on. You can purchase paper and envelopes in bulk, then use the paper cutter at the local copy shop to cut it to the sizes you need. With a few carefully chosen rubber stamps and colored markers, anyone can make beautiful and unique cards and stationery for personal use or to give as gifts. Use postcards whenever possible. This way you'll not only save the cost of the envelope, but you'll save on postage too.

Subscription—large-print newspaper

A great gift for a senior or someone with impaired vision is a subscription to the *New York Times* large-print edition. This edition is published weekly and provides a summary of the week's news. Cost is up to $3.30 per week, depending on the method of shipping. To order go to http://homedelivery.nytimes.com and click on "Select a Subscription."

Subscription—magazine

Go to a magazine stand and select a magazine you know someone would enjoy, maybe because of a hobby or a secret desire to sail or skydive. Wrap the current copy of the magazine with a note saying, "Look forward to this all next year!" Be sure to mail in the subscription card with a check.

Wood for sharing

Share a cord of firewood with a neighbor. Announce the gift in a card tucked between several logs wrapped with a wide ribbon. If possible, stack the wood between your properties.

Wrapping—box lids

If you use a plain-colored box, wrap only the lid. It saves paper and makes the gift easier to open. If the box is not plain colored, wrap the box and lid separately. It's easier to open and allows the box to be reused.

Wrapping—construction paper decorating

Wrap a gift in plain white paper and decorate with curved shapes cut from red, yellow, and blue scraps of construction paper or other colored paper. Use a glue stick to attach them.

Wrapping—large baby shower gift

Wrap a large baby shower present in a crib sheet or baby blanket, and secure with

colorful diaper pins. Attach a rattle too.

Wrapping—organization, flower shipping boxes

Ask a nearby flower shop for their shipping boxes from long-stem roses. The boxes are the perfect length to store wrapping paper rolls, and you will be recycling boxes that usually get broken down and discarded.

Wrapping—organization, paper caddy

Store rolls of wrapping paper in the legs of old pantyhose. This will prevent your paper from getting wrinkled and torn between uses, and you won't run the risk of ruining any of the paper by having to tape the rolls.

Wrapping—organization, paper-towel holder

Store rolls of tape and ribbon on a paper-towel holder.

Wrapping—paper tablecloth for oversize gifts

Don't waste time and expensive wrapping paper trying to cover an oversize package with regular-size wrapping paper. Instead, buy a colorful paper tablecloth. It works great, and you'll have enough paper to wrap a refrigerator—depending of course on the size of the refrigerator—for just a couple of bucks.

Wrapping—paper, brown

Brown paper is not just for mailing packages. Dressed up with stickers, doilies, fancy ribbon, and such, it's a wonderfully inexpensive way to wrap gifts. You can either purchase craft paper in a roll or recycle brown grocery bags. Cut them open and lightly iron them on the nonprinted side. (A very light misting with spray starch will help iron out stubborn wrinkles and folds.)

Wrapping—paper, cutting

A coupon-clipping tool works beautifully to cut wrapping paper quickly.

Wrapping—paper, kids' artwork

Save your kids' drawings and use them to wrap gifts. Tape several together if the package is large. This will especially be a big hit with grandparents.

Wrapping—paper, matched with the gift and recipient

Find paper that's appropriate for the gift or recipient. For example, wrap a cookbook with pages from a beautiful food magazine or use sheet music for a music lover's package.

Wrapping—paper, removing creases and wrinkles

To remove creases from folded or wrinkled wrapping paper, lightly press them out with your iron set on the lowest setting. Don't steam the paper. For persistent wrinkles, spray the wrong side lightly with spray starch. (Not recommended for waxed or foil papers.)

Wrapping—ribbon alternatives

Visit a decorator fabric shop, upholstery supply store, or

sewing supply store and look for braids, cords, tiebacks, fringes, and tassels to use instead of ribbon. Bolt ends are often sold as remnants at just a fraction of their retail price.

Wrapping—ribbon from paper

Cut strips of wrapping paper and curl it with the edge of a scissors blade the same way you would curling ribbon. This requires a gentle touch so the paper ribbon does not tear, but the final effect is really nice.

Wrapping—with garbage bag

If time is short or gift wrapping is especially difficult, use a white plastic garbage bag (two, if they are too transparent) tied with a great big bow. With presents, as with people, it's what's inside that counts!

Wrapping—with glue stick

Instead of using clear tape to wrap gifts, keep a glue stick handy for sealing packages. Costs less, dries fast, and

looks great for professional "no-tape" ends and seams.

Wrapping—with handkerchief

Wrap odd-shaped small packages in a handkerchief.

Wrapping—with lunch bags

Purchase pastel and brightly colored paper lunch bags to decorate and use for gift bags. Wrap the gift in tissue and place it in the bag. Fold the top of the bag down and punch two holes through the layers. Thread a ribbon through the holes, then tie a bow or add curly ribbon.

Wrapping—with scarf

Place a gift box diagonally on a square scarf and tie opposite corners together at the top. Tie again with gold cord or ribbon.

Wrapping—with shoe boxes

Turn ordinary shoe boxes into colorful gift boxes. Use a utility knife to cut simple designs like stars on the sides and top of the box. Paint the box with brightly colored acrylic paint. Wrap the gift in tissue paper of a contrasting color, and let it show through the cutouts.

Wrapping—with spray paint on carton

If the gift is really large, don't waste yards and yards of pricey paper. Just spray-paint the carton and add a bow.

Wrapping—with unique materials suited to the gift

Use a road map to wrap up a gift for the traveler. Wrap a woman's present in a piece of fabric or a pretty scarf. Tape together several weeks' worth of newspaper crossword puzzles for that crossword aficionado in your life. The Sunday comics make great wrapping, especially for kids and teenagers.

6

Health and Beauty

Bandage care

To keep a finger bandage dry and secure, pull a small balloon over it before you bathe or wash dishes.

Calcium absorption

Don't drink sodas together with calcium-rich foods or supplements. If your soft drink contains phosphoric acid (and most do), it will block absorption of calcium into the bloodstream.

Canker sores—prevention

Prevent canker sores by adding 4 tablespoons of plain yogurt to your diet each day.

Canker sores—remedy

Try applying a wet, black tea bag to a nasty canker sore. The tannin acts as an astringent and will relieve the pain and promote healing.

Exercise—golf club burn

A round of golf burns well over 1,000 calories if you

walk and push the clubs on a wheeled cart for 18 holes. That's the equivalent of running 6 or 7 miles, depending how long it takes you to get those 18 holes in!

Exercise—health club memberships

Try the club before you join. Most offer several free visits or short, low-cost trial memberships. Join with a group of five or more friends, and at some clubs you'll save as much as 35 percent. Pay a year's dues in advance to save up to 20 percent (make sure the club has a reasonable likelihood of still being in business a year later). Ask about new member perquisites, such as a free session with a personal trainer. Also, if you need to take a long-term break for travel or other reasons, ask the club to freeze your membership and start it up when you return.

Exercise—strengthen your immunity

Want to beat the common cold? A brisk walk or exercise at a moderate level has been associated with strengthening the immune system. On the other hand, extremely strenuous exercise can actually lower immunity to colds and flu. So, take a walk but take it easy.

Exercise—winter motivation

Stay motivated to stick to your exercise program during the winter months: Put on your swimsuit and stand in front of the mirror once each month.

Eyes—emergency eyeglass repair

Here's an emergency repair for the missing screw in your eyeglasses: Insert a wooden toothpick through the hole in the hinge. Break off both ends of the toothpick, and you're ready to go.

Foot massager

Give your tired feet a mini massage by rolling them back and forth over an ice-cold soda or juice can.

Hair—barrette cleaning

Use isopropyl rubbing alcohol to remove hair spray buildup from barrettes. Some mega-hold hair sprays cause metal barrettes to tarnish. To avoid, allow hair spray to dry before putting in barrettes.

Hair—buildup remover

To remove a buildup of minerals, conditioners, sprays, mousses, and gels, here's a cheap alternative one professional hairdresser we know uses on her own hair: Wash hair with a gentle shampoo, rinse in cool water, and towel dry. Saturate hair with apple cider vinegar (not white vinegar, it's too harsh). Wrap hair in a plastic cap or plastic wrap, and heat with a blow dryer for 10 to 15 minutes. Rinse hair thoroughly and shampoo again.

Hair—coloring not just for men

A woman we know colors her gray hair with a popular product, Just for Men. It produces identical results, costs half as much, and lasts twice as long as a similar product sold for women.

Hair—condition with mayo

Slather mayonnaise on your hair. Wrap your hair in plastic wrap or a small plastic bag, and heat with a hair dryer. Leave on for 30 minutes. Shampoo and rinse well.

Hair—control with lemon and lime juices

The combination of lemon, which closes the hair cuticle, and lime, which is slightly emollient, helps break up static electricity to end flyaway hair. Mix together 1 teaspoon lemon juice, ½ teaspoon lime juice, and 1 cup water. Pour into a plastic spray bottle. Spritz on clean, damp hair. Do not rinse. Style as usual. Keeps for up to 5 days in the refrigerator.

Hair—dye alternative

As a color pickup for drab brown hair, rinse it with

strong, stale coffee. Then rinse with cool water.

Hair—residue remover

Mix 1 tablespoon baking soda with the amount of shampoo you use for one hair washing, and shampoo your hair with the mixture. This removes residue buildup and leaves hair shiny and bouncy. Repeat about once a month. This is a cheap substitute for very expensive commercial products that do the same thing.

Hair—shampoo, half-price

Read the instructions on most shampoo bottles: Apply, lather, rinse, repeat. Don't "repeat." Your shampoo will last twice as long.

Hair—shampoo, inexpensive

Don't be a shampoo snob. In a *Consumer Reports* test of 132 brand-name shampoos, the lowly cheap brands from the supermarket rated just as high as the pricey salon brands.

Hair—spray buildup remover, control dandruff

To remove stubborn hair spray buildup and to control dandruff, mix one package lemon Kool-Aid with 2 quarts warm water (don't add sugar). Wet your hair and pour on the mixture. Work well into your hair, leave on for several minutes, and follow with regular shampooing. The citric acid is the key ingredient.

Hair—spray can clogs

Ordinary rubbing alcohol will unclog the spray nozzle of a hair spray container that even hot water hasn't cleared. Just dip the nozzle into the rubbing alcohol, let it sit for a few minutes, wipe off, and spray.

Haircuts—for kids

Learn to cut your kids' hair. Ask an expert to teach you or get a step-by-step DVD or video download. It's not difficult but learn well. We don't want any goofy-looking kids out there.

Heating pad

Here's how to make an effective, inexpensive heating pad. Take a clean sock (a man's tube sock with no holes works best). Fill halfway with about 5 cups of uncooked white rice. Tie a knot in the top. Warm in a microwave on high at 30-second intervals until desired heat is reached. (Caution: Rice can burn, so watch it carefully.) This heating device will conform well to any body part and can be reused many times. Just make sure to keep it dry.

Hot-water bottle

Fill a 2-liter soda bottle about 6 inches from the top with hot water. Screw the top on tightly. Wrap the bottle in a towel, and snuggle up with your very wonderful, yet cheap hot-water bottle. A smaller bottle with just warm water works well for an older child.

Ice pack, with rice

Instead of paying big bucks for fancy ice packs, do this:

Freeze raw rice in a freezer-weight resealable plastic bag. To use, wrap it in paper towels. It conforms well to most body parts, such as backs and sprained extremities, and stays cold for at least 45 minutes. Use gallon-size bags for backs and legs, pint-size and snack-size for boo-boos. Double bag to discourage accidents, and don't leave packs unattended with children.

Ice pack, with rubbing alcohol

Make your own flexible ice packs. Pour ¾ cup water and ¼ cup rubbing alcohol into a resealable plastic bag, and close. Put the bag into another bag, seal, and freeze. You will have a slushy bag of ice whenever needed for sprains, headaches, or other ailments because alcohol doesn't freeze. Label clearly.

Jewelry—allergic to earrings

If earrings leave your lobes sore, chances are you are allergic to nickel silver, which is an alloy in many types of jewelry. Apply a coating of clear nail polish to the earring posts and backs or clasps, and other parts that come in contact with your skin. Only surgical steel and platinum are free of nickel silver; even 14- and 18-karat gold earrings can contain some of this alloy, to which many people are highly sensitive. You will need to reapply the polish after several wearings.

Makeup—blush color

To find the right shade of blush, check the color of your skin after exercising and try to match that color. Blush should add a healthy glow, not introduce a foreign color.

Makeup—economy line

If you love a particular high-priced cosmetic line, ask for the name of their economy line. For example, Lancôme (available in department stores) also produces the L'Oreal line (available in drugstores). Research cosmetic lines online or call the customer service department of your favorite line to inquire.

Makeup—eye makeup remover

Use a no-tear brand of baby shampoo to remove eye makeup. Ophthalmologists encourage contact lens wearers to do this to reduce protein buildup on their lenses. Apply with a cotton swab in a brushing motion while holding your eyelid taut. Rinse thoroughly.

Makeup—lipstick palette

Don't toss the last ½ inch of lipstick in the tube. Do what professional makeup artists do. Using an orange stick or other clean implement, transfer what's left of the lipstick from the bottom of the tube to one section of a compartmentalized medication container (the kind with a little space for each day of the week, available at drugstores for less than $2). Use a lipstick brush to apply. As you accumulate colors, fill each of the compartments, and soon you will have a portable lipstick palette.

Makeup—mascara caution

Don't use waterproof mascara on a regular basis. It's hard on the eyelashes. But water-soluble types really smudge, especially in sweltering heat. Here's a reasonable compromise: Use a waterproof version only on lower lashes, because that's what usually smudges.

Makeup—curling first, then mascara

Use your eyelash curler before applying mascara. Otherwise, lashes could stick to the curler and break off.

Makeup—pencils

Long lip liner and eyeliner pencils are awkward to use and don't fit into small handbags. Solution: Break the pencil in half; sharpen both pieces. Now you have two manageable pencils for the price of one.

Makeup—remove with baby wipes

Use baby wipes to remove makeup. They're made for

sensitive skin and won't cause dryness or irritation.

Makeup—test samples

Before purchasing a new cosmetic or skin-care product at the counter in a department store, request a sample you can test for a few days before making a decision.

Medical facilities—ask questions before you choose

Inquire about specific hospital fees before you are admitted. Fees do vary considerably from one hospital to the next. Why pay for the availability of kidney machines and heart-transplant teams if you are having knee reconstruction? While you're in an inquiring mode, ask what rating the hospital received the last time it was examined for state accreditation.

Medical facilities—avoid Fridays

Friday is the most expensive day to check into the hospital. Hospital labs usually close for the weekend, and you may waste 2½ days and a lot of money just waiting for the labs to open on Monday. If you must be admitted for surgery, insist that you go in the day of the surgery. An early admittance will run up your bill and is usually for the convenience of the staff, not the patient.

Medical facilities—cash discounts

Whenever undergoing a dental or medical procedure for which you will eventually pay, inquire about a cash discount. Do not be timid about expecting as much as a 25 percent discount when you pay by check or cash at the time the procedure is done. Never be afraid to ask.

Medical facilities—examine bills

Carefully examine hospital bills even if you have full insurance coverage. If you go in for a knee reconstruction and are billed for infant nursery time, put up a fuss. A good consumer scrutinizes every charge. Report all discrepancies to the hospital, physician, and insurance company.

Medicines—aspirin miracle

Research suggests that one aspirin tablet, at a cost of 1 cent, taken every other day helps reduce risk of heart attack, certain kinds of strokes, cancer of the gastrointestinal tract, and possibly Alzheimer's disease, among other serious ailments. (See your doctor before beginning such an aspirin regimen.)

Medicines—call around for prices

Most pharmacies will quote prices over the phone. Call around until you find the best price. Or go online and compare prices at sites like Drugstore.com and TheOnline Drugstore.com. You won't believe how the prices will vary.

Medicines—doctor samples

Every doctor's office is flooded with all kinds of expensive prescription samples, also known as "stock bottles."

When required to take a medication, be sure to ask your doctor if he or she might have samples for you to try. Asking for sufficient samples to make sure the medication is right for you is especially wise, particularly if you might be allergic to it. Don't hesitate to ask again every time you go to the office. Doctors can also write a prescription for a stock bottle to be filled at the pharmacy for patients unable to afford the prescription.

Medicines—measure correctly for kids

Don't use tableware spoons when giving medicine to a child. Teaspoons and tablespoons in your silverware drawer may not hold the correct amount of liquid. A tableware spoon that's off by even 1 milliliter (0.0338 fluid ounce) could mean you're giving the child 20 percent more—or less—of the recommended dose of medicine. Use a proper measuring device, either one provided with the medicine or purchased separately, such as a measuring spoon, syringe, or oral dropper. Ask the pharmacist for a complimentary calibrated measuring device for dispensing liquid medications.

Medicines—numb your kids' taste buds

You may be able to make unpleasant-tasting medicine a bit more palatable for your children. Have them suck on a small piece of ice until their tongues are numb (this will probably occur once the ice melts), then give the medicine. Follow with more ice. The cold dulls the taste buds just long enough to render the medication tasteless.

Medicines—prescription and over-the-counter equivalents

Ask for generic prescriptions, which cost less yet by law must have the same chemical makeup and potency as brand-name drugs. Also, buy generic nonprescription pain medication. You can purchase ibuprofen (the active ingredient in Advil) for less than half the cost of name brand. The same goes for Tylenol. It is acetaminophen. Consult your pharmacist when in doubt.

Medicines—split those tablets

If your doctor prescribes, for example, 50 milligram (mg) tablets, ask about changing that to the 100 mg version so you can break the tablets in half to accomplish the 50 mg dosage. If this is possible, you will save a lot of money, because the difference in price between 100 mg and 50 mg will usually be negligible. You can purchase a tablet splitter for just a few dollars at any pharmacy. Caution: Some pills' delivery systems may be affected by splitting them in half. Check with your doctor or pharmacist first.

Midday pick-me-up

Use a cosmetic sponge to soak up some of your favorite after-bath splash. Put the sponge in a small, resealable plastic bag, and toss it into your purse or briefcase. Now you can freshen up before an important meeting or at the end of a long, tiring day.

Nails—broken

Tea bag paper can mend a broken nail instantly and easily. Cut the paper to fit the nail, then coat with clear nail polish.

Nails—buffing

Buff your fingernails rather than polish them, because it's quicker and cheaper. Apply a bit of petroleum jelly as a buffing compound, which will also soften cuticles.

Nails—polish bottle trick

Keep the top of a nail polish bottle from sticking shut by putting cooking spray on a cotton swab and wiping it around the neck of the bottle before closing it.

Nails—polish fix

Smudge your polish while giving yourself a manicure? Not a

problem. Do what the professionals do. Put a drop of polish remover on the pad of your thumb, and rub it lightly over the smudge until the spot is smooth. Reapply polish.

Nails—polish prep

Scrub your fingernails with white vinegar, rinse, and dry. Now apply your nail polish. It will adhere better and last longer.

Nails—polish rolling

Don't shake nail polish before using. Shaking whips bubbles into the product, which will cause chipping later. Instead, turn the bottle upside down and gently roll it between your palms.

Perfume—overdose fix

When you overdo it with your perfume, saturate a cotton ball with rubbing alcohol and wipe it where you put the perfume. The alcohol will cut the scent without altering it.

Perfume and cologne—refrigerate

Refrigerate your cologne, and it can last for as long as 2 years. If a fragrance is exposed to heat, air, or sunlight, it immediately begins to change.

Remedies—bee sting pain

To soothe bee stings, immediately wet the spot and cover with salt.

Remedies—chicken pox itching

If your children get chicken pox, and an oatmeal bath is in order, save a lot of money by making your own oatmeal bath product that is similar to Aveeno. Take old-fashioned rolled oats and a clean, old knee-high nylon. Place a handful of the oats into the stocking, tie a knot in the end, and let it sit in the bathwater. Squish the bag of oatmeal to activate it more quickly.

Remedies—hiccups

Eating a teaspoonful of sugar gets rid of hiccups in a flash.

Remedies—insect bite itching

Make a paste of baking soda and water and rub it on insect bites to relieve the itch.

Remedies—splinter removal, sunburn relief spray

To reduce pain while you are trying to remove a splinter, spray the area with a dab of sunburn relief spray. The topical anesthetic will numb the area and reduce the pain.

Remedies—splinter removal, teething gel or ice cube

Before removing a splinter from your child's finger, apply some teething gel to the area around the splinter and wait a few seconds for the skin to get numb. Gently remove the splinter with tweezers. If you don't have teething gel available, put an ice cube on the splinter. It will briefly numb the area and allow the splinter to be removed. Follow with a first-aid antibiotic ointment such as Neosporin.

Skin—astringent

Instead of purchasing an expensive brand-name astringent to add to your skin-care regimen, use witch hazel, an old standby recommended by skin professionals for decades. It's available over the counter at drugstores and performs as well as any brand of astringent, no matter how expensive.

Skin—baby oil before sunless tanning lotion

Smooth baby oil onto your skin, and allow it to penetrate before applying sunless tanning lotion to achieve a more even, lighter tanning effect, especially on elbows and feet.

Skin—calloused feet

Crush 6 aspirin tablets and mix them with a tablespoon each of water and lemon juice; work into a paste. Apply the paste to calloused spots or dry skin on your feet. Put each foot in a plastic bag and wrap with a warm towel. Sit for 10 minutes with your wrapped feet elevated. Caution: If you are diabetic or have circulatory problems, special care of your feet is essential. Get a doctor's guidance for all questions regarding foot health.

Skin—deodorant alternative

Rubbing alcohol is an effective deodorant for both underarms and feet, because it kills odor-causing bacteria, dries quickly, and becomes odorless. Apply in a fine mist from a spray bottle or with a cotton ball. Spritz your feet and the insides of your shoes with rubbing alcohol in a spray bottle to refresh and eliminate foot odors.

Skin—elbows

Elbows get lots of wear and tear, and they really show it. Here's the perfect way to give them the attention they deserve: Cut a lemon in half and rest an elbow in each part for at least 10 minutes. (Sure, you'll look ridiculous and that's why you're not going to do this in the middle of an important meeting or while sitting in church.) The lemon juice will remove the stains that make elbows look dirty. Jump in the shower, do the regular stuff, and then use those lemon halves for a final body scrub. Towel dry, follow with lotion, and you'll think you've just visited an expensive spa.

Skin—exfoliate

Mix ½ to ⅔ cup granulated sugar with the juice of one lemon to form a paste. While showering, invigorate your skin with the paste. Rub heels and elbows with the inside of the lemon.

Skin—facial mask

Use milk of magnesia for a soothing facial mask. Spread it on your face, being careful to stay away from your eye area. Leave on for 30 minutes, rinse with warm water, then pat dry.

Skin—facial scrub

Baking soda mixed with a tiny bit of water makes an excellent facial scrub.

Skin—herbal bath

There's nothing like a relaxing, naturally scented bath to revive a tired mind and body. Fill a piece of cheesecloth with fresh rosemary, tie it up with string, hang the bag from the faucet, and run the water over it into the tub.

Skin—inexpensive care products

A reader asked a doctor friend what he learned during his dermatology rotation concerning expensive skin- and facial-cleansing products. He informed her that the best products are not the most expensive. Dermatologists recommend Dove or Lever 2000 for cleansing and Lubriderm lotion for moisturizing. Both products are sold over the counter at drugstores and most grocery stores.

Skin—instant face-lift

Here's how to give yourself an instant "face-lift" and beauty treatment: Mix 1 teaspoon each of baking soda and olive oil to form a paste. Gently massage it into your skin, rinse well, then pat dry.

Skin—itching, acne medication

One of the most soothing topical treatments for bug bites, poison ivy, rashes, and the like is your teen's over-the-counter acne medication. It will dry the infected area and reduce itching.

Skin—itching, baking soda bath

Dissolve ½ cup baking soda in bathwater to soothe skin irritations from sunburn, insect bites, poison ivy, hives, chicken pox, and itchy rashes.

Skin—moisturize hands while you work

Keep a pump dispenser of hand cream in the kitchen. When you're washing dishes, apply the cream before putting on rubber gloves, and you'll get a quick hand-softening treatment as you work.

Skin—moisturize with petroleum jelly

Apply a small amount of petroleum jelly to your skin nightly. It's a natural moisturizer and is especially effective on extra-dry areas, such as elbows, heels, and knees.

Skin—on tired feet

Freshen tired feet and soften skin easily and quickly: Add 4 tablespoons of baking soda to 1 quart of warm water. Pour into a large container, and soak your feet for 10 minutes.

Skin—scrubber

Put leftover pieces of soap into a mesh produce bag to make an effective scrubber for feet, elbows, and hands. If the bag is fairly large, fold or cut it down to a delicate, dignified size.

Skin—sunscreen roll on

Sunscreen won't spill and will be much easier to apply if it's transferred to a roll-on deodorant bottle. Squeeze the neck of an empty bottle with pliers so the ball pops out. (Watch out because it can really fly.) Clean the bottle, pour in the sunscreen, and pop the ball back in.

Teeth—baking soda for toothpaste

An inexpensive toothpaste substitute that dentists endorse is plain old baking soda. Wet the brush and dab it in the powder. The cost is a fraction of what you'll pay for toothpaste, and if you can handle the taste, or lack thereof, you'll save a lot of money. Check with your dentist.

Teeth—dental schools

College and university dental hygiene programs are excellent places to get your teeth cleaned. Do an internet search to determine if your local university or community college has a dental school facility.

Teeth—orthodontic rubber bands

Anyone wearing orthodontic appliances with replaceable

rubber bands should get a fresh supply of bands often, especially following an illness. When reaching into the bag of bands, the wearer will contaminate the supply, which could mean recurrences of the illness.

Teeth—prevent dental problems

Finish meals and snacks by rinsing your mouth with water. It's fast, it's easy, it washes out substantial quantities of bacteria and food, and it's free.

Teeth—tea for fluoride

If your water lacks fluoride, drink teas. Black tea delivers more fluoride than fluorinated water.

Teeth—toothbrushes, hold pencil-style

Brandish your toothbrush with a pencil-style grip rather than a racket-style grip. Foreign research shows that the pencil grip gets teeth as clean but causes less gum damage.

Apparently this grip promotes a vibrating motion more than a stroking one.

Teeth—toothbrushes, replace or disinfect

When family members have been ill with colds, flu, and other illnesses, make sure you replace toothbrushes often, or thoroughly disinfect them. Toothbrush germs can be destroyed by storing the brush, bristles down, in a glass of antiseptic mouthwash. Replace the mouthwash every few days.

Toiletries and grooming— beauty schools

Take advantage of the inexpensive beauty services available at a local cosmetology school. Students are carefully supervised, conscientious, and eager to please. Be nice but firm about your expectations and desires. If you're a bit nervous, try a low-risk procedure, such as a wash-and-style or a manicure. The students who will be graduating soon are very qualified. The savings are fantastic.

Basically you'll pay only for the materials, not labor.

Toiletries and grooming—buy unscented in men's department

Buy men's toiletries if possible when it comes to such things as unscented deodorant, shaving foam, and hair coloring. Products specifically for men are significantly cheaper ounce for ounce. Go figure.

Toiletries and grooming—keep wipes moist

Keep towelettes and baby wipes moist by storing the container upside down.

Toiletries and grooming—pain-free eyebrow plucking

Put some over-the-counter oral anesthetic solution on your eyebrows 5 minutes before you pluck them. This will prevent the pain.

Toiletries and grooming—razor sharp

If you carefully dry your razor after each use, it will stay sharp much longer than if you simply rinse and leave it.

Walker caddy

Tie the handles of a plastic grocery bag to the arms of a walker. The bag will remain open and can be used to carry everything from eyeglasses to tissues to medication.

7

Holidays and Special Occasions

Baby shower—food gifts

Here's an idea for a unique way to welcome the baby and help the new parents in a big way. Instead of the usual baby gifts, invite the guests to bring a prepared dish, casserole, dessert, and so on, completely prepared and frozen for the guest of honor's freezer. Request that each dish have the recipe attached to it, which can be put into a small photo album during the shower. You'll be able to present the expectant parents with a unique cookbook along with a freezer full of food. It's fun and inexpensive and will give your friends precious time to spend with the new baby instead of in the kitchen.

Birthdays—cake candleholders

Use creamy mint patties as birthday cake candleholders. Just make a hole in the center of each patty and fit the candles in. Place candles and patty on top of the cake.

Birthdays—cake writing like a pro

Use a toothpick to sketch letters onto a frosted cake before you try to write "Happy Birthday" or another message with icing. If you make a mistake, smooth the top and start again. When you're happy with your lettering, simply pipe icing along the sketched lines.

Birthdays—child's dress-up party

Collect dress-up clothes, old shoes, sweaters, and jewelry from friends, relatives, thrift shops, and garage sales. Launder and disinfect everything. Let the girls get all gussied up as they play dress-up at the birthday party. Follow with a fashion show just before refreshments. Allow the little guests to take their outfits home as party favors.

Birthdays—party favor photos

Take a picture of your birthday party child with each guest, holding the gift that guest brought. Have double prints made, one for your child and one to include with a thank-you note. This way, you have a record of who gave what, and each guest has a memento of the party.

Birthdays—party snack shack

Set up a snack stand with hot dogs, popcorn, soda, peanuts, and candy. Give each guest play money to buy treats.

Birthdays—teen girl pampering

For a teenage girl's birthday, make up a fancy coupon redeemable by her and her best friend for an afternoon of pampering at the local beauty school. The coupon can include a haircut or trim, braiding, hot-oil treatment for hands, pedicure, manicure, and so on. Total cost for an afternoon of pampering will be very affordable and should be paid for ahead of time.

Birthdays—teen party

Take the birthday party group to the mall, armed with a

camera. The assignment: The group sticks together, and each party guest "shops" until they find the gift they'd buy for the birthday girl or boy if money were no problem. But instead of purchasing it, the group snaps a photo of the gift, the "giver," and the guest of honor. When every gift has been properly photographed, continue the party with pizza, soda, ice cream, and other planned events. Download the photos to your computer and assemble a photo album on one of the many photo websites.

Christmas—adopt a needy family

Adopt a needy family for the holidays. Make a special shopping trip or have a gift-making session when each member of your family buys or creates a present for the person in the adopted family who is closest in age.

Christmas—after, catch the sales for every holiday

Be sure to take advantage of post-Christmas sales. While you're picking up deeply discounted wrapping paper and other items, look for red candies and paper goods that will work for Valentine's Day, green items to help celebrate St. Patrick's Day, and red, white, and blue items for Independence Day.

Christmas—after, donate living tree

Buy a living tree to use for the holidays, and then donate it to a local park or forest once the Christmas season is over. First call your state or local parks and forestry commission to find out where the tree could be planted after the holidays. Other organizations that might enjoy a new tree to add to their landscape are libraries, churches, and schools.

Christmas—after, make list of holiday supplies

After the holidays, make a list of the items you won't need to buy next year, such as bows, wrapping paper, ornament hooks, greeting cards, and the like. Attach it to your

Christmas card list. The reminder is then easy to find once the holiday season rolls around.

Christmas—after, make pine needle pillow

After the tree is undecorated and ready to be thrown out, strip off the needles while wearing gloves. Then put the needles into a pillow slip and cover it with a pretty pillow cover. The scent will last all year and will keep the spirit and anticipation of Christmas alive.

Christmas—after, make plans for next year

Get the family together during the week after Christmas. Review your holiday plan and the goals you met. Ask everyone what they liked best and least about the holidays and what they would like to do differently next year. Take notes.

Christmas—after, postpone party for a week later

Rather than overschedule, host a party the week after Christmas when the house still looks great and you don't feel as rushed.

Christmas—after, recycle bows and make like new

Don't throw away those wrinkled gift bows. You can reuse them by placing the bows in the dryer along with a damp washcloth. Set the machine on "fluff" cycle for 2 minutes. The bows will come out looking like new.

Christmas—after, recycle cards for charity

Once the season is over, don't throw out the cards you received. If you don't plan to use them yourself to make postcards or gift tags, send them to St. Jude's Ranch for Children, a residence for abused children. The kids at St. Jude's make new cards out of your old ones and sell the cards to support the ranch. For more information or to place an order for cards, call 877-977-7572. Send your cards to St. Jude's Ranch for Children,

Recycled Card Program, 100 St. Jude's Street, Boulder City, Nevada 89005.

Christmas—after, recycle packaging for packing

As you unwrap gifts this year, save discarded paper, ribbon, and packing material to use as packing material next year.

Christmas—after, save piece of tree for Yule log

Save a piece of the Christmas tree trunk to burn as next year's Yule log. Tell the family the legend behind the Yule log. Long ago, people brought home the largest log they could find, usually ash in England and birch in Scotland. They decorated it with a sprig of holly, placed it in the fireplace, and lit it with a piece of the log saved from the previous year. It was hoped that it would burn throughout the 12 days of Christmas. In many households, the lady of the house kept the kindling piece under her pillow. It was thought this

provided year-round protection against fire. If you don't have a fireplace, bring home a festive cake called a Buche de Noel that's in the shape of a Yule log. Share the cake on Christmas Eve with the whole family—or take on a challenge and make a Buche de Noel yourself!

Christmas—after, Twelfth Night celebration

Give your family a post-Christmas treat by celebrating Twelfth Night on January 6. Also known as the Feast of Epiphany, this Victorian tradition celebrates the day when the three wise men arrived in Bethlehem with their gifts for the Christ child. Children are given three gifts from the Magi before a gala dinner. Afterward, a Twelfth Night cake decorated with figures of kings is served. The child who receives the piece containing the silver coin baked into the cake becomes "king" or "queen" of the family for the whole year!

Christmas—attend a church recital

Go to a recital at a local church. Many choirs perform Handel's *Messiah* and other seasonal favorites.

Christmas—attend a parade

Take the family to see a small-town Christmas parade.

Christmas—attend a school pageant

Attend a Christmas pageant at your local elementary school, even if you do not have children in the school.

Christmas—caroling

Caroling spreads cheer throughout your neighborhood. Take a thermos of hot cocoa to keep everyone warm.

Christmas—Christmas Eve

Before going to bed on Christmas Eve, turn out all the lights and light lots of candles. Read Luke 2 from the Bible to your family, then join hands and sing "Silent Night."

Christmas—decorate a senior's home

Brighten an elderly neighbor's day by helping her decorate her home for the upcoming holiday.

Christmas—decorate children's rooms

Instead of decorating the outside of your home, decorate each child's room and get them excited about the holidays. Help your children make red and green paper chains from construction paper to hang all over the room. Not only is this activity less time-consuming than attempting a big exterior display, it may also establish a special tradition your children won't forget. Plus you won't have to say "time for bed!" twice when your child can nestle among the enchanting lights of her very own bedside boughs.

Christmas—decorating, apples and evergreens

Pile red apples on a bed of evergreens, and tuck in some tiny Christmas balls.

Christmas—decorating, banister

Wind strands of tiny white Christmas lights and greens around and up the banister. Add large plaid bows.

Christmas—decorating, bedroom doors

Wrap your child's bedroom door with gift paper to transform it into a giant package.

Christmas—decorating, candles

Using candles is a simple and natural way to decorate for Christmas. If all you have are pine-tree greenery and candles, you have all you need. Use candles lavishly, and light them as often as possible. Nothing will turn your home into a softer, more beautiful place faster than candles. Just make sure you never leave candles lit while unattended!

Christmas—decorating, candy

Fill a glass container with holiday candy and top with a lid or a circle of gift wrapping or foil. Tie with a ribbon and set on a table.

Christmas—decorating, car

Attach a wreath and big red bow to the front grill of the family car. Hang a fun ornament from the rearview mirror.

Christmas—decorating, card display on window

Display all your holiday cards so they add to your home's decor. Cut a piece of string just a bit longer than the length of a front window and attach the string to each side at the top of the window. Hang the cards from the string by folding them over the string so the front of the cards face out. Once full, the string will drape ever so slightly to give a beautiful valance effect across the top of the window.

Christmas—decorating, card display with ribbon streamers

Tape, tie, or staple Christmas cards to ribbon streamers to hang for display.

Christmas—decorating, centerpiece with ivy

Create a simple centerpiece. Trail greens or ivy down the center of the table, then add fresh fruit or holly for color and craft-store pearls for sparkle.

Christmas—decorating, centerpiece with ornaments

For an instant table dress-up, heap shiny Christmas balls of all sizes in an elegant glass bowl. Place near candles and allow the light to bounce off all the shiny surfaces of the centerpiece.

Christmas—decorating, centerpieces with filled bowls

Use crystal or cut-glass bowls of different sizes to make a holiday arrangement. Fill one bowl with Christmas balls—either place them upside down to hide the hangers, or tie a small bow on each. (This is a great way to use damaged ornaments.) In another bowl, combine fresh fruit with ev-ergreens. In a third bowl, add holiday-scented handmade or purchased potpourri. Place votive candles in the smaller bowls.

Christmas—decorating, cranberry balls

Cover small Styrofoam balls with white glue and attach fresh cranberries. Allow to dry, attach a ribbon, and hang the balls on the tree.

Christmas—decorating, cranberry garlands

String garlands of cranberries on thin wire or heavy nylon thread or fishing line, because the berries can become quite heavy.

Christmas—decorating, doghouse

Put Christmas lights and a small wreath on the doghouse.

Christmas—decorating, doormats

Paint a bright red "bow" on a doormat. Add a painted tag with your family's name.

Christmas—decorating, doors

Decorate doors with Christmas trees cut from white foam-core board. Pin, tape, or glue on bright ornaments and garlands of beads.

Christmas—decorating, doorway

Drape a long rope of greens (tied together with narrow-gauge wire) over the front door. Attach a red velvet or satin bow in the middle and weave matching ribbon through the garland like a streamer. As a finishing touch, place a poinsettia plant on each side of the doorway.

Christmas—decorating, gift tree

Create a gift tree. You'll need 30 to 50 (depending on the size of your tree) small boxes of all sizes and shapes (empty Jell-O boxes are perfect), wrapping paper, and coordinating curling ribbon. Wrap each box with paper and curling ribbon. Tie the "gifts" to the tree, starting with the small ones at the top and ending with the larger

ones toward the bottom. You can use different patterns of wrapping paper or wrap every gift in the same paper and ribbon. This is especially dramatic with gold or silver foil packages and small white lights.

Christmas—decorating, golden accents

Gold, one of the gifts the wise men carried to Bethlehem, is a symbol of generosity. For a truly glittering Christmas, recycle miniature pumpkins and squash from Halloween and Thanksgiving by spraying them with gold paint. Place them throughout the house or use them in centerpieces, garlands, and topiaries. Gild walnuts, pinecones, bay leaves, dried flowers, apples, pomegranates, pineapples, lemons, and grapes. Wear gloves, a dust mask, and glasses or goggles when spraying.

Christmas—decorating, greenery kept fresh

Evergreen garlands and wreaths generally last about

3 weeks. To keep them fresh, mist with water regularly.

Christmas—decorating, guest bath

Decorate the guest bath by wrapping a tissue box like a gift.

Christmas—decorating, guests welcome

Keep one room sparkling clean just for visitors, and don't let anyone in it before you have guests.

Christmas—decorating, luminaries in bags

Line your walkways, drive, or other areas on your property with luminaries made from small paper bags filled with 2 inches of sand and a votive candle in the center.

Christmas—decorating, luminaries in punched tin

Make punched-tin luminaries that can be kept from year to year. Rinse out an opened tin can and pinch all rough edges flat and smooth. Fill the can with water and freeze. When the ice is solid, remove the can from the freezer. Using a permanent marker, draw designs around the sides of the can, making sure the design does not come within 1-inch of the bottom. Place the can on its side on a towel so it won't slip. With a nail and hammer, punch holes along the design lines you've drawn. Leave about ½ inch or so between each punch. Then allow the ice to melt and drain. Place a votive candle in each can and line your sidewalk. Light your luminaries every night during the holidays.

Christmas—decorating, mantel

To make a gorgeous, yet inexpensive, holiday display for your fireplace mantel, lay sprays of evergreens across the top, thread a string of white lights on green wire through them, and nestle some of your collectibles, ornaments, or pinecones amid the greens.

Christmas—decorating, miniature live tree

Decorate a tiny live tree with fruit ornaments and ribbon, and set it on the kitchen table or countertop.

Christmas—decorating, mirrors for an extra glow

Hang extra mirrors around the house during the holidays to add to the glow and multiply the special effects of your decorations.

Christmas—decorating, mirrors with tinsel garland

Wrap a tinsel garland around the bedroom or bathroom mirror.

Christmas—decorating, mistletoe

Hang mistletoe in every single door of your house.

Christmas—decorating, outdoor broom people

If you're fresh out of oversize Santas for the yard and have no snow for snowmen, make a family of "broom people" to warm the hearts of passersby. Stick the broom handles into the lawn. Cut white circles for eyes from felt or white cardboard, and draw black dots in the center for the pupils. Glue these "eyes" to the bristle part of the brooms. Top with real hats and earmuffs; tie scarves around the handles. Let your imagination go wild, not your pocketbook.

Christmas—decorating, outdoor light ties

Tie outdoor lights to trees and posts with strips cut from the legs of old pantyhose.

Christmas—decorating, photo display

Display some great family Christmas pictures from years past in a special photo album or in a location where your family and guests can enjoy them.

Christmas—decorating, pinecones

Fill a basket with large pinecones interspersed with

clusters of delicate baby's breath, then thread tiny white lights throughout, hiding the wires under the pinecones.

Christmas—decorating, place mats

Make special holiday place mats with your kids. All you need is a box of crayons and light-colored vinyl place mats. Help the kids draw holiday designs and write their names on the place mats. After the holidays, simply wipe the mats clean with a good all-purpose liquid cleaner. Some traces of color may remain, so make sure you don't use your very best place mats.

Christmas—decorating, plants with twinkle lights

Put white twinkle lights on your large houseplants.

Christmas—decorating, refurbish what you have

Instead of buying new decorations, have your kids help refurbish old ones. Give life to a wreath by adding fresh ribbon. Glue glitter on faded ornaments. Or go back to old standards like popcorn-and-cranberry garlands and construction-paper chains.

Christmas—decorating, serving tray decoupage

Decoupage a serving tray with last year's Christmas cards (they're probably sitting somewhere in a drawer), and set it on your coffee table.

Christmas—decorating, snowflake made from a berry basket

Cut the bottom out of a plastic berry basket, trim into the shape of a snowflake, coat with glue, and dip into glitter.

Christmas—decorating, soaps

Make holiday soaps with appropriately shaped candy molds. Melt a bar of soap in the top of a double boiler (20 to 30 minutes at medium heat) until it's soft enough to pack into the molds. Spoon soap into molds, freeze for 20 minutes, and pop out.

Christmas—decorating, Spanish moss

Cover the mantel or a wide windowsill with a bed of Spanish moss. Tuck in ivy, holly, pinecones, and a few gilded nuts and fruit.

Christmas—decorating, tablecloth

Sew small brass jingle bells along the hem of a tablecloth.

Christmas—decorating, table napkins

Dress up your napkins by tying each with a ribbon and a small bell.

Christmas—decorating, window art

Let your kids turn one of your windows into a holiday canvas. Mix powdered tempera paints (available at an art supply store or crafts store) with clear dish-washing liquid until they acquire the creamy consistency of house paint. If you have premixed tempera paints, stir in a bit of the dish soap. Use individual plastic containers (margarine tubs are perfect) to mix and separate the colors. Cover the window sash with masking tape and spread newspaper on the surrounding floor. Then let the window artists take it away. If you are using a large picture window, help the kids design a mural. Dad and Mom can get into the act by painting the hard-to-reach sky. Windows with individual panes offer a great opportunity for a Christmas montage of a snowflake, a bell, candy cane, Christmas tree—one design per pane. When it's dry, the paint will come off easily—just wipe with a dry paper towel.

Christmas—decorating, window frames

Surround window frames with greens and strings of outdoor lights.

Christmas—decorating, wreath from backyard greenery

Make a wreath from greenery you find in your own backyard and let the children decorate it.

Christmas—decorating, wreath with gumdrops

Make a gumdrop wreath. Either buy a Styrofoam wreath or cut one out of a piece of Styrofoam. Use toothpicks or stiff wire to attach red, white, and green gumdrops to the wreath, or use multicolor ones to resemble Christmas tree lights. Top off the wreath with a big bow.

Christmas—decorating, wreath with popcorn and cranberries

Bend medium-gauge wire into the shape of a heart or wreath, then thread with popcorn or cranberries. Top with a bow.

Christmas—digital year in review

A digital record makes a very special holiday greeting or gift. Put together a movie with highlights of the past year. You might include birthday celebrations, summer vacation footage, sporting events, a school play, and other special moments from throughout the year. A festive way to end the video might be to gather the family and sing, "We Wish You a Merry Christmas." A movie like this will bring joy to faraway family members long after Christmas has come and gone.

Christmas—dinner by candlelight

Buy a big candle for the dinner table. Light it every night at dinner during the holidays.

Christmas—dinner by tree light

One night a week during your family's holiday season, eat dinner by the light of the Christmas tree.

Christmas—do for others

Actions speak louder than words, so go caroling at a retirement home as a family; make sandwiches for the homeless; or take toys, clothes, and canned goods to a charity. Or take a nondriver to the grocery store, the mall, a holiday service, or local Christmas program. Involve the kids in the entire process so they understand, and doing good deeds becomes second nature.

Christmas—emergency cleanup

Try this "5-Minute Emergency Cleanup for Unexpected Guests." Put all the clutter from the floor and tabletops into a large box or basket. Hide the basket or box. As you circle the room collecting clutter, use a rag to wipe up any crumbs or obvious dust. Pick up newspapers and magazines and neatly stack them on the coffee table. Spray some pine- or cinnamon-scented room freshener. Pick up any towels on the bathroom floor. Hang some, throw the rest in the tub, and close the shower curtain. Wipe the sink. Pull out a special basket (prepared ahead of time and stashed under the sink) with a couple of pretty holiday towels and guest soaps tucked in it, and place the basket on the vanity. Turn off a few lights (to hide the dust) and sit in the glow of the Christmas tree.

Christmas—empty nester blues

Feeling a little blue because your nest is empty this year? Invite a family with young children to a tree-trimming party.

Christmas—gather one day later

If you find it nearly impossible to gather together all of your married children and their families on Christmas Eve or Christmas Day, consider a new tradition of spending the day after Christmas together. This will give you an additional day to prepare, and because this day is typically free of other intrusions, you'll be able to spend a more relaxed time together.

Christmas—gently used toys for children with none

Every Christmas Eve, have your children leave some of their old toys near the fireplace for Santa to take to children who don't have any toys. Once the kids are asleep, hide the toys and then deliver them to a worthy charity later.

191

Christmas—goodies for local heroes

Take a basket of holiday good-ies to your local fire or police station.

Christmas—jingling shoes

Tie jingle bells to everyone's sneakers.

Christmas—learn it in many languages

Teach the family to say "Merry Christmas" in another language each year.

Christmas—miniature trees

Make miniature Christmas trees for a great holiday fam-ily activity. Glue the wide ends of sugar ice cream cones to a large sheet of cardboard. Spread green icing over the cones, and then decorate them with assorted candies such as M&Ms, gumdrops, and Life Savers. Let the kids come up with new decorating ideas for the "family forest."

Christmas—movie night with friends

Invite friends over to watch classic Christmas movies like *Frosty the Snowman*, *A Charlie Brown Christmas*, *How the Grinch Stole Christmas*, *Rudolph the Red-Nosed Reindeer*, *It's a Wonderful Life*, *Miracle on 34th Street*, and others. Refreshments can be as simple as eggnog and Christmas cookies.

Christmas—neighborhood story

Instead of sending holiday cards to your neighbors, start a new tradition: Organize the Bentley Street Christmas Book (use the name of your street or neighborhood). Begin a story (fictional) in a notebook, at-tach a routing slip with the name of each family on your street, and then send it around the neighborhood with direc-tions for every family to add a sentence or paragraph. When the story comes back to your family, add an appropriate ending. Edit as necessary, print out the story on your computer, and assemble it into a simple book, one for each family who contributed. Have a neighborhood get-together and read the crazy tale. This will bond your neighbors and promote goodwill all through the year.

Christmas—photo testing

Taking family photos? Do some trial runs first with an instant or digital camera. Wear different clothes and makeup colors to see which you like best.

Christmas—photo tradition

Every year, take a holiday photo of the family in the same pose in the same spot.

Christmas—reading at bedtime

Instead of reading the usual bedtime stories, during the month of December read to your children about Christmas customs in other countries, and include other wonderful holiday stories available at your local library.

Christmas—reading Christmas cards

Reserve opening the day's Christmas cards until dinnertime. Read the messages aloud and remind the kids how the family knows these people.

Christmas—reading party

Carve out a quiet hour or two for a storytelling party with the entire family. Read classic Christmas stories aloud.

Christmas—Santa boot prints

Little ones will believe Santa was actually in their home if you make boot prints with baking soda. Just dampen the bottom of a pair of boots, dip them into baking soda, and make tracks leading from the chimney to the tree and then to the cookies and milk. Make sure the cookies and milk are properly consumed. The baking soda will vacuum up easily.

Christmas—Santa booth photos

If the Santa booth allows you to take your own photographs

(most do, but be sure to inquire ahead of time), take your camera when your kids visit with the old gent. Instead of ordering duplicates of the photo, take it to a quick-print shop and have colored photocopy enlargements made for about $1 each.

Christmas—Santa visit success

If you take your kids to see Santa, here's a way to save time and aggravation shuffling in long lines like cattle: Stay away from overcrowded malls. Instead, check smaller department stores or neighborhood centers. Santa Claus will probably be visiting in a less hectic atmosphere.

Christmas—saying thanks candle

Buy a large white candle (3 by 8 inches is ideal). Starting at the top, carefully carve 25 evenly spaced "stripes" around the candle with the point of a knife. At a designated time each day (dinnertime or bedtime), starting on December 1, light the candle and decide on

something you are thankful for as a family. Allow the candle to burn down one stripe each night until Christmas.

Christmas—see the neighborhood lights

Take a nighttime walk in your neighborhood to enjoy the holiday lights. It's fun to see decorations up close and personal.

Christmas—socializing reality check

Be realistic about how much you can do. You don't have to see everyone between Thanksgiving and New Year's, for example. Save some get-togethers until after the holidays, and you'll have something to look forward to.

Christmas—vacation starter

On the last day of school before Christmas vacation, tie red and green balloons to the mailbox to welcome your children home.

Christmas—"We missed you" photo

Photograph your family for the friends and family members who can't attend your special event or holiday gathering. Download the photos to your computer and have copies printed. Mail them along with a note describing the event to those who are missed.

Christmas cards—send personal notes throughout the year

If you have a very long Christmas card list and feel rushed to write the personal notes you love so much, divide your list over four or five holidays such as Valentine's Day, Easter, Halloween, Thanksgiving, and Christmas. Explain that this is your annual greeting. To keep your records straight, color code every name in your address book to denote on which holiday you wrote the note.

Christmas cards—send postcards instead

Send postcards instead of traditional Christmas cards. They are cheaper to mail and can be made by the clever sender by recycling last year's cards.

Christmas games—board games

Get out the board games and have an ongoing family tournament during December.

Christmas games—jigsaw puzzle

Start a giant jigsaw puzzle at the beginning of your season. The goal is that it be finished by Christmas Day. Keep it out on a table in a well-lit area so everyone can work on it whenever they want.

Christmas games—"Pin the Red Nose on Rudolph"

Make a "Pin the Red Nose on Rudolph" game board. Draw Rudolph's head on a big poster board and cut red noses out of construction paper. Use loops of tape to attach the nose.

Christmas gifts—cookie cutters

A simple cookie cutter in a holiday shape of a star, tree, or gingerbread man can make a great little gift. Lay the cookie cutter in the middle of a piece of clear cellophane. Fill the center of the cookie cutter with tiny candies such as jelly beans. Gather the cellophane and wrap with a bow.

Christmas gifts—cookies for kids' groups

Bake Christmas cookies for your child's team or group. To save time, make the slice-and-bake variety and decorate with ready-made frosting.

Christmas gifts—emergency

Be prepared for surprise guests and keep some gender-generic gifts (candy or comics for kids, candles or calendars for adults) wrapped and at the ready. Use color-coded wrap, stickers, or ribbon to help select the right gift for the age of the recipient.

Christmas gifts—for college students

Send a Christmas basket to a college student on the first

of December. Include holiday music, decorations for the dorm room, Christmas cards, stamps, and red and green pens.

Christmas gift tags—backup

Just in case the tag falls off packages under the tree or while in transit, write the name of the recipient on the back or bottom of the wrapped gift.

Christmas gift tags—cookie cutters as patterns

Using holiday-shaped cookie cutters as patterns, cut tags from file folders or other heavy card stock. Decorate with stickers, markers, or rubber stamps.

Christmas gift tags— skip the gift tags

Use a marking pen that writes on glossy surfaces to write directly on gift wrapping. Sharpie is a popular brand; check stationery and art supply stores. Now you can skip gift tags entirely.

Christmas gift tags—with free color paper scraps

Call or stop by a local print shop and ask for any scraps of colored paper they are discarding. Around the holidays you'll end up with lots of green and red scraps. Cut the green paper in the shape of holly leaves, add tiny red berries cut from the red scraps, and you have beautiful gift tags. Make blue stars and yellow bells. The possibilities are endless.

Christmas gift tags—with photos

Instead of writing the recipient's name on the tag, attach a childhood photo. It's fun for the kids to try to match the grown-ups to the pictures.

Christmas gift wrapping— color-code dots for snoopers

When wrapping gifts, outsmart kids who are prone to snooping. Instead of using name tags, put a color-coded

self-stick dot on each package so only you know who it's for.

Christmas gift wrapping— large gifts

A car, or even a bicycle, can be "wrapped" by tying an oversized gift tag to a piece of string. Leave the tag under the tree and run the string to where the gift awaits.

Christmas gift wrapping— newspaper comics

Don't buy gift wrapping. Start saving the comics from the Sunday papers in the summer and by Christmas you'll have a good supply. You can also use foreign newspapers or fashion ads.

Christmas gift wrapping— penny accents

Wrap a box in brown paper, then hot-glue rows of pennies to the outside in a symmetrical design, randomly or in the shape of a Christmas tree. Tie with a copper-colored or white ribbon.

Christmas gift wrapping— scented packages

Just before you seal up a box for shipping, sprinkle in some pine-scented potpourri. When the carton is opened, the whole room will smell like Christmas.

Christmas gift wrapping— shoelace ties

Use new, colored, or patterned shoelaces to tie up small packages. Add jingle bells for that special touch. (Note: Packages with any string on the outside are not suitable for shipping.)

Christmas gift wrapping— special area

Set up a gift-wrapping area. Drape a card table with a large tablecloth that hangs to the floor. Hide wrapping supplies under the table for quick retrieval.

Christmas gift wrapping— velvet gift sacks

Sew little pouches of red or green velvet, then put small gifts inside and tie with a holiday ribbon.

Christmas gift wrapping—wall art

For the price of wrapping paper and ribbon, you can decorate your entire home in a truly spectacular way. Gift wrap all of the framed paintings on your walls. The effect is stunning. Tip: Wrap only the fronts and sides to use less paper.

Christmas parties—back- to-back to save time

If you're having two holiday parties or get-togethers at your home, schedule them back-to-back. Serve an identical (or at least similar) menu. It takes the same amount of time to make a double batch. Bonus: All your serving pieces will be out and your house will be clean.

Christmas parties— cookie decorating

Plan a cookie decorating event with your kids. Hint: Bake

the cookies early in the day. At party time, set out various toppings and frostings. If you've invited friends, let each child take home a batch of goodies.

Christmas parties—cookie favors

Copy your favorite cookie recipes on cards, then wrap colorful cellophane around a couple of freshly baked samples, insert a recipe card, and tie everything with a bright red ribbon. Give one to each guest as a favor.

Christmas parties—cutting costs

To cut back on entertaining costs, hold a joint party with a friend or relative. You can split the labor and the expense. Or have a caroling party and just serve cookies and hot drinks.

Christmas parties—food organizing

Organize your refrigerator for easy access to the food you'll be using most. Put all the appetizer or salad supplies together in a container or on a tray, labeled and ready to use.

Christmas parties—for singles

Getting together with a group of friends who are also single is a great way to celebrate Christmas. How about hosting a party and having everyone pitch in to bake cookies, prepare cards, and wrap gifts? Some activities are a lot more fun to do in a group than alone. The evening could end with an ornament swap.

Christmas parties—progressive

Instead of everyone in your circle of friends hosting a separate holiday party, make plans to have a progressive dinner. The dinner party moves from one house to another, starting with hors d'oeuvres at the first stop, appetizer or soup at the second, main course at the next, and dessert and coffee at the last. It's an enjoyable way to share the burden and the glory, and you get to see everyone's holiday decorations.

Christmas parties—seating arrangements

If you have so many in attendance at your Christmas dinner that you must have two tables or more, have everyone get up and exchange places between dinner and dessert.

Christmas stockings—filled with stockings

Don't know how to fill the stockings hanging by the chimney with care? Fill them with stockings! Everyone loves argyles, tube socks, running socks, or knee-highs. Stockings filled with stockings are fun and practical.

Christmas stockings—New Year's Day

Start a new tradition. Even though Santa fills all the stockings on Christmas Eve, leave them hanging full and untouched until New Year's Day. This helps to relieve the feeling of overdose on Christmas morning and is a nice way to celebrate the new year.

Christmas tree—decorating, base

Don't forget to decorate the base of the tree. A pretty tablecloth; a yard of lace, satin, or silk; an arrangement of potted plants; or even a collection of dolls and stuffed animals can make your tree look unique.

Christmas tree—decorating, fast-food toys

All year, save the toys your kids receive with fast-food meals. Use the toys to decorate a small artificial tree by tying them on with ribbons, but allow the kids to take the toys off and play with them. This will help make your fancy tree with fragile decorations a little less tempting.

Christmas tree—decorating, lighting tips

Use lots of lights. If your tree is loaded with your collection of different ornaments, limit the lights to one color to help tie everything together. If the tree is sparse, lights in a variety of colors and shapes will help fill things out.

Christmas tree—decorating, lights that sparkle

To make your tree sparkle, use lots of miniature lights. To figure out the minimum number you need, multiply the tree's width in feet by 8, then multiply that figure by the tree's height. For example, a 4-foot-wide tree that's 5 feet tall would require 160 lights (4 x 8 = 32 x 5 = 160).

Christmas tree—decorating, ornament alternatives

If you don't have a huge collection of ornaments, fill out the tree with Christmas cards, candy canes, ribbons, bows, tinsel, and snowflakes cut from paper doilies. Tiny boxes covered with gift wrapping can look surprisingly elegant. Hang gingerbread men, cinnamon sticks tied with bows, and seashells. To add glitter, hang walnuts, pinecones, bay leaves, or blown eggs spray-painted gold or silver.

Christmas tree—decorating, ornaments made of cardboard

Make paper ornaments out of cardboard. Trace cookie-cutter shapes or draw designs on the cardboard freehand. Color the shapes and cut them out. Punch a hole at the top and pull ribbon or string through the hole.

Christmas tree—decorating, ornaments made of clay

Make clay ornaments. In a saucepan, stir together 2 cups baking soda and 1 cup cornstarch, add 1¼ cups water. Cook over medium heat, stirring constantly, until mixture is the consistency of moist mashed potatoes. Turn out on a plate and cover with a damp cloth until cool enough to handle. Roll to ¼-inch thickness. Cut shapes with cookie cutters. Use a drinking straw or toothpick to make holes at the top of each ornament. Allow to dry and harden on a flat surface overnight. Paint, decorate, then protect with a shiny glaze; you can use a clear acrylic spray found at

201

craft and home improvement stores.

snowflakes over the branches of the tree.

Christmas tree—decorating, ornaments made of cookies

Any recipe for crisp rolled cookies can be used to create cute and edible tree decorations. Simply roll and cut the cookie dough as usual, but before baking, use a drinking straw to make a hole near the top of each cookie. Repeat if hole closes during baking. When cookies have cooled, thread ribbon through the holes.

Christmas tree—decorating, ornaments made of glue

Draw free-form stars and snowflakes in varying sizes on waxed paper with white glue that dries hard (like Elmer's White Glue). Sprinkle with glitter, covering the glue completely. Allow to dry for 2 days. Then, starting at the points and working in, carefully peel away the wax paper. Hook the stars and

Christmas tree—decorating, ornaments made of paper

Cut out pictures from magazines, greeting cards, or wrapping paper and glue them to circles of construction paper or cardboard. Attach loops of ribbon to ornament backs, and hang them on the tree.

Christmas tree—decorating, ornaments made of pipe cleaners

Help very young children make Christmas ornaments out of red and green pipe cleaners. Twist them into the shapes of candy canes, stars, and trees, and hang them on the tree or decorate packages.

Christmas tree—decorating, ornaments made of tin

Hang "tin" ornaments cut from foil pie plates on a tree or bush near the house, and watch them sparkle.

Christmas tree—decorating, popcorn garlands

String popcorn garlands with stale popcorn—it's easier to handle.

Christmas tree—decorating, process

Attach strings of lights from the bottom up. Concentrate them on the bottom two-thirds of the tree, and then gradually thin them out toward the top. Attach lights first, garlands next, then ornaments.

Christmas tree—decorating, process for hanging ornaments

Work from the inside out when hanging ornaments. Put some large, shiny ones on the innermost branches of your tree to reflect light and eliminate dark spots. Hang your most attractive ornaments at eye level on the outermost branches.

Christmas tree—decorating, snowflakes made of paper

Let kids make paper snowflakes out of white or silver paper doilies. Fold each into eights and cut designs into all three sides of the wedge. Each one will turn out differently. Attach a ribbon loop to the back or just tuck the snowflakes into the tree branches.

Christmas tree—decorating, stickers

Place star, tree, or other holiday stickers back-to-back along a wire or ribbon. Wind these with the garland through the branches of the tree.

Christmas tree—decorating, trunk brightener

To brighten the center of the tree, wrap the trunk with foil or garlands of gold tinsel.

Christmas tree—is it fresh?

Test a tree for freshness by running your hand gently over a branch. Needles should bend, but stay on. Pick up the tree and thump the trunk. A few brown needles may fall off, but the green ones should stay on.

Christmas tree—nontraditional

Instead of a traditional evergreen tree, bring a potted tree in from the garden or terrace for the holidays or decorate any indoor plant or tree with small ornaments. Small red ribbons on a Norfolk pine, masses of white lights on a ficus, or colorful popcorn and cranberry garlands covering any plant can be very festive.

Easter baskets

Tackle boxes, backpacks, bicycle baskets, school utility boxes, and even a bike helmet can all be used as Easter "baskets." It's a fun way to give an otherwise dull gift.

Formal wear—rent or borrow it

Rent, don't buy, formal wear. Bridal gowns, evening gowns, and other formal wear are usually high-priced—and worn once. So rent or, better yet, borrow. For men, tuxedo rental prices vary tremendously, so check around.

Harvest—jack-o'-lanterns, cutting

When cutting a jack-o'-lantern, don't cut the top of the pumpkin for a lid but instead cut an opening around the bottom. No more reaching down inside! Simply lift the pumpkin by its stem, and light the candle.

Harvest—jack-o'-lanterns, with flashlight

Using a flashlight in the bottom of a jack-o'-lantern is safer than using a candle. Or line the bottom of the pumpkin with aluminum foil, and put a string of tiny exterior Christmas-tree lights inside. Run the cord from a hole in the back of the pumpkin.

Harvest—personalized pumpkins

During pumpkin-growing season next summer, use a pen or other pointed tool to scratch kids' names into your pumpkins when they're about softball size or slightly larger. The name will heal over but leave scars as the pumpkins grow. Because pumpkins grow so fast, kids can watch almost daily to see their names appear in the skin.

New Year's Day—make a family movie

Preserve holiday memories digitally every year on New Year's Day. Do impromptu interviews with family members about the past year and special events, with the primary goal of capturing how your kids have grown and matured in the past year. Close each movie with a shot of the entire family, taken in the same spot year after year.

New Year's Eve—forget the past

While sitting around the fire (great reason to turn off the television), take turns writing down past events you'd like to forget and toss them into the fireplace.

New Year's Eve—give thanks

On New Year's Eve, ask each family member to light a candle and think about the events of the past year for which they are most thankful.

Parties—beverages, iced in child's pool

Fill an inflatable child's pool with ice to hold canned drinks for a big group of guests. Place balloons or flowers in the pool to decorate.

Parties—beverages, iced in fish tank

An impeccably clean, large fish tank filled with lots of shaved ice makes a fun cooler for fruit juice bottles, cans of soda, or pitchers of punch.

Parties—beverages, punch bowl fun

Add these big, hilarious ice cubes to your party punch: Fill a new pair of surgical gloves (nonpowdered) with water, and tie each one closed with rubber bands. Place them in the freezer. When they are frozen, peel back the gloves and add the frozen "hands" to the punch bowl.

Parties—beverages, punch bowl ice ring

Make an ice ring for your punch bowl with fruit juice or sherbet instead of water. It looks pretty and it won't water down the punch as it melts.

Parties—beverages, punch that's not red!

Never serve red punch. It stains carpeting.

Parties—cheering crowd recording

Make a recording of the cheering crowd when you attend a sporting event. Then next time a family member who's done something terrific walks through the door or the guest of honor arrives at a party, play the recording to help offer congratulations.

Parties—coffee and dessert, not dinner

Instead of a full-fledged dinner party, host an adults-only coffee party, with each couple contributing a dessert. This way everyone brings something really special, and the emphasis is on being together.

Parties—decorating, centerpiece with frosted fruit

Frosted fruits are a delicious-looking centerpiece and are simple to make. Simmer apple jelly with a little water, let cool, then brush over fruit. Roll the fruit in granulated sugar to coat.

Parties—decorating, centerpiece with winter candles

Set white votive candles in a clear, glass bowl filled with coarse salt to make an inexpensive "candles in the snow" centerpiece.

Parties—decorating, votive candles and mirrors

Increase the effectiveness of votive candles by placing them on squares of mirrored glass.

Parties—face paint base

Zinc oxide ointment (available at drugstores) is a perfect

makeup base for face painting at parties because it is pure white and creates a kind of "canvas" once applied and allowed to dry.

Parties—face paint recipe

Mix cold cream with cornstarch and water until you form a paste. Add food coloring for the color you want. No cold cream handy? Substitute with a white flour and vegetable shortening or corn syrup mix. Just eyeball it, then adjust until you have the consistency of paint.

Parties—food, buffets for large groups

If you are having a large group in for a meal, consider a buffet. Just be sure to choose dishes that can be served at room temperature and will still look good after sitting out for an hour or so.

Parties—food, cake decorator

A clean, squeezable mustard bottle is great for decorating cakes. Just fill the bottle with the color icing you want, screw on the top with the pointed tip, and get to work on that cake.

Parties—food, cupcake freezer trick

Bake and freeze cupcakes ahead of time, making plenty if you need them for several occasions in the near future. On the day you need to take them to your event, frost the cupcakes while they're still frozen and then pack them for the trip. They will defrost just in time for the party and will have that just-baked taste.

Parties—food, customize plain cake

To get the benefits of a custom-decorated cake at a highly reduced price, ask the bakery to layer, fill, and frost the otherwise plain cake of your choice. You'll end up with a "blank canvas" cake you can bring home, decorate, and customize to your heart's content.

Parties—food, ice cream ready to go

Before a child's party, scoop ice cream into paper cupcake liners and store the treats in the freezer. Now you can serve the ice cream in its little cupcake paper liner on the plate with a piece of cake, or roll the ice cream ball out onto the plate and discard the paper. Serving will be quick and easy because the hard work is done.

Parties—food, ready-made appetizers

Don't be afraid to use prepared foods. Put a store-bought appetizer on your finest china, garnish it with herbs, and no one will know the difference.

Parties—food, realistic recipes

Be realistic about the menu. Don't choose recipes that are too elaborate or require last-minute preparation. If you have time to cook only one really blowout course, make it dessert because that's the last impression everyone will take home.

Parties—food, spread out the goodies

When you're hosting a party, arrange the appetizers, snacks, and beverages on several tables. This keeps everybody circulating instead of gathered around the food. You could also ask guests who seem a little shy to pass appetizers; doing so helps to break the ice.

Parties—games, family crossword puzzle

You'll have a fun game to play at your next family party when you create a crossword puzzle using unique family information. For a child's party, use information about friends and classmates, and keep it appropriate for the age group.

Parties—invitations

Make original party invitations instead of buying cards at the store. Making them as a craft project involves your child in planning his or her party. And it can be as much fun to make invitations by hand as to receive them. You might be able to get scraps of heavy colored paper stock from a local printer. Call ahead and ask them to save usable scraps for you.

Parties—outdoor lighting with portable candles

Fill a kid's wagon with sand and place candles in it for movable light at an evening outdoor party.

Parties—remember the absent

When someone can't be with you to celebrate a special occasion, have everyone at the event hold up a poster that reads "We miss you!" Take a picture and mail or email it to the absentee.

Parties—table, easy dessert display

Cakes, cookies, and other baked goods look elegant when served on a pedestal plate. If you don't have one, create your own by putting a dinner or cake plate on top of a short, wide drinking glass or sturdy vase.

Parties—table, for unmatched dishes

If you don't have adequate matching flatware and dishes for a large group—and most people don't—just mix and match. Tie everything together with matching napkins.

Parties—table, place card names

When preparing place cards for your next dinner party, write the guests' names on both sides of the cards so that those across the table can read them too.

Parties—table, place cards with photos

Put a small, framed photograph of each person at his or her place instead of traditional place cards.

Parties—table, plate decorating

To celebrate a birthday, anniversary, or other big event, use a tube of cake-decorating gel or your own icing in a clean, squeezable mustard bottle to write your message, such as "Congratulations" or "Happy Birthday" around the edge of the dessert plates. This works especially well when you don't have an entire cake to decorate, you are serving pie or ice cream, or you want to make a low-cal dessert look more festive.

Parties—table, serving dishes

Use unusual serving dishes. Put crudités in brightly colored mugs or bread in a shiny metal colander.

Parties—table, set the day before

Set the table the day before with everything, including platters to make sure it all fits and looks attractive. Cover with a clean sheet to keep dust-free.

Thanksgiving—prepare for Christmas now

Before Thanksgiving, give all family members who'll attend a ticket to write down their current interests, hobbies, and Christmas gift requests. The rule is: No Ticket, No Dinner. (Make sure they know this is all in fun.)

Valentine's Day—easy heart-shaped cake

No special pan is required for this cake. Using your favorite recipe or box mix, bake one round layer and one square layer, then cool and remove each from the pans. On a large tray, platter, or aluminum-foil-covered cardboard, place the square layer with its corners pointing up, down, right, and left so it looks like a diamond. Slice the round layer in half. Place one half on each of the two adjacent sides of the square layer. Frost and decorate as desired.

Wedding—bride's feet saver

Buy a pair of white sneakers and decorate them with lace, pearls, and white satin ribbon. At your wedding reception, go from your high heels to these comfy shoes. Your feet will thank you.

Wedding—decorated cake at a good price

If you are planning a wedding, contact a cake-decorating class in your city. Coordinate with them to get a cake at an amazing price.

Wedding—shower, for the mother-of-the-bride

Gifts for this nontraditional event might include a gift certificate to have her hair done for the wedding; bubble bath and other soothing remedies; a lace handkerchief for potential tears; frames for wedding pictures; a memory book to record the details of the occasion; writing paper and stamps; lingerie; and some books by her favorite authors for after the wedding.

Wedding—shower, to fill the newlyweds' pantry

Give the future bride and groom a "fill-their-cupboard" wedding shower. Each guest copies a favorite recipe or dinner menu onto a recipe card, purchases the nonperishable ingredients to prepare the dish or meal, and wraps them up as a unique gift. Newlyweds will be thrilled to have their cupboards filled with the ingredients and specific directions for how to make favorite tried-and-tested meals.

8

Home

Appliances—coffeemaker timer

Rather than purchase an expensive automatic coffeemaker with a built-in timer, buy a model without the timing device. Pick up an appliance timer at the home improvement center (the kind used to turn lamps on and off) for about $10, plug your coffeemaker into it, set the time, and you'll have a quality, timed coffeemaker that costs a lot less than the built-in variety. And it will work equally well.

Appliances—dishwasher, energy savers

Select the "energy save" option on your dishwasher, run it only once a day (at night), and allow the dishes to air-dry rather than use that expensive heat-dry portion of the cycle.

Appliances—dryer repair

If your clothes dryer seems to take twice as long to dry a standard load, try these two tips before calling the repairman: (1) Go outside, remove the vent cover, and clean out any lint that missed the trap and has become stuck at the vent opening. (2) Pull the entire dryer away from the wall. This will alleviate a possible "kink" in the accordion tubing, which can impede efficient operation.

Appliances—dryer vent

If your home is dry during the winter, and you have an electric dryer (never do this with a gas dryer), you can detach the vent pipe from the outside vent, cover it with a piece of cheesecloth or nylon stocking to serve as a lint filter, and redirect that moist hot air back into your house. Come summer, return the vent to its normal position. You can buy a heat diverter attachment at your local hardware or appliance store and install it yourself. There is a lot of moisture in that diverted heat, so you need to keep an eye out for condensation and mildew. This technique is *not* advisable in areas with humid winter climates or for homes with humid indoor air.

Appliances—freezer, count the cost

Think twice about buying a separate home freezer. It can be convenient, but it takes a lot of savvy food management to make it really pay for itself. If a freezer makes economic sense for you, a chest style costs less to run than an upright model.

Appliances—freezer, energy saver

Be sure to keep your freezer packed full to consume the least amount of energy. As your store of food is depleted, fill the gaps with plastic jugs filled with water. You'll accomplish a keep-it-full technique and have a good supply of fresh water in the event of a power failure.

Appliances—iron, water refills

Keep a plastic ketchup bottle full of water on your ironing board for handy refills.

Appliances—refrigerator coil maintenance

Vacuum the coils at the bottom or back of your

refrigerator frequently to prevent dust from building up around them. Dust makes the refrigerator kick on more often, as does keeping it too close to the wall. Refrigerators and freezers need room to breathe or else they can get too hot, run too often, and guzzle too much energy.

Appliances—refrigerator warmer setting

Turn your refrigerator to a slightly warmer setting when you go away for more than a day. As long as the door stays closed, food won't spoil. Just don't forget to restore it to its colder setting when you return!

Appliances—vacuum cleaner, hose on hose

Attach pantyhose with a rubber band over the end of your vacuum hose when cleaning drawers or searching for a tiny lost object like a contact lens or earring back. The small item cannot be sucked into the nozzle, but you'll find what you've been looking for

because it will stick to the hosiery.

Appliances—washing machine, pantyhose filter

If your washing machine drains into a laundry sink, attach one leg of an old pair of pantyhose to the end of the washing machine drain hose to catch lint and prevent clogged drains.

Appliances—water heater, blanket

Insulate your water heater with a blanket manufactured just for this purpose to reduce heat loss. On an electric heater, this could save $20 a year.

Appliances—water heater, empty house

Turn off the water heater when your house is empty, whether it's for a weekend or a week's vacation.

Appliances—water heater, size

Match your water heater size to the needs of your family.

If you are constantly heating enough water to service a family of eight and your nest is empty, you're wasting a lot of money.

Appliances—water heater, timer

A $30 timer on your water heater will pay for itself in saved energy in less than a year. The unit turns the water heater off while you sleep and then back on again in plenty of time to heat water for morning showers. Also consider taking advantage of off-peak electric rates. Call your utility company for more information.

Bathroom—moisture

Learn a plumber's trade secret and hide a few pieces of charcoal in your bathroom to absorb moisture and odor.

Bathroom—not down the toilet!

Don't throw dental floss or colored toilet paper or colored tissues down the toilet. The insides of sewer pipes are very rough, and dental floss has a tendency to stick to the pipe and accumulate over time. Colored toilet tissue might look good, but it doesn't break down as readily as white toilet paper and could cause problems down the line.

Bathroom—shower curtain hooks

To prevent shower curtains from slipping off the hooks, alternate the direction each hook faces.

Bugs and such—ants, repelled by lemon juice

Squirt lemon juice on windowsills and doorways. Ants hate it and will absolutely refuse to come into your home.

Bugs and such—ants, repelled by spices

Drive ants from the kitchen by sprinkling shelves or windowsills with cinnamon, cloves, or baking soda. Put these ingredients into crevices too, and reapply occasionally.

Bugs and such—ants, repelled by water and vinegar

Repel ants by washing countertops, cabinets, and floors with equal parts water and vinegar.

Bugs and such—catch with tacky flyswatter

For fruit flies and other tiny flying insects that a regular flyswatter seems to miss, put a few strips of double-backed tape on your flyswatter.

Bugs and such—catch with tape

Don't squash a bug that is crawling on your wall, drapes, or anywhere else it can stain. Just "apply" a strip of clear tape. The bug adheres to it and can be disposed of.

Bugs and such— cockroach deterrent

Cockroaches often enter homes through plumbing holes under the kitchen or bathroom sinks. Plug these tightly with rags or steel wool and you'll cause a permanent traffic jam on that roach freeway. The same trick keeps mice at bay too.

Bugs and such—cockroach killer

Mix ¼ cup shortening with ⅛ cup sugar. In a separate container mix ½ pound powdered boric acid (available at pharmacies) and ½ cup flour; add to shortening mixture. Stir well with enough water to make a soft dough. Form into small balls the size of marbles, and hide in those out-of-the-way places roaches love to hide. This recipe works far better than commercial products. Just make sure you keep this out of the reach of children.

Bugs and such—fruit flies

Set out a small dish of vinegar that contains a few drops of detergent to repel fruit flies.

Bugs and such—keeping out of food

Insects are attracted to the glue in cardboard cartons and brown paper bags, so when you keep things stored in them, it's the same as inviting the bugs to a banquet. Seal items in plastic before placing them in cardboard boxes and paper bags.

Bugs and such—mothproofing

Make sachets of dried lavender or equal portions of rosemary and mint. Place in closets, drawers, or closed containers to mothproof garments.

Bugs and such—moth repellent

Here's an easy and inexpensive way to make a moth repellent. Purchase a bag of cedar chips from a pet supply shop—a large bag is only a few dollars. Put 1 or 2 cupfuls into resealable plastic bags and poke small holes in them. Hang the bags in your closets and drawers. The lovely, fresh scent repels.

Bugs and such—natural repellents

Fill vases with geraniums or eucalyptus. Bugs stay away from their scents.

Bugs and such—silverfish

To get rid of silverfish, put about ¼ inch of flour in a small, straight-sided glass. Run a strip of adhesive tape on the outside of the glass from bottom to top. Silverfish will travel up the tape and drop into the glass, but they won't be able to get back out. Place one of these traps in each room where you've seen silverfish.

Candles, dripless

To make new candles dripless, soak them in a strong saltwater solution for a few hours, then dry well.

Candles, warped

To straighten those droopy, warped candles, dunk them in a pan of warm water until they are just pliable enough to bend back to their original shape.

Candleholders—easy candle removal

Coat the inside of a candleholder with a tiny amount of

petroleum jelly to ensure easy removal of the candle.

Candleholders—removing wax

Remove wax from candleholders by placing them in the freezer until the wax freezes and snaps off.

Candleholders—tight

Fit a candle into a really tight holder by holding the bottom end of the candle under hot tap water. It should soften just enough so you can firmly place it in the holder.

Cleaning—deadlines

Invite company over at least once a month so you'll be forced to clean up. Keep the bathtub clean so you can hide clutter in it at a moment's notice.

Cleaning—dejunk schedule

Dejunk drawers and closets in one room each week until you're done. Prepare one box for charity, one for items in

need of repair, and one for a garage sale.

Cleaning—neighborhood exchange

Don't sell your kids' outgrown bicycles, skates, or sports gear at a garage sale. You may not raise enough money to replace it in a larger size. Instead, organize a neighborhood exchange. You'll be surprised to find out how many of your neighbors are in the same boat.

Cleaning—quick magnetic pickup

Pick up spilled nails, screws, or pins with a strong magnet wrapped in a paper towel. When the spilled items attach to the magnet, gather the towel corners over the pieces and pull that tidy bundle away from the magnet.

Communication—chalkboard from window shades

Paint an ordinary window shade with chalkboard paint and mount it on the wall in front of your garage workbench or in your utility room. When you need to make a note, just pull it down.

Communication—memory assistant

If you're worried about remembering something, wear your watch on the wrong wrist. It doesn't look as silly as a piece of string tied around your finger, but it works just as well.

Communication—mirror notes

Leave reminders for family members by writing notes on the bathroom mirror with a dry erase marker, available in all kinds of colors at office supply stores. It wipes right off with a tissue, and it's sure to be seen. If a note is not erased for some time, use a bit of rubbing alcohol on that tissue to wipe it away without a trace.

Communication— voicemail for reminder

If there's something you absolutely have to do when you get home, just call your answering machine and leave a message for yourself. That's probably the first thing you'll check.

Communication—welcome map for new owners

When you move, leave a "neighborhood guide" for the new homeowners. Include items such as a map of the surrounding area, and names and phone numbers of the best babysitters and trustworthy repair companies.

Crafts—art display

To display posters, maps, or children's artwork on the wall without marring the art or the wall, put a dab of toothpaste at each corner of the paper and press it onto the wall. Sounds goofy, but it works really well, and you end up with an undamaged, minty-fresh wall.

Crafts—artist paintbrush protection

Slip tiny artist paintbrushes into drinking straws to protect them.

Crafts—clay

Mix 2 cups baking soda, 1 cup cornstarch, and 1½ cups water. Heat in a saucepan over medium heat, stirring constantly. Mixture will become thin and smooth at first. Cook, stirring constantly, until mixture is too thick to stir. Turn the mixture out onto a cookie sheet to cool. Cover with a damp cloth. When cool, knead until smooth. Store in a tightly closed plastic bag in the refrigerator for up to 2 weeks. Clay will harden at room temperature. Most items made with this clay will be dry after 24 hours. If desired, you can preheat the oven to 350°F, turn it off, and then put the clay into the oven to dry, turning the pieces occasionally.

Crafts—glue caps stuck on

If your glue cap keeps getting stuck to the tube, coat the inside with petroleum jelly and it will open easily.

Crafts—restringing beads

Use dental floss for restringing beads.

Decorating—black touches

A touch of black adds punch to any decor. But use a light hand. A lamp shade, needlepoint pillow, or area rug is all it takes.

Decorating—bookends

Go to the home improvement store and pick up a pair of glass blocks to use as bookends. They are heavy enough to hold the books and small enough to fit on a shelf. Because they are clear, they go with any décor.

Decorating—dye to change your look

When redecorating, remember Rit dye. Light-colored curtains, bedspreads, and throw rugs can be dyed a darker shade of another color and will give a room an entirely new look. Remember to wash these items separately in cold water. Drying in the dryer or direct sun will fade the colors quickly, so remember to allow time for air-drying indoors or in a shady place.

Decorating—headboard

Use a length of picket fence as a headboard. Cut it to size, stain or paint it to coordinate with your room, and bolt it to the wall or bed frame.

Decorating—lamp shade pizzazz

Brighten up a boring lamp shade. Sponge or stencil designs on the shade with fabric paint.

Decorating—paint, custom-blend

If you have miscellaneous quantities of leftover paint sitting around, you can pour it all into one container for your own custom blend. As long as you are careful to mix only latex with latex or oil-base with oil-base, it won't matter if you mix flat, glossy, and semigloss. If your garage is a typical one, it won't be hard to come up with a full gallon that easily covers an average-size bedroom. You'll achieve the best results if you mix colors that are similar. Store tightly sealed paint cans upside down to extend usable life.

Decorating—paint, goofs for sale

Most home improvement centers, paint stores, and hardware stores have bins of "goofs"—gallons and quarts of high-quality paint in custom colors that have been tinted wrong. Typically these items are available at near-giveaway prices. A gallon of paint is plenty for the typical-size kid's room or bathroom. There's nothing wrong with the paint or the colors—it's just that for some reason the color didn't exactly match someone else's expectations.

Decorating—paneling

If you want to give a room with dark wood paneling a new look but a complete remodel is not in the budget right now, consider painting the paneling. First treat the paneling with a paint de-glosser. This will remove all grease, dirt, and the high gloss. Next apply a coat of white primer and follow with regular wall paint. This is a very inexpensive way to re-decorate a room. Check with the paint professional at your home improvement center regarding the kind of products that would be best for this job.

Decorating—photograph rooms for reference

If you have a wall arrangement you are fond of or a furniture arrangement that works particularly well, photograph it to use as a reference when you change your decor for the holidays or you move.

Decorating—pictures, groupings on walls

To hang a group of pictures, try arranging them on a big piece of butcher paper first.

When you have a grouping you like, trace around each frame with a pen, and mark where to put the nails. Tape the paper to the wall and nail through the marks; then remove the tape and paper.

Decorating—pictures, hanging

This is the formula that professional picture hangers use: (1) Measure up 60 inches from the floor. (2) To this, add half the height of the framed picture. (3) Subtract the height of the wire (the height of the triangle that the wire would form if the frames were actually hanging in place). This magic number is the distance from the floor at which you should nail the picture hook regardless of the height of the ceiling or even your height.

Decorating—pictures, prevent marks on the wall

Put masking tape on the backside of the corners of a picture to keep them from marking the wall.

Decorating—pillows

To save money on decorative pillows that match your room's decor, you can stitch them yourself from elegant cloth napkins.

Decorating—quilt tablecloth

A baby-size quilt draped over a plain table rather than hidden in a drawer can give a room an instant face-lift.

Decorating—repaint appliances

If you have a home appliance that runs well but is simply the wrong color, have it repainted at an auto body shop. This type of finish looks great, holds up well, and isn't terribly expensive.

Decorating—shop with a photo album

Fill a purse-size photo album with paint, fabric, and wallpaper samples organized by room. Take the album when you go shopping or to garage sales, and you'll take the guesswork out of finding co-ordinating accessories for your home.

Decorating—shower curtain

Give your current shower curtain a brand-new look. Remove the rings, slip pieces of ribbon through the holes, and tie the curtain to the rod with big bows.

Decorating—wallpaper, not over wallpaper

It is best not to apply wallpaper over wallpaper. Proper adhesion of the new paper to the old paper can present a problem, and even if you can finally get it to stick, years later the layers will be very difficult to remove.

Decorating—wallpaper, removal

To remove wallpaper, mix equal parts white vinegar and hot water. Dip a paint roller into the solution, and apply until the paper is thoroughly wet. After two applications, most paper will peel off in sheets. Patience is the secret.

Decorating—window boxes inside

To show off your plants, hang a window box under the window, inside the room.

Doorstop

If you would like a nice-looking and functional door-stop but don't want to spend a small fortune, fill a tin box that has a lid (the kind that holds cookies or candies at holiday time) with dried beans. You can choose a size and style to coordinate with your room's decor for a fraction of the cost of a ready-made doorstop. What a simple way to add a unique and functional decorator item to any room in the house.

Drain—jewelry drop

If you drop an earring or pin down the drain, attach a small magnet to a stiff piece of twine or wire, put it down the drain,

and use it to attract the item and pull it out.

Drawer—liners

Place mats, because they're washable, make excellent drawer liners.

Faucets—leaky

Until you can get that leaky faucet fixed, tie a piece of fabric, long enough to touch the drain, around the faucet. The water will run down the fabric, eliminating that annoying drip.

Fireplace—bellows

Empty, squeezable plastic bottles can serve as bellows; use them to fan a wood or charcoal fire.

Fireplace—logs from newspaper

Make homemade fire logs for the fireplace. Stack some folded newspaper, alternating the folded sides, until the stack is about 1 inch high. Don't use colored comics or advertisements. Roll the stack as tightly as you can. Hold it together with wire or by slipping over each end a small tuna fish (or similar size) can from which you've removed both the top and bottom. Don't use string because it will burn off and the paper will fly all over the place. When rolled and secured, thoroughly soak the "logs" in water and set them outside to dry completely. Burn with can rings in place.

Fireplace—logs starter

For a fireplace log starter, stuff the cups of a paper egg carton with lint from the dryer. Melt paraffin or an old candle, and pour the wax over the lint in each section and allow it to harden. To use, place one of these neat fire-starters under the logs. Light it and it will burn for about 20 minutes.

Fireplace—wood in the bag

When gathering kindling or pieces of wood from outdoors for the fireplace, carry them into the house in a brown grocery bag. Place the entire bag and its contents into the fireplace and light the bag. This prevents that inevitable trail of wood dirt and debris that always follows the person carrying wood into the house, and it's a tidy way to start a fire.

Floors—area rugs

Instead of buying finished area rugs, purchase a remnant from a carpet store, have it bound, and save a bundle. The carpet store can either bind it or refer you to someone who can.

Floors—carpet bargain

If you are not in a big hurry and are fairly flexible as to color and quality, let the carpet stores in your area that offer "Complete Satisfaction Guaranteed" know that you would be interested in purchasing the carpeting someone else rejected. Many times when new carpet is installed, the homeowner for one reason or another is not completely satisfied with some aspect of the carpet and takes advantage of the carpet supplier's satisfaction guarantee. You should be able to make a real bargain on the like-new goods, including installation.

Floors—carpet indentations

Here is how to make those carpet indentations rebound: Place an ice cube in each indentation. Let it melt, then wait about 12 hours before blotting up the moisture. Gently pull up the carpet fibers using a kitchen fork.

Floors—rocking chair marks

If a rocking chair is wearing the finish off your wood floor, put a strip of adhesive-backed weather-stripping tape on the runners.

Flower frog

Wad up a mesh produce bag and stuff it in a vase. It will act as a "frog" to hold fresh or artificial flower arrangements.

Flowers—artificial flower base

To hold artificial flowers in place, pour salt in the container, add a little cold water, and arrange the flowers. As the salt dries, it will solidify and hold the flowers.

Flowers—bouquet alternative

If you forget to pick up flowers for the table, set a houseplant in a basket and add a pretty ribbon.

Flowers—daffodils

Place daffodils in a separate vase of water for half a day before combining them in a bouquet with other flowers. They excrete a sap that clogs the stems of other flowers.

Flowers—longer lasting

Here's a remarkable method for greatly increasing the useful life of freshly cut flowers. Add ¼ teaspoon of bleach to the vase water. Recut flower stems at an angle to encourage absorption and arrange them in the bleach water. Place them in a cool, dark place for several hours, then put out on display. (Flowers should be angle-cut and the water refreshed daily.) The bleach retards the growth of bacteria in the water, which causes flowers to wilt much more quickly.

Flowers—plants on their own

If you must leave small potted plants unattended while on vacation, push a needle threaded with wool yarn into the soil, and put the other end in a jar of water. The plants will stay moist through this wicking system.

Flowers—refrigerate

Put cut flowers in the refrigerator when you're at work, asleep, or otherwise unable to enjoy them. This will extend their indoor life.

Flowers—roses, drying

Don't throw away wilted roses; dry them instead. They can almost always be salvaged by hanging them upside down, stems and all, and putting them in a dark, dry place. It takes 1 to 2 weeks, but when they're good and dry, they are absolutely gorgeous. Just spray them carefully with shellac or craft glaze and use them in wreaths, vases, or give them as gifts. Dried roses cost up to $12 per half dozen in craft stores.

Flowers—roses, longer lasting

To keep cut roses looking beautiful longer, remove the roses from the vase and refill the vase with fresh warm water and one crushed aspirin every day. Angle cut a tiny bit from the bottom of each stem and quickly plunge it into the vase. This makes the roses open more slowly.

Flowers—stem extenders

To give stemmed flowers more length for an arrangement, slide the stems into drinking straws before putting them into an opaque vase. If you need to shorten any stems afterward, just snip off the bottom of the straws.

Flowers—stem trimming

Cut flower stems on a slant with a knife. Angled cuts permit absorption even when the stem rests on the bottom of the container. To aid water intake, scrape stem ends for about an inch; split woody stems with a knife or mash with a hammer. Plunge stems into water immediately after cutting. Remove excess and damaged foliage as well as foliage below water level. Fill the container with clean water; refresh as often as possible by holding the vase under the faucet and flushing with tepid water until the old water is forced out.

Flowers—stem trimming, with lukewarm water

Hold cut flowers under lukewarm water as you trim the stems. It gives them a surge of water they don't get if you cut first, then put them in water. Put heavy and tall stems in the

vase first, and use lighter ones to fill out the arrangement.

Furniture—bookcases

If you don't have a free wall for a bookcase, try squeezing a compact library around a doorway. Find a home for cookbooks in the same way by encircling a kitchen window with shelves.

Furniture—built-in shelves

You'll gain shelves without sacrificing floor space if you break into the wall and install built-in shelves between the studs (vertical structural supports). If you have no idea what this means or would entail, you probably are not a good candidate for this tip. But if you do know how to handle basic home remodeling jobs, go for it!

Furniture—foam cushions

To replace a foam cushion that has been removed from a zippered cover, place the cushion in a plastic garbage bag and insert the bag open-end first into the cover. The cushion will slide right in. Once in place all you have to do is pull out the bag, leaving the foam perfectly in place.

Furniture—moving

When moving heavy furniture across the room, protect an uncarpeted floor by first placing a soft-sole slipper, thick sock, or the bottom half of an empty milk carton under each leg of the furniture. The piece will slide across the floor easily without scratching or damaging the floor.

Furniture—reupholster

If you have a lovely old couch you don't want to part with, consider having it redone at an upholstery school for a fraction of a professional upholsterer's price. There is a fee, plus you'll be expected to purchase fabric through the school. Plan on students taking a little longer to complete the job—their work is done under the supervision

of teachers. Research "Upholstery Schools" online, or call the industrial arts divisions of your area high schools and colleges.

Furniture—sofa cushions don't slide

To keep your sofa cushions from slipping and sliding, place a bath mat or square of foam rubber under each cushion.

Fuse box

If your switches are mislabeled in your electrical circuit box, or they were labeled in pencil that has become too faint to read, plug in a small radio to an outlet in a room. Turn up the volume so you can hear the music in the room while you are standing at the circuit box. Flip all the circuit breakers until the music stops. Remember that circuit then repeat for each of the outlets in that room. Label the circuit breaker accordingly, then repeat the procedure for all the rooms in your house.

Garage sale advanced pricing

Price all items you put aside for a future garage sale before you store them away. Doing the pricing ahead of time will make preparing for the actual sale a breeze.

Garage sale ambience

Take time to create the right sale ambience. Play upbeat music; you want to make an inviting atmosphere. Make sure your best and biggest items can be easily seen by folks who drive by to do a quick curbside survey.

Garage sale coffee

People will stay longer and be in a better mood if you serve coffee, and—who knows—you might even sell the coffeepot.

Garage sale displays

Create an inviting display. Your knickknacks should not look cluttered. Put them against a dark background

and arrange the tables so the sale goods can be easily viewed without customers' movements becoming restricted. Hang clothing items to make them visible.

Garage sale for early birds

Avoid negotiating with early birds. If a buyer is hot for an item at 6 a.m., chances are you'll get your asking price before the day is over. Be nice but firm. Offer to take their phone number. If the item hasn't sold by day's end, do not hesitate to call.

Garage sale giveaways

When advertising your garage sale, mention you'll have "giveaways." This conveys a spirit of generosity on the part of the seller.

Garage sale guidelines

Be ready to begin your sale an hour before the advertised start time. Keep the doors of your home locked while you are having your sale. You'll

231

get the best prices if your merchandise is clean and well displayed. Have batteries available so shoppers can confirm that items such as toys and radios work.

Garage sale permit

Check with your city hall to see if you need a permit to hold a garage sale. The last thing you'll need is the police showing up to shut you down just when things are picking up.

Garage sale pricing

For fairly new items in good condition, charge a quarter of what you originally paid for them.

Garage sale profit margin

Decide on the price of each item and then mark it up 20 percent. This allows room to negotiate with a customer, and you'll find most yard-salers love to bargain.

Garage sale seasonal merchandise

Seasonal merchandise sells best. If it's spring, haul out that old lawn mower, gardening tools, and so on. People buy what they can use now, not what they're going to have to store in their own garages.

Heating and cooling—air conditioner, location

If you have an option, install window air conditioners in north- or east-facing windows. South- and west-facing windows receive more sun and will make the unit work harder.

Heating and cooling—air conditioner, proper size

Make sure your window air conditioner is the proper size. An oversize unit will use more energy than necessary and will not dehumidify properly. If you're in the market for a window air-conditioning unit, choose the size you need to cool only one room. Window units aren't designed to cool more than one room.

Heating and cooling—air conditioner, relief

To keep your air conditioner from having to work harder than it should in the summer, cook outdoors or prepare cold meals to avoid heating your kitchen. Place heat-producing appliances such as lamps and TVs away from the thermostat. Change or clean the air-conditioning filter once a month during the peak season. Don't forget to clean the filters on window units. They're behind the front panel. Clean them with soap and water.

Heating and cooling—air conditioner settings

Set your thermostat on the highest comfortable setting. Raising the temperature just 2 degrees will reduce cooling costs by 5 percent.

Heating and cooling—air-conditioning and the cook

You can reduce your air-conditioning use by preparing oven-cooked meals in the cool of the day. When it's time to eat, simply reheat the entrée in the microwave or toaster oven.

Heating and cooling—air-conditioning, blockage

If you have central air-conditioning, make sure your registers for supply and return air are not blocked by furniture or drapes.

Heating and cooling—air leak test

Here's how to check for air leaks. Shut the doors and windows in your home. Move a lighted candle around the perimeters of the doors or windows. If the flame flickers, you have an air leak. Plug it with caulk and weather stripping.

Heating and cooling—blinds behind drapes

Hang blinds behind drapes to help keep the room warmer in winter, cooler in summer.

Heating and cooling—buy heating oil and firewood in summer

Buy heating oil off-season. Start checking prices in the spring.

233

Typically you should be able to take advantage of the lowest prices from July to September. The same applies to firewood.

Heating and cooling—fabric wall hangings

A quilt or decorative rug will insulate interior walls, keep your room cozier, and allow you to turn down the thermostat a few degrees in the winter without a noticeable difference.

Heating and cooling—insulation, free or low-cost

Take advantage of your community's free or low-cost programs for insulating your home. Check with your utility companies or community action center to see what might be available to you. You may be pleasantly surprised.

Heating and cooling—light exterior colors are best

Light colors on the outside of a house reflect the sun's rays, reducing the temperature inside. If your cooling bills are higher than your heating bills, consider white or light-colored roof shingles when you replace your roof.

Heating and cooling—programmable thermostat

A programmable timer thermostat is really worth its weight in gold. Reasonably priced, it will pay for itself in no time at all in reduced heating and cooling bills.

Heating and cooling—window coverings

During the winter daylight hours, open all drapes and window coverings on the side of your home that is receiving the most sunlight (all day on the side facing south). When the sun goes down, be sure to close all window coverings to retain the natural heat.

Home office—funky envelope

Need to mail something but you don't have an envelope that's large enough? You can use a small paper bag. If it is larger than 6 by 9 inches, you will need to add additional postage. The maximum size allowable is 6⅛ by 11½ inches. The top can be folded down to meet length requirements and stapled or taped.

Home office—out of glue

Clear nail polish makes a good emergency glue for small items like stamps, recipe clippings, and so on.

Home office—packaging material

When mailing something breakable to family or friends, use intact rolls of toilet tissue as filler to cushion the item. It's lightweight and inexpensive filler—and something the recipient can use. If you remove the center cardboard tubes, the rolls become more compressible.

Home office—pencil sharpener

In a pinch you can sharpen a pencil on a piece of sandpaper, if you work at it for a few minutes.

Home office—recycling with style

For just a few bucks you can order a rubber stamp that reads something like: "Personally Recycled by (your name)." Now you can collect paper that has been printed on one side only, like computer run, flyers, and junk mail. Just cut it to size, stamp it, and you have your own personalized notes and stationery.

Jar lids—stuck

To loosen a stuck jar lid, hold the jar upside down and pour warm vinegar around the neck at the joint between the glass and the top.

Jar lids—tight

When you can't remove a tight lid from a jar, this handy hint may do the trick: Take a heavy-duty rubber band, put it around the lid, and twist. Because the rubber band gives you something to grip, the lid should come off easily.

Kitchen—funnel

Cut off the bottom of a clean plastic quart or liter soda bottle and use the top as a funnel.

Kitchen—glass, chipped

Keep a fingernail sanding block (available from a beauty supply store or drugstore cosmetic counter) on hand. Use it to sand, polish, and smooth out chipped corners and edges of glassware and glass baking dishes. With just a few minutes of gentle sanding and polishing with the block, the jagged dangerous edge or corner will be smoothed out and the glass piece will be restored to usefulness.

Kitchen—glasses, stuck together

To separate two stacked glasses stuck together, put cold water into the inside glass. Place both glasses in warm water up to the rim of the outer glass. Remove the glasses from the water, then gently pull them apart.

Kitchen—plastic wrap, clingier

Plastic wrap will cling better if you moisten with a bit of water the rim of the bowl or pan you are covering.

Kitchen—plastic wrap, end finder

When you can't find the end of the plastic wrap, put a piece of clear tape, sticky side out, around your index finger. Run your taped finger around the roll until the wrap lifts up.

Kitchen—plastic wrap, in the freezer

Store plastic wrap in the freezer. The cool air will keep it from clinging to itself and makes it a lot easier to work with.

Kitchen—ring hook

Install a small hook near your kitchen sink to hold rings, watches, or other jewelry you remove when washing, cleaning, or cooking.

Kitchen—scale

Here's how to make sure your kitchen measuring scale is accurate: Place 9 pennies on the scale. They should weigh 1 ounce.

Kitchen—splatter guard

Lay a washable rolling window shade in the space behind your range top. When you cook, pull the shade up and attach to a mounted cup hook to protect the wall from splatters.

Kitchen—trash can liners

Store the roll of tall kitchen bags in the bottom of your kitchen trash receptacle. Now no one has a reason not to put a new bag in when the full one is removed.

Kitchen—vegetable bin liners

Place paper towels in the bottom of vegetable bins to absorb water.

Kitchen—wooden bowls and cutting boards

Freshen wooden bowls and cutting boards. Sprinkle the surface with salt and rub with half a lemon.

Lighting—dimmers

Add dimmers to switches on overhead lights. Soft light uses less electricity and creates a more appealing environment in a room.

Lighting—on or off?

When leaving the room for under half an hour, you should leave the compact fluorescents on, and when leaving for under 5 minutes, leave incandescent lights on.

Lighting—three-way bulbs

Use three-way bulbs. They are more efficient, provided you use the lower wattage whenever possible.

Lighting—timers

Install timers or motion detectors rather than leaving lights on all night. This will ensure that you use lights only when necessary and will greatly reduce your electric bill.

Linens—bed coverlet

Cutwork and lace bed coverlets can be expensive. Use a lace tablecloth instead. A 70-by 90-inch oblong cloth will fit a full-size bed.

Linens—herbal fragrance

For a subtly sweet-smelling table setting, put cinnamon, raspberry, orange, or lemon herbal tea bags in the drawers where you store your table linens.

Linens—napkins, no creases

To store cloth napkins without creases, wrap and store them around a cardboard tube.

Linens—napkins, sturdy for kids

Washcloths in lieu of paper napkins are a tidy and environmentally friendly alternative for messy young eaters.

Linens—pillowcases

Pillowcases are very expensive, so you might want to consider making your own set. When buying new sheets, pick up a fitted sheet and two flat sheets, making sure the second flat is queen-size, regardless of the size of the bed you will be outfitting. Out of the queen-size flat sheet, you will be able to make three sets of pillowcases. By analyzing a commercially made pillowcase, it is easy to measure, create a pattern, and see how it is put together.

Linens—sheets, full to queen

You don't need all new bedding if you replace your old double bed with a queen-size one. Lay a full-size flat sheet on your new queen-size mattress. Fold a hospital corner (this has a pleated rather than gathered look) at all four corners and pin them in place. Stitch elastic completely around the pleated corners. You will have a queen-size fitted sheet. Buy coordinating flat queen-size sheets when you see them on sale. Make extra pillowcases from the full-size fitted sheets.

Linens—sheets, queen to king

Buy queen-size top sheets for king-size beds. King-size top sheets are usually way too big and require a lot of tucking in. Queen-size flats work great on most king-size beds and are a lot cheaper. Note: All sheets vary in size, and it seems the better the quality, the more generous the amount of fabric.

Linens—table linens, on a hanger

Use a multiple shirt hanger to organize place mats, cloth napkins, and folded tablecloths. Hang it in the entry closet, and they'll always be neat and wrinkle-free.

Linens—table linens, spritz to protect

Spray table linens with a fabric protector a few days before you plan to use them. The inevitable spills will be less likely to stain, and spills will simply bead up so you can remove them quickly.

Linens—table runners, no creases

Use the cardboard tubes from rolls of gift wrapping paper to store crease-free, freshly ironed dresser scarves and table runners. Simply lay the tube over one end of the item and roll it up. Secure with a piece of ribbon or string.

Linens—table runners, unique

Use a pretty muffler or scarf as a unique table runner.

Linens—unique with fabric paint

A touch of washable fabric paint, available at craft and fabric stores, can customize plain-Jane napkins, place mats, or tablecloths into fabulous accessories that coordinate with your dishes, floors, or wall coverings.

Linens—vinyl wrinkles

To remove the wrinkles from a new plastic or vinyl tablecloth, toss the tablecloth in the dryer with a damp cloth (for moisture), set on the lowest heat possible, and let tumble for only a minute or two. To be on the safe side (putting plastic in a clothes dryer sounds like a fire hazard just waiting to happen), do not leave it unattended. Stand there for the short time it takes to do this, and personally take out the beautifully wrinkle-free tablecloth.

Locks—lubricate them

Graphite from an ordinary soft pencil can be used to lubricate a resistant lock. Rub the key across the pencil point, then move it in and out of the lock several times.

Mice—trap them

Use peanut butter as bait for your mousetraps. You can reset the traps and catch several mice before you need to add more bait.

Moving—move midweek

If you're moving, do it on a weekday. Fees can be as much as 50 percent higher on the weekend. Pack everything yourself and save at least 10 percent. Most movers provide cartons.

Odors—air freshener with eucalyptus

Available at a reasonable cost from many florist shops, eucalyptus makes a unique bathroom air freshener. Simply place fragrant eucalyptus stems in a vase and add enough water to cover about 2 inches of the stem bases.

Odors—basements and garages

Fill a net vegetable bag with charcoal and hang it in the musty basement or damp garage to absorb odors.

Odors—bathrooms

Keep an open, shallow dish of baking soda behind your toilet to absorb odors.

Odors—fireplace

Remove ashes often for optimum fireplace performance. Each time you remove the ashes, place a shallow pan of baking soda in the fireplace. Leave it overnight to absorb unpleasant fireplace odors.

Odors—fragrant home

Here are several ideas for a home, sweet home: (1) To make your house smell sweet, sprinkle cinnamon on a pan and warm it on the stove. (2) To fill your home with the smell of citrus, throw a handful of orange peels in a pot of boiling water. (3) Each time you clean a room, place a few drops of a fragrant oil on a lightbulb, or spray the room with a fresh potpourri scent to give the house a nice smell and to leave a subtle sign that this room is clean! (4) To make your own carpet and room deodorizer, mix 1 cup Epsom salts with a few drops of perfumed oil. Spread the mixture on waxed paper to dry. Store in an airtight container. To use, sprinkle the grains on the carpet, allow to stand for a few minutes, and vacuum as usual. (5) Don't throw away lemon rinds or old spices. They make fabulous room deodorizers. Simply place them in a pot of water and bring to a low boil. The scent is better than any potpourri you can buy.

Odors—linen closets

Keep your linen closet smelling fresh. Spray cotton balls with your favorite fragrance. Once dry, stash them into closet corners and shelves.

Odors—suitcases

To restore a musty suitcase, fill it with crumpled newspaper, then close it up. Change the paper every 2 to 3 days until the odor is gone.

Odors—vacuum with cinnamon

Place a cinnamon stick in the vacuum bag before vacuuming

to naturally deodorize your home.

Organization and storage—bathroom, magnet metal corral

If you often misplace tweezers, manicure scissors, and nail files, try this trick: Attach these items to a large magnet placed on the inside of your metal medicine cabinet.

Organization and storage—bathroom, shoe bag

Hang a shoe bag on the back of the bathroom door. The pockets are perfect for washcloths and toiletries and other small items that cause such a clutter problem in the bathroom.

Organization and storage—bed-making storage

For quick and easy bed-making, keep linen sets together. For each set, fold and wrap a top and bottom sheet and one pillowcase together. Then stick them all in the matching pillowcase and store

in a drawer right next to the bed.

Organization and storage—blankets

Eliminate the question of where to store extra blankets. Keep them between the mattress and the box spring.

Organization and storage—bowls and lids

To save space and promote neatness in the kitchen, nest all plastic storage containers, and place the lids in a resealable plastic bag. Hang the bag of lids from a hook inside a door.

Organization and storage—broom

Cut the fingertip from an old rubber glove and slip it over the end of your broom handle. Now it won't slip when leaned against the wall.

Organization and storage—bureau instead of table

If you have a table with no storage space by the front

door, replace it with a bureau that has drawers galore.

Organization and storage—CD container

Keep your compact discs neatly organized by storing them in the perfect-sized container—an empty shoe box. Place them upright in the box so the titles are visible, and you'll be able to easily flip through them to find the ones you're looking for. The box can be covered with contact paper or painted.

Organization and storage—closet's top shelf

Attach a mirror to the closet ceiling so you can keep track of top-shelf contents.

Organization and storage—clutter in a bag

Take a large brown grocery bag and load into it all the clutter that's driving you nuts. Stash it in a cupboard or another out of the way place. If family members are missing

something, send them to the bag. Anything not retrieved in 2 to 3 weeks can be considered a likely candidate for the trash—just in time for another clean sweep of the house.

Organization and storage—cords

Keep extension cords neat. Stuff the looped cords into individual cardboard tubes.

Organization and storage—cosmetics in desk organizers

Check out those acrylic desk organizers you see in office supply or art stores. They're ideal for cosmetics, brushes, and nail polish, and much cheaper than the same thing sold to hold cosmetics.

Organization and storage—cubbies

Here's an uplifting idea: Don't forget to look up for extra storage. A row of cubbies (storage boxes) attached to the wall over coat hooks is one example of found space. Other logical locations are above a washer or dryer, chest of drawers, medicine cabinet, or window.

Organization and storage— family in-boxes

Decorate a colored file folder or plastic in-box for each of your children. When they come home from school, have them place important papers, forms, and other school information in their special place. And they'll know where to find the papers and items they need to return to the teacher the next day.

Organization and storage— flowerpots as storage

Paint small terra-cotta flowerpots pastel colors and place on a small tray in the bathroom to hold makeup, soaps, and other small items.

Organization and storage— hide your valuables

Spray-paint the inside of a mayonnaise jar white. Store it in the refrigerator as a hiding place for money and valuables.

Organization and storage— in the luggage

Suitcases, which spend the greater portion of their functional lives completely useless and taking up space, should be considered for storing almost anything, from holiday decorations to out-of-season clothes.

Organization and storage—jewelry

Keep your earrings, small bracelets, and necklaces in the separate compartments of a plastic ice tray. The tray fits in a dresser drawer so jewels stay neat and out of sight.

Organization and storage—jewelry box

Don't throw out that old tarnish-retardant silver chest designed to store silverware. It will make a wonderful jewelry box. Earrings clip to the band designed to hold knives; chains, rings, and brooches fit nicely in the open spaces; and you won't have to worry about tarnish because of the specially treated material that lines this type of chest.

Organization and storage—keys

Keep a pretty, decorative bowl on a table near the front door to hold house keys. You'll always know exactly where they are.

Organization and storage—ladder

Nail a sturdy, old leather belt to the garage wall. Store the ladder by wrapping the belt around its top step and buckling it closed.

Organization and storage—lost and found

Keep a lost-and-found basket in a central location where family members can stash things they find lying around the house and also look for things they've lost.

Organization and storage—roll under the bed

Attach casters to the bottom of an old dresser drawer and use it for storage underneath a bed.

Organization and storage—shoe storage bags for small stuff

The perfect solution for organizing all the little stuff that clutters the rooms in your home is a large, clear plastic shoe storage bag—the kind with lots of pockets. All of its contents are clearly visible, neatly separated, and easily portable. Hang one on the back of the door in the nursery, kitchen, bedrooms, and bathrooms.

Organization and storage—table leaves

Store extra table leaves in the closet behind your clothes. They won't take up room and will be out of sight and protected from scratches.

Organization and storage—table pedestal

Top a new trash or garbage can with a piece of plywood and cover it with a piece of floor-length fabric to turn it into a lamp table. The receptacle provides a fairly large storage space for Christmas decorations or other infrequently used items.

Organization and storage— under-the-bed box

Keep a cardboard storage box in each bedroom (under the bed is good), and use it to collect outgrown clothes and toys. Full boxes means it's time for a yard sale or a trip to the Salvation Army or consignment store.

Organization and storage— velcro the remote

Attach an adhesive-backed Velcro strip to the side of your TV and another to the back of the TV remote control.

Packing—sealing boxes

Before you tape shut a box, run a piece of string along the path where you'll be placing the tape. Press the tape over the string and seal the

box, leaving a bit of the string hanging loose. When it's time to unpack, just pull on the string to rip the tape.

Photos—clean with rubbing alcohol

If photos have marks (even permanent marker), sticky stuff, dirt, or they are stuck together, clean them with 91 percent or more rubbing alcohol, and then carefully pry them apart. Dry them printed side up and not touching other photos. Anything less than 91 percent alcohol will ruin the photos because it contains too much water.

Photos—keep memories with a camera

Does this sound familiar? You've made a commitment to dejunk your life. Suddenly you and your family get hit with the sentimental bug. Instead of hanging on to all that stuff, why not take a photograph of the special items? A photo of the giant stuffed animal that was your daughter's favorite when she was three will take up a lot less room in the photo album than in the attic. The picture will call up the same memories as the item itself, and you'll be freed emotionally to get rid of the things that are cluttering your life.

Photos—magnetic photo album nightmare

The warmth from a hair dryer can loosen photos that have become stuck within the pages of a magnetic photo album.

Safety and readiness—ceiling work on bucket stilts

If you need to do some work on the ceiling, 5-gallon buckets make good, stable stilts. Remove or tape down the wire handle on each bucket, turn the bucket upside down, make a foot stirrup out of duct tape, and off you go. You don't want the tape to stick to your shoes, so double it, sticky side to sticky side, on the part that your foot slides under.

Safety and readiness—disaster "Go Bags"

Every household needs a Go Bag. This is a collection of items you may need in the event of a disaster that requires you and your family to be self-sufficient when all services are cut off. And because you may need to evacuate, your Go Bag needs to be packed in an easy-to-carry container like a suitcase on wheels. Then each family member needs to have a backpack that contains enough basic supplies to last for 72 hours—all packed and ready to go. Each backpack should contain a change of clothing, including underwear, socks, and a jacket or sweater; some food and an emergency lightweight blanket; copies of personal documents that are sealed in zip-type plastic bags such as photo ID, emergency phone numbers, social security numbers, insurance cards, and so on. When it's time to evacuate, each person grabs his or her backpack and a gallon of water and gets out. The larger family Go

Bag or box should be compact enough to carry easily and should fit in the trunk of the car—a vehicle whose gas tank is never less than half full.

Safety and readiness—fake vent for valuables

Cut a hole at the approximate location and size of a heat vent in the wall, and attach a vent cover. Paint it to match all the other heat vents, and you'll have a great hideaway for your treasures.

Safety and readiness— fire extinguisher

Everyone in the family needs to know how to operate a portable fire extinguisher. Just remember the word PASS. P: pull the pin to release the locking mechanism. A: aim low, at the base of the fire. S: squeeze the handle. S: sweep the spray from side to side, as if you were hosing down a sidewalk.

Safety and readiness— holding nails in place

If you can't hammer a nail without hammering your fingers in the process, use the tines of an old fork instead of your fingers to hold the nail in place.

Safety and readiness—out-of-area contact person

Every family needs to identify a friend or relative who lives in another state to be their disaster point person, and then keep that person's phone number and contact information with them at all times. Now instruct all of your family members to call this person to check in with their location and conditions. Long-distance phone service is often restored sooner than local service.

Safety and readiness—prevent a child's being locked in

Toss a towel over the top of a bathroom door so it won't close completely. This way, little ones are less likely to lock themselves in.

Safety and readiness—smoke detector battery changes

Fire safety officials remind us to change the batteries in our smoke detectors and home security systems every 6 months. Get into the habit of changing batteries when the time changes in the spring and again in the fall. But don't throw away the old batteries. They still have lots of life remaining and can be used in radios, toys, pagers, and so on.

Safety and readiness—surge protector for computer

Voltage spikes and surges through the power lines can fry the electronics of your computer and printer. A good surge protector is far better insurance for your machines than an extended warranty policy. You just plug your computer into the protector, it's quite inexpensive, and it's available at any computer or hardware store.

Safety and readiness—water

You don't have to live in "hurricane" country to get hurricane prepared. Disasters can hit anywhere, which means water could be in short supply. For flushing toilets and showers, line 30- to 45-gallon garbage cans with those large contractor plastic bags available at home improvement stores. Then, fill the garbage cans with water. Most people forget that three weeks without electricity means three weeks of no water if your supplier has not attached a generator to pump it to the houses.

Scales—for the home

Here are three scales worth their weight in gold in any home: a 25-pound scale in the laundry room so wash loads are right; a 5-pound scale in the kitchen to measure food portions for serving, freezing, and storing; a 300-pound scale for weight control. The kitchen scale also serves to weigh mail. No more wasting stamps trying to make sure you have enough postage.

Sewing—bedsheets for extra-wide yardage

Buy flat bedsheets instead of yardage. Buying sheets on sale gives you extra-wide yardage at a fraction of the cost of yard goods. They're perfect for making curtains, tablecloths, napkins, pillows, nightclothes, and crafts.

Sewing—dryer sheets for appliqué

Another use for dryer sheets: Use these sheets, new or used, as interfacing when appliqué-ing a quilt. They form the layer between the cutout and the quilt top. They keep the quilt fresher longer between washings and airings, add increasingly lightweight insulation, and extend the life of the quilt.

Sewing—lazy Susan for notions

Put a lazy Susan on your sewing table to store your notions. Now everything you need is just a spin away!

Sewing—machine dusting

When the bobbin apparatus in your sewing machine needs dusting, blow the dust out by aiming quick bursts of air from an empty squeeze bottle.

Sewing—magnet for pins and needles

Keep a magnet in your sewing box to pick up pins and needles that fall on the floor.

Sewing—make your own washcloths

The next time you see cotton bath towels on sale, buy one and give this a try: Cut it into 8 washcloths. Either serge the edges or use a zigzag or over-lock stitch on a regular sewing machine. You should be able to make loads of wonderful washcloths for a fraction of the cost of ready-made.

Sewing—mend with newspaper

Slip a folded newspaper through the leg or sleeve of the garment you're mending so you don't sew through both layers.

Sewing—needle sharpening

Sharpen a sewing machine needle without removing it from the machine by "stitching" through a sheet of fine-grain sandpaper.

Sewing—pincushion of soap

An unwrapped bar of soap makes a terrific pincushion. Bonus: Needles and pins that have been stuck in soap will glide through fabric.

Sewing—stuffing made easy

Cut clean, used pantyhose in rings and use as stuffing for pincushions, pillows, and children's toys. The fabric is washable and can easily be coaxed into tight corners.

Sewing—thread color choices

A good rule of thumb is to use a thread that is one shade darker than the fabric you

are working on. Thread has a tendency to fade more quickly than solid materials.

Sewing—threading a needle

If you have trouble threading a needle, wet the end of the thread and draw it across a bar of soap. The thread will stiffen and slip right through the eye of the needle. Or, draw the end of the thread across a wax candle first.

Shelf lining—adhesive-backed shelf paper

Put adhesive-backed shelf paper in the freezer for about an hour before using. The frozen paper will be less limp and easier to apply. Smooth it out with a blackboard eraser or dry squeegee.

Shelf lining—bath rug

Use an old bath rug to line the cabinet under your bathroom sink. It will soak up spills and leaks, and is easy to clean. Just toss it in the laundry.

Shelf lining—contact paper

The warmth from a hair dryer can remove contact paper from a shelf. If there's any glue left behind, use rubber-cement thinner, Soilove, or WD-40 aerosol lubricant.

Shelf lining—freezer or butcher paper

White freezer or butcher paper is perfect for lining kitchen and bathroom cabinets because it is sturdy, extra wide, and quite inexpensive. Place the coated side up to make for easy clean-ups, and use thumbtacks to hold down the corners.

Shelf lining—vinyl flooring

Use pieces of vinyl flooring to cover shelves. This product can be cut to size and is easily removed when you want to clean. Vinyl flooring is also very durable and comes in a variety of colors and patterns. Put the vinyl in the sun to soften it before cutting. Do not glue or attach the vinyl in any way; just lay it on the shelf.

Sound of music

Put a clock radio in every bedroom. Instead of the buzzer, set them all on the same radio station that plays lively music, and your family will get up to surround sound each morning.

Vinyl records

To straighten a warped vinyl phonograph record, place the record between two pieces of sturdy glass and set the glass in direct sunlight for 2 hours.

Windows—cord hiders

Put self-stick plastic hooks on the wall or window frame next to drapes and blinds. Keep any loose cords looped around the hooks.

Windows—curtain rods, unique

Instead of the typical drapery rod, hang curtains from a copper pipe or a sturdy tree branch set on brackets.

Windows—curtain rods, wide

Many window valances are hung on 2½-inch rods rather than the typical skinny ones. If you don't want to spend money to get the wider ones, update your skinny rods. Cut 2½-inch strips of wood from an old piece of paneling and use a hot glue gun to attach the strips to the skinny rod. Attach the rod to the existing hardware, which should still be in place on the wall. New valances can be slipped right over the rod.

Windows—curtains, sheer

To hang sheers and curtains quickly and easily, insert a table knife—blade-first—into the open end of the curtain rod. It will act as a guide and sheers will glide onto the rod without snagging.

9

Kids and Babies

Art and crafts—artist smocks

Old pillowcases can be turned into inexpensive smocks for kids to use when finger painting or doing other messy stuff. Just cut a hole on each side for the arms and a large one at the top for the head.

Art and crafts—dried-up markers

Are your children's markers starting to dry out? Dip the tip of the marker in water or vinegar for 5 to 10 seconds. Blot excess liquid, and you have just given a marker a new lease on life.

Art and crafts—edible finger paint recipe

You'll need one envelope of unflavored gelatin softened in ¼ cup warm water, 3 tablespoons granulated sugar, ½ cup cornstarch, 2 cups cold water, and food coloring. Mix sugar and cornstarch. Add water and cook over low heat, stirring constantly until thick. Remove from heat and add the softened gelatin. Divide into as many portions as you have colors (four or five is best). Add food coloring to each portion.

Art and crafts—face paint recipe

Ingredients: 1 teaspoon cornstarch, ½ teaspoon water, ½ teaspoon cold cream, and food coloring. Mix the first three ingredients, and blend well. Add food coloring a drop at a time until you get the color you want. Store in small covered containers. Paint chubby little faces with a small paintbrush. Allow paint to dry. Remove with cold cream.

Art and crafts—make a family history book

Write a book of your family's history. Let the kids write and illustrate their own personal chapters.

Art and crafts—make a flannel board

Cover a large piece of cardboard with flannel, using glue, staples, or tape. Cut shapes from felt, such as rectangles, squares, triangles, circles, trees, letters, numbers, and so on. Kids will spend hours creating scenes and pictures by sticking the felt to the flannel.

Art and crafts—make big crayons

Clean out a small, flat can. A tuna can works well. Preheat oven to 250°F. Fill the can halfway with crayon pieces that you would normally throw out. Don't forget to remove any paper. Place the can in the oven until the crayons melt in about 20 minutes. Once the crayons are melted and the colors have run together (don't stir or you'll introduce a new Crayola color: mud), take the can out of the oven and cool the mixture in the refrigerator until hard. Pop the crayon out of the can, and your kids will have a big, new rainbow crayon.

Art and crafts—make edible necklaces

Tiny fingers can easily thread Cheerios or Fruit Loops onto a length of yarn. Tie a knot in one end, and twist a bit of tape on the other end so it is easier to handle.

Art and crafts—make place mats

Cover your kids' drawings with clear adhesive-backed

contact paper, and use them as place mats. You can also give these great works of art to their grandparents as gifts.

Art and crafts—paint palette

Use plastic or Styrofoam trays (like the ones vegetables or fruit are sometimes packed in) as palettes for mixing paint colors. They won't leak, and they are especially good for kids' projects.

Art and crafts—paint pots

Save old muffin tins or egg cartons for kids' painting sessions.

Art and crafts—play-and-eat dough recipe

Here's an alternative recipe in the event your little one likes to eat more than play. Mix ½ cup smooth peanut butter with ¼ cup powdered sugar. Can be stored in a tightly closed container on the pantry shelf.

Art and crafts—play dough recipe

In a large pot combine 3 cups flour, 1 ½ cups salt, and 6 teaspoons cream of tartar. Stir in 3 cups cool water, into which you have mixed 3 tablespoons vegetable oil and food coloring of choice. Stirring constantly, heat over medium heat. Keep stirring until the mixture coagulates and begins to pull away from the sides of the pan, or for about 5 minutes. Turn onto a cutting board and cool slightly. Once you can touch it, knead it until it is smooth and has the right feel. Store in an airtight container.

Art and crafts—shaving cream finger painting

Dress each kid in an old shirt, apron, or pillowcase smock. Squirt out a small amount of shaving cream on the kitchen table. The kids can then "paint" on the table, and after rubbing for several minutes, the shaving cream will disappear. Test the tabletop ahead of time for any adverse effects.

Art and crafts—sidewalk chalk recipe

Mix together 1 cup plaster of Paris, 4 tablespoons water, and food coloring, and blend to a toothpaste consistency. Pour the mixture into cookie cutters placed on waxed paper to make fun shapes, and pour it into toilet tissue tubes covered on one end with waxed paper secured with a rubber band. Allow chalk to thoroughly dry. Remove from cutters or cardboard tubes.

Bathing—baby

Smear a tiny bit of petroleum jelly above your baby's eyebrows to channel soapy water and shampoo away from her eyes.

Bathing—food coloring

Kids sensitive to bubble bath but still want a fun and festive bath? Add a few drops of food coloring to the water and presto! Green, blue, or whatever color you want. It doesn't stain and they love it.

Bathing—goggles for shampooing

You can turn an unpleasant situation into a really fun time if you let your child wear swim goggles while you shampoo and rinse his hair.

Bathing—lotion warmer

Lotion can be cold on a baby's skin after a nice warm bath. Warm it up by floating the closed bottle of lotion in the bathwater with baby.

Books—covers

Instead of buying expensive, laminated book covers for paperbacks, children's books, or booklets, use clear contact paper. It is much cheaper and performs equally well.

Cleaning—baby bottles

To clean the gook that sometimes accumulates in the bottom of plastic baby bottles, drop a teaspoon of regular rice and a few tablespoons of hot water into the bottle. Apply the lid and shake vigorously.

Repeat as necessary. The kernels of rice act as tiny scrubbers to clean even the tightest spots inside the bottle.

Cleaning—rake to gather toys indoors

Keep a small plastic yard leaf rake for quickly picking up all those tiny toys kids love to scatter. Rake them into a pile. Now you can quickly sort and put away.

Cleaning—stuffed animals

To freshen up a stuffed animal that can't be laundered, give the toy a "shower" with baking soda. Sprinkle it on, work it in, allow to sit for a while, then shake well or vacuum the baking soda away.

Clothes and shoes— mark the right shoe

Mark your toddler's right shoe with a special mark like a heart or star. You'll be able to teach right from left while you teach how to put shoes on the correct feet.

Clothes and shoes— securing mittens

If your kids keep losing their mittens, do this: Sew a button to each mitten, and teach them how to button their mittens or gloves to a buttonhole in their coat or jacket when they take it off. No buttonholes? Make two in a concealed but convenient place on the inside of the coat.

Clothes and shoes—trace feet for right-size shoes

Every few months trace your kids' feet on paper, cut out, and carry with you. If you run into an outrageous shoe sale and the kids are not with you, you can fit shoes nearly perfectly using the drawn image.

Decorating—room redo

If the cost of redecorating a child's room with matching sheets, comforter, pillow shams, dust ruffle, and drapes sends you over the edge, here's a way to reduce that cost: Buy sheets in the pattern you want, then buy an extra set that matches exactly or coordinates nicely. Cover the box springs with the extra fitted sheet, which eliminates the need for a bed skirt. Use the extra flat sheet to make curtains and or a valance and throw pillows. Two additional flat sheets would make a perfect duvet if you have even minimal sewing skills.

Decorating—sleep under the stars

Instead of buying plastic stars or stickers for your child's ceiling, dab glow-in-the-dark paint on the tip of a dowel and randomly tap the ceiling in your child's room, reapplying paint as needed. The dots won't show during the day, but at night these "stars" glow and even seem to twinkle. A cheap and easy way to surprise a child.

Diaper rash

Instead of buying expensive diaper rash ointments, purchase store-brand zinc oxide from the drugstore. It works great to prevent and treat diaper rash and is very inexpensive. Always consult your pediatrician about any unusual condition that does not clear up quickly.

Entertainment and activities—bubbles recipe

Bubble recipe: Thoroughly mix 1 cup water, ⅓ cup Joy dish-washing liquid (must be Joy), and ⅛ cup white corn syrup. Use with a bubble blower.

Entertainment and activities—create a carnival

Summer boredom set in? Have your kids help you create a carnival. Using resources such as *Family Fun* magazine, design a selection of simple games kids will like, such as shooting cotton swabs through straws to knock down paper cups, water balloon tosses; make a golf club with a sponge tied to a stick, and so on. Make game tickets on your computer or draw by hand. Have your kids help with setup and include some fun food, such as popcorn in paper bags or homemade popsicles. Set up prizes picked up from the local thrift shop and "price" each with the number of tickets needed to win. Invite some friends, blow up some balloons, and have a ball.

Entertainment and activities— designer birthday party

Here's a great idea for a young girl's birthday. Buy inexpensive fabrics for the young guests to cut and create fancy dresses. You won't need to sew, just tie and pin with safety pins. Hold a fashion show to allow the guests to model their creations.

Entertainment and activities—dress up

Go to a thrift store and purchase old clothing, jewelry, shoes, hats, scarves, and purses, or ask for donations from friends and relatives. Select things that can easily be laundered and disinfected. Put everything into a special box

or costume trunk. Little ones love to dress up.

Entertainment and activities— garden hose phone

Insert a clean, tight-fitting funnel at each end of a garden hose. One child can speak into the "transmitter" funnel, while the other listens through the "receiver" funnel at the other end.

Entertainment and activities—indoor sandbox

Here's a cheap, indoor, rainy-day activity for preschoolers. Pour coarse cornmeal into roasting pans or small boxes to make indoor "sandboxes." Provide plastic utensils, toy soldiers, cars, trucks, and small wooden blocks to use in the "sand," and you will have created hours of fun. Keep the vacuum cleaner on standby.

Entertainment and activities—indoor tennis

You'll need one leg from a clean pair of old pantyhose,

a wire coat hanger, masking tape, scissors, and blown-up balloons. Bend the hanger into a diamond-shape and straighten the hook to form a handle. Slowly pull the hose over the hanger until the top point of the diamond fits into the foot portion. Now wrap hose tightly around the handle, making sure the sharp end is well padded. Tape the hose to the handle. Use balloons instead of a ball to play tennis indoors. This is easy, quick, and lots of fun for little ones.

Entertainment and activities— make a playhouse

Get a big cardboard box and cut holes for a door and windows. Let the kids color the box. Help them draw flowers at the bottom, shutters on the windows, maybe curtains on the windows. The possibilities are limitless. Washer, dryer, or other large boxes are ideal.

Entertainment and activities—occupied baby

Keep a stack of family photos at your baby's changing table.

Babies who can focus love to study the pictures, which will buy you enough time for a quick, noncombative diaper change. Just make sure these are photos you don't mind getting crumpled.

Entertainment and activities— rainy-day surprise video

Videotape or make a digital film of the kids in action during one fine summer day, then put the movie away for a rainy-day surprise for the kids.

Entertainment and activities— toys during phone calls only

If your kids cut up and misbehave when Mom's on the phone, here's a solution: Keep a large bag of small toys hidden until phone time, at which time the toys are taken out of the closet and dumped on the floor. The children are so excited with their "new" toys that Mom can have a pleasant conversation.

Equipment—booster chair

Start with old magazines of the same size, and stack

them to the desired height to properly boost your little one. Bind them together with strong tape, such as duct tape. Make a simple fabric cover that can be easily removed for laundering.

Equipment—chalkboard

Instead of buying an expensive chalkboard for your kids, for less than $20 you can purchase a piece of clear plywood and chalkboard paint available at any paint store. Paint according to instructions.

Equipment—kid's bulletin board

Need a bulletin board for a child's room? Use an old-fashioned game board—a relic from the age before electronic games took over. A no-longer-used Monopoly board is colorful and decorative for hanging on a playroom wall.

Equipment—nursery security viewer

Check on your sleeping infant without making noise or waking her up by installing a security door viewer in the nursery door.

Fear of the dark

If your children are fearful of the dark, send each to bed with a small flashlight. For the first few nights, they might flash it on and off until they fall asleep, but after the novelty wears off, they will keep it nearby for emergencies. Funny how that works, but it does. And for the cost of a few batteries, it's a great way to help children with their fear of the dark.

Food and meals—cereal mugs

Serve cereal to little kids in large mugs instead of easy-to-tip cereal bowls. The handle helps kids control the messies.

Food and meals—mealtime tray

Use a muffin tin as a food tray for a picnic outside, snacks during a movie, or for a sick child. Paper cupcake liners can hold the different foods.

Games and puzzles—make puzzles for toddlers

Glue brightly colored pictures from magazines or books onto pieces of cardboard. When dry, draw lines shaped like puzzle pieces over the pictures. Cut the pieces out and teach little ones how to put puzzle pieces together. For very young tots, cut into only two or three pieces.

Games and puzzles—map puzzles

Make inexpensive map puzzles to help your kids learn geography. Paste any map (world, country, state, or county) onto a sheet of poster board. Allow to dry. Cut into puzzle-shape pieces. For a map of the United States, cut along state borders.

Games and puzzles—memory game

Collect two identical copies of each family member's photo, and glue them to the lids of frozen-juice cans. On the opposite side of every game piece, glue a paper circle with the game's title, such as "Reese's Memory Game." To play, lay out all pieces with photos face-down. The child turns over one piece, names the family member, then attempts to locate its matching piece. Before long your child will recognize by face and name all family members, even those who live far away. Even a toddler can play.

Games and puzzles—new puzzles

When your kids get a new puzzle, number the box and put the same number on each puzzle piece. This way, if the pieces are accidentally mixed in with another puzzle, the kids can return the pieces to their proper place.

Games and puzzles— part replacements

Don't throw that game or toy away because some parts are missing. You can get a complete set of Monopoly money, 32 little green houses, a Boggle timer, Clue weapons, or Sorry! tokens at www.Hasbro.com. Hasbro owns Parker Brothers and other game and toy companies, so check on their website for more information. If you need Mattel or Fisher-Price game or toy replacement parts, visit www.Mattel.com.

Games and puzzles— playing-card holder

Tiny hands can hold playing cards if you make a holder from two plastic lids. Use margarine lids or the plastic tops from cans of potato chips. Simply line up the lids and secure them with a brass fastener or a button sewn on with sturdy thread. The cards just slip into the hairline space between the two lids.

Games and puzzles—rent video games before buying

When your kids want a new video game, rent it first to see if it's the appropriate age and skill level for them. You'll avoid spending big bucks on a game they may never play.

Hair—tiny ponytails

Tiny rubber bands from the orthodontist office are perfect to hold ponytails in an infant's fine hair. Just one twist and that pony will stay all day.

Memories—memory quilts

If you've saved lots of your kids' baby clothes and blankets, here's a terrific idea for what to do with them. Make quilts for each child from pieces of their old baby clothes.

Memories—when you're away

Leave a camera or camcorder with your babysitter so the next time your child does something new and special, you won't have to miss it.

Memories—YOU, the journal

Not into keeping detailed baby books? That's okay. Instead write your child a detailed letter for his or her birthday, citing the milestones of the past year. Keep each one, and by the time the child is grown, you'll have an excellent life journal.

On the go—10-gallon tub

A 10-gallon storage tub makes a great baby bathtub for home or travel. Just load it up with bath toys, towels, washcloths, and other items. If on vacation, you're ready to give your little one a bath in familiar surroundings without having to sit in a questionably "clean" motel bathtub.

On the go—bubbles

Keep a bottle of bubble solution and a couple of wands in your purse. You won't believe all the times you'll be able to pull that out to keep the kids happily occupied while waiting.

On the go—crayon tote

Metal bandage containers make great on-the-road crayon holders. Small enough to carry in your bag, the containers can be pulled out any time you want to keep little hands busy.

On the go—lunch prep

If you have older kids in school and little ones at home, pack everyone a lunch. This way if you have to run out unexpectedly, you and the little ones have lunch all ready to go. No need to spend on fast food.

On the go—packing for kids

When traveling with small children, put one day's outfit (shirt, pants, socks, underwear) into a gallon-size ziplock bag. Seal partway, push out air, and seal the rest of the way to make it very compact. This saves space in the suitcase and allows you or your child to find their clothes without rummaging through everything. Keeps everything nice and clean too.

On the go—portable swimming toys

Use a large mesh laundry bag to carry your kids' toys to and from the beach or public pool. When you return home, hose down the bag and hang it outside or over your tub so the toys can air-dry.

Organization and storage— double-decked closet

In the children's closets, install a high clothes rod for seldom-worn dress clothes and a lower one for everyday items. The lower one should be positioned so the child can easily reach it.

Organization and storage— laundry

If your children wear different sizes of similar underwear, socks, and T-shirts, doing the laundry can be enough to send you to the funny farm because everything looks alike. Clearly, your family needs to get color-coded, and the sooner the better. Pick up a variety of fabric paints so you have a different color for each member. Mark the toes of socks and the labels on underwear and T-shirts with the owner's color. Now folding and sorting laundry will be so easy, even the kids can do it.

Organization and storage— make up complete outfits

If you iron your kids' school and play clothes (or even if you don't), place complete outfits on hangers with socks, barrettes, belts, and other accessories tucked in a pocket. This saves a lot of time and frustration when it's time to get up and get ready to go.

Safety—high-chair security

Keep baby from sliding around in the high chair. Line the chair seat with a small rubber bath or sink mat. Cut to fit if necessary.

Safety—security whistle

When going to an unfamiliar or crowded place, give small children a whistle to blow should they become separated from you.

Safety—wading pool

To keep a child from slipping in a plastic wading pool, on the bottom affix nonslip adhesive shapes designed for the bathtub.

School—assignment book

If your child is forgetful about homework and household chores, get a special notebook for writing down assignments. This will give your youngster an incentive to keep track of homework, just like Mom and Dad jot down appointments in their special books.

School—first-day-of-school security photo

Help youngsters eliminate first-day-of-school jitters by taping a family portrait or photo of a pet to the notebook or lunch box your child takes to school.

School—free supplies

Keep your eyes open at the office. Instead of throwing away outdated three-ring binders, pocket folders, un-printed computer runs, and other useful supplies, bring them home for the kids'

school supplies, or donate them to your local school. Company logos can be covered with popular stickers or vinyl-paint designs.

School—high school ring

Before spending a lot on a high school ring for your student, check with local jewelry stores. Most people do not realize that local stores offer a wider variety of styles for at least two-thirds less than the on-campus company's price. Since this item commonly carries a price tag of $200 to $300, it pays to shop around.

School—home reading lessons

If your kids love to help out in the kitchen, let them read the recipe as you cook. This way, they get a reading lesson and learn how to follow directions, and you get to spend more time with them.

School—homework totes

Don't discard cardboard tubes from waxed paper and plastic

wrap. Give them to your kids to carry homework like maps and art projects back and forth to school.

Teaching responsibility— during school vacations

To keep skills sharp during school vacations, give kids schoolwork and chores each day. To improve their enthusiasm, decorate a big cardboard box and write Mom's Really Fantastic Prize Box on the outside. Fill the box with assorted small toys, and small packages of mints or candy bars, and so on. This will stop the nagging and the groaning.

Teaching responsibility— lost winter wear

Most kids go through stages when they lose every hat, scarf, and pair of gloves they own. So the next time cold-weather gear goes on sale, buy a few extras and hide them away. Whenever they can't find their winter wear, allow them to rent a substitute for, say, 50 cents. You'll make a few bucks

in the beginning, but plan on business dropping off considerably as your kids quickly become responsible.

Teaching responsibility— setting a table

Teach your kids to set the table by taping a diagram to the refrigerator. While you cook, they set and learn. Teamwork in action.

Toys—documented age range

Use a permanent marker to write the suggested age range on children's toys. This makes figuring out which toys are ready to be donated a snap and eliminates the confusion and clutter of keeping unwanted toys.

Toys—doll clothes for less

Newborn-size clothes from garage sales make great clothes for large baby dolls. They are better quality and a fraction of the price of new doll clothes.

Toys—make bowling pins

Empty 2-liter soda bottles make great bowling pins for kids. Put a little sand or some pebbles inside the bottles to make them more stable and use a lightweight playground ball as a bowling ball. Best used outdoors, in the basement, or in a clear area such as the kitchen floor.

Toys—road for toy cars

Make a roll-up roadway for the kids to drive toy cars along. On a piece of canvas, draw or tape out highways and byways with markers or electrical tape. Draw traffic signs, buildings, trees, gas stations, parking lots, and so on. When it's time to stow the roadway, you just roll it up.

Toys—swap

Start a toy-swapping club with other families. Trade toys your kids have outgrown or no longer use. Plan a really special trade during the first part of December. Young children don't care whether new toys are actually new or not.

10

Laundry

Bleaching—no chlorine

If you want to keep your white laundry stain-free and brilliantly white without using chlorine bleach, here's the secret: Fill the washing machine with the hottest water available. Add 1 cup Cascade automatic dishwasher powder and 1 cup washing soda (you can find this in the supermarket laundry section). Add washable whites and allow to agitate for a few minutes. Turn the machine off and allow to soak at least 3 hours (overnight is fine). Finish the cycle and dry as usual.

Bleaching—use half

You can cut the amount of chlorine bleach used in your wash by half when you add ½ cup baking soda to top-loading washing machines or ¼ cup to front loaders.

Candle wax—remove from tablecloths

To remove candle wax from a tablecloth, use a dull knife to scrape off as much wax as possible. Place the fabric between two blotters or facial tissues and press with a warm iron. Apply laundry stain treatment.

Wash with detergent in the hottest water that is safe for the fabric.

Color setting

White vinegar sets the color in washables. The first time you wash dark and bright colors, add 1 cup of white vinegar to the wash water.

Colorfastness

Will your new blue blouse run in the wash? Take a light-colored, wet washcloth and rub an inside seam of the blouse. If any color rubs off, the garment will run. Hand wash or dry-clean instead.

Corduroy

Keep corduroy looking brand-new. Wash inside out and according to label directions. If necessary, iron corduroy inside out to avoid crushing the pile.

Delicates—baby shampoo

Instead of using expensive cold-water detergents for delicates and fine sweaters, use baby shampoo. The results will be the same, and the cost is considerably less.

Delicates—hand washables in the shower

Take your delicate items that require hand washing into the shower with you. Instead of laundry detergent or Woolite, wash them with your shampoo.

Delicates—in a pillowcase

Machine wash hosiery and other delicate items in the washing machine by first putting them into a pillowcase and closing it with a safety pin.

Dryer—air-dry instead

Dryer lint is visual proof of just how destructive drying is to clothes. And if that's not enough, the heat causes gradual shrinking (expect even your preshrunk garments to lose another 5 percent). Whenever possible, air-dry your clothing. You'll cut energy costs and prolong the life of your garments. When you do use the dryer, turn dress garments inside out to minimize the pilling on the outside.

Dryer sheets—dispenser

Mount a paper towel holder next to the clothes dryer to dispense a roll of fabric softener sheets for easy access. And keep an empty tissue box close by to stash the used dryer sheets, which can be recycled.

Dryer sheets—use more than once

There is no need to throw out your fabric softener sheet after one use. One sheet will work just fine for two or even three loads of laundry.

Dryer sheets—use washcloths instead

As a cheaper substitute for dryer sheets, dampen an old washcloth with liquid softener, throw it in the dryer with a load of clothes, and you'll have static-free, good smelling, soft laundry. Wash and dry the cloth every couple of loads so it will continue to absorb the solution.

Drying—bathroom rack

Create a convenient drying rack in your bathroom. Install an adjustable tension-type shower curtain rod or two over the center of the tub at a height that is easy to reach but well out of the way when you shower. Drips will go down the drain instead of all over the floor.

Drying—comforter or pillow

When drying a comforter or pillow in the clothes dryer, toss in a couple of clean tennis shoes. They will bounce around on the items and keep them from bunching up.

Drying—cut the time, use extra spin

When you have a heavy load in the washing machine, such as towels, reset the machine for an extra spin dry. The drying time will then be reduced considerably.

Drying—cut the time, with dry towels

A dry towel in the dryer with a very damp load will speed drying time. The towel will absorb a lot of the moisture.

Drying—dry several loads at once

Don't dry only one load of laundry. Do several loads if you can, one right after the other. It takes a lot of energy to get the dryer from room temperature to hot, so while it's at that level, take full advantage and save energy.

Drying—marks from clothes rack

If the bars of your wooden clothes-drying rack leave brown stripes on your clothes, you can solve the problem easily by covering the bars with aluminum foil.

Drying—outdoor hangers

Protect the clothes you hang outdoors from taking off in a strong wind: Put each piece of clothing on two hangers, hooks reversed, to keep the hangers from falling.

Drying—plastic shower curtain

Yes, you can dry a plastic shower curtain in the dryer. Set the temperature to low and add one or two dry towels. Common sense says plastic in a clothes dryer presents a potential fire hazard. So don't even think about walking away. Stand there for the 2 minutes it takes to remove the wrinkles and dry the shower curtain.

Drying—unmentionables

Heat deteriorates hosiery and misshapes bras, so air-dry whenever possible.

Ironing—emergency board

Need an emergency ironing board? Use a kitchen bread-board covered with a dish towel.

Ironing—lightly scented

If you do not like to spray perfume directly onto your

clothes or skin, try giving your ironing board a squirt or dab before pressing your blouse, trousers, or skirt. The steam from the iron draws just the whisper of the scent, and it clings to the fabric all day.

Ironing—out of time

If you run out of time before you finish ironing, stuff any clothes you've dampened into a plastic bag and store the bag in the refrigerator. This prevents mildew and saves the time it would take to dampen them again.

Ironing—pleats

Use bobby pins or clothespins at the bottom of each pleat to hold it flat while you iron.

Lint—on corduroy

To remove lint from corduroy garments after laundering, take them out of the dryer while they're still damp and brush vigorously with a clothes brush. The next time you wash the items, keep them lint-free by turning them inside out before laundering.

Lint—on dark clothes

Use a bit of white vinegar in the final rinse water to keep lint from clinging to dark clothes.

Mending kit for laundry room

Create a mending kit for the laundry room. Thread several sewing needles with basic colors, stick them into a pincushion, and hang it near the dryer.

Odors—baking soda in the hamper

Sprinkle baking soda into the laundry hamper to minimize odors from soiled clothing.

Odors—perspiration in clothes

Perspiration odors in washable clothing can be removed by wetting the affected areas and rubbing in baking soda before laundering.

Odors—smoke in clothes

When washing smoky-smelling duds, add 1 cup baking soda to the wash cycle. If laundering doesn't do the trick, check whether your dry cleaner offers a treatment that removes smoke odor. This treatment does cost more than regular cleaning, but it might be worth the cost if the clothes are of particular value.

Pillows

Hand wash foam-filled pillows in mild detergent, then roll them in a towel and squeeze out excess water. Machine drying could cause a fire, so always air-dry foam-filled pillows away from heat.

Presoak manually

Instead of using the presoak and prewash cycles on your washing machine, which use additional water and energy, use the regular cycle but turn it off after the clothes agitate a few minutes. Let them soak for an hour or overnight, and then resume the rest of the cycle.

Pretreat collars and cuffs

Use shampoo to pretreat dirty collars and cuffs. Scrub gently with an old toothbrush. Shampoo is meant to clean body oil, which is exactly what that ring is.

Rugs—in a pillowcase

Cotton and synthetic braided throw rugs are generally machine washable in cold water on a gentle cycle. The agitation of the machine, however, can be hard on these types of rugs, so to keep them intact, put the rug into a pillowcase and close it with a safety pin. Throw the rug, case and all, into the washing machine for a gentle yet effective cleaning. Be sure to test that the rug is colorfast prior to laundering.

Scorch marks from white cotton

The best way to remove scorch marks from white cotton is with 3 percent hydrogen peroxide, which acts like bleach. Using an eyedropper, saturate the scorched area, and allow to sit for 15 to 20 minutes. Repeat until the marks have disappeared, then flush the fabric with water.

Socks—keep in bags

No more lost socks. Make each family member—even the baby—a drawstring sock bag to keep in his room. All dirty socks go in, and the bag is thrown into the wash. After drying, the bag, still full, is returned to its owner intact.

Socks—pin them

Pin kids' dirty socks together before dropping them in the laundry. The time invested will be more than returned when you're sorting laundry later.

Stains and spots—basic solution for fabrics

Mix 1 cup Cascade (powdered) and 1 cup Clorox 2 with very hot tap water in a large pail or container. Soak stained articles overnight. Wash as usual.

Stains and spots—blood

Presoak bloodstained clothing in cold or warm water for at least 30 minutes. If the stain remains, soak in lukewarm ammonia water (3 tablespoons ammonia per gallon of water). Rinse. If the stain still remains, work in detergent and wash, using fabric-safe bleach.

Stains and spots—cocoa and chocolate

To remove cocoa and chocolate stains, scrub the stained area immediately with cold water. Apply laundry stain remover to area and wash as usual.

Stains and spots—coffee

The key to treating coffee stains is to get at them as quickly as possible. If the garment must be dry-cleaned, don't waste any time getting it to the cleaner. If it's washable, immediately rinse it in cold water and apply a good prewash treatment as soon as possible. Wash the garment in warm, soapy water, then rinse and allow it to drip-dry.

Don't put it in the dryer just in case all the stain didn't come out, which sometimes happens with coffee, and you need to repeat the process.

Stains and spots—deodorant

Vinegar applied to clothing stained by deodorant removes the spots from most fabrics. Soak the soiled area in the vinegar, then launder the garment as usual.

Stains and spots—fruit, berries, and juice

Stains in fabric from fruits, berries, and juices should be sponged immediately with cold water. Then if it's safe for the fabric, hold the garment over the sink and pour boiling water through the stain. Follow by working laundry detergent into the stain and rinse.

Stains and spots—grass, with rubbing alcohol

Pretreat minor grass stains on washable fabric with full-strength rubbing alcohol. Rub gently and launder as usual.

Stains and spots—grass, with shampoo

To remove grass stains from clothes, spot-treat the stain with a shampoo made for oily hair.

Stains and spots—ink, with borax mixture

Place the ink-stained fabric over several thicknesses of paper toweling. Combine 1 tablespoon white vinegar, 1 tablespoon milk, 1 teaspoon lemon juice, and 1 teaspoon borax in a small bowl, and "paint" the spot. Wait for a few minutes, then sponge the area with cool water. Repeat until the stain is gone.

Stains and spots—ink, with hair spray

Aerosol hair sprays, because they contain a high concentration of acetone, will remove some ballpoint ink stains from clothing. Try this: Hold a rag under the fabric to blot the ink that comes through on the other side, then aim and spray. Remember this tip when

278

you're at the office and get an ink stain. Someone usually has hair spray, and the key to beating an ink stain is to tackle it as quickly as possible.

Stains and spots—ink, with milk

A quick, easy, and cheap way to get ink spots out of washable clothing is to soak the stain in milk. Wash as usual.

Stains and spots—last-ditch effort

After you've tried every method you know to remove impossible stains such as mildew from fabric, try this: Use a cotton swab to apply a commercial mildew stain product such as Tilex directly to the stain. Let stand for about a minute and wash immediately. This will work on colorfast or white fabrics but will leave a huge bleach mark on noncolorfast items. This is a last-ditch, severe action—so beware.

Stains and spots—lipstick

Use hair spray to remove lipstick stains from clothing.

Spray it on, let it sit for a minute or two, and wipe carefully. Launder as usual.

Stains and spots—makeup

Here's a wonderful prewash treatment for cleaning makeup from collars: Mix equal amounts of white vinegar and liquid dish-washing detergent like Dawn or Joy. Rub into the soiled collar or other soiled spots, and toss into the washing machine. Launder as usual.

Stains and spots—mildew on white fabrics

To remove mold or mildew stains from most white fabrics, soak the garment for an hour or so in a solution of 1 tablespoon vinegar, ½ cup liquid bleach, and 2 quarts hot water. Wash and dry the garment as usual.

Stains and spots—on Little League uniforms

Clay dirt from baseball fields gets on clothes and uniforms and is just about impossible to remove. Try this: Brush off any dry clay remaining on the fabric. Treat heavily stained areas with your laundry stain treatment and then soak the garments overnight in a solution of enzyme-action detergent (like Biz), following package directions. The next morning, launder the clothes. If stains remain, repeat the whole process. Or, if the fabric is white, use chlorine bleach as a last resort.

Stains and spots—on wool and silk

An excellent spot remover for wool and silk is Murphy's Oil Soap, which is available in the household cleaning section of the supermarket. Use directly on the fabric and allow it to soak in. Always test on an inconspicuous spot like an inside seam. Wash as usual. Murphy's is also great for cars, floors, and, of course, wood furniture and cabinets.

Stains and spots—paint, tar, and rubber cement

Soften hardened paint, tar, and rubber cement on washable fabrics with petroleum jelly. Launder fabrics treated in this way immediately after application.

Stains and spots—perspiration

To remove perspiration stains, add 4 tablespoons of salt to 1 quart hot water, and sponge the fabric with the solution.

Stains and spots—rust

To remove rust stains from washable fabric, shake ordinary table salt on the stain and wet with lemon juice. Allow to set overnight, then wash normally.

Stains and spots—sunscreen

That ring around the collar on shirts and blouses may be your sunscreen, so make sure you pretreat it with a stain treatment that is designed to break down and remove grease and oil. Wash as usual, using the warmest water that is safe for the fabric. Don't put the garment in the dryer before checking to see if all the stain has been removed. If the stain remains, the heat from the dryer may set it. Repeat treatment as necessary.

Stains and spots—yellowed fabric

Denture-cleaning tablets will remove yellow stains from fabric. Find a container big enough to hold the stained fabric. Fill the container with warm water and the number of tablets according to the ratio described on the package. After the tablets dissolve, add the stained item to the solution and soak until the spots are gone.

Stains and spots—yellowed linens

To remove that disgusting yellow from old linens that are supposed to be white, dissolve ¼ cup automatic dishwasher detergent (such as powdered Cascade) in a large stainless steel (not aluminum) pan filled with boiling water. Carefully add linens and allow them to soak, off of heat, for 8 hours. Rinse and launder as usual.

Starch—spray, cornstarch

Dissolve 1 tablespoon cornstarch in 1 pint of cold water. Place in a spray bottle. Shake well before using. Clearly label the contents of the spray bottle.

Starch—spray, make your own

If you use a lot of spray starch around your house, you've likely discovered those aerosol cans of spray starch don't last very long. Cheaper and better, purchase concentrated liquid starch such as Sta-Flo and mix it in a spray bottle, 1 part starch to 2 parts water. In this way a 32-ounce bottle of starch equals 3½ cans of aerosol starch for a fraction of the cost.

Washing—baking soda boost

Add ½ cup baking soda to the laundry wash cycle, and you can expect your liquid laundry detergent to get a boost in its enzymatic and cleaning action.

Washing—cut suds when hand washing

Cut excess suds when hand washing clothes by adding a splash of vinegar to the rinse. Rinse again in plain water.

Washing—in coin-operated laundry

When at the laundromat, place a small refrigerator magnet on each washer and dryer you're using. No more embarrassing mix-ups.

Washing—inside out means longer wear

Reduce fading and pilling. Turn clothing wrong side out before washing and drying to reduce friction on the right side of the garment.

Washing—water temperature

The bulk of your laundry is only minimally soiled. Modern-day detergents clean very well with cold water as well as warm. Your colors will last longer, too, if you use cold water. The average family can save several hundred dollars per year by switching to cold water when possible. And always rinse clothes in cold water. The temperature of the rinse cycle does not affect cleaning. Exception: Health professionals recommend that bedsheets and towels be laundered in 130°F water to make sure nasty bacteria and stubborn germs are properly laid to rest.

Waste not—measure detergent

Measure detergent for both washing machine and dishwasher. If you just dump it in, you are probably using way too much.

Waste not—stiff laundry = too much detergent

If items come out of the laundry stiff, you're probably using too much detergent. Don't use more than the manufacturer advises, and add a cup of vinegar to the rinse water to help soften your clothes.

Waste not—use the last bit of liquid laundry soap

When using the last quantity of liquid laundry soap, fill the empty bottle all the way to the top with water and replace the lid. Shake vigorously, and use the entire contents with your next load of laundry. You'll get one last wash from a bottle that normally would have been thrown away.

11

Money and Finances

Banking—ATM safety

When using the automatic teller machine, always wait for the "Welcome" prompt to signal that your transaction is over, and then take your card. Leaving prematurely may allow the next customer to continue making transactions in your account.

Banking—checks, buying

Don't buy checks through the bank. You can save 50 percent of what they charge by ordering through an independent source like Current, 800-848-2848 (Current.com), or Checks-in-the-Mail (checksinthemail.com), 800-733-4443.

Banking—checks, deposit safety

Before you take a check to the bank, write on the back "for deposit only" followed by your signature and account number. If the check is lost or stolen before you can get it to the bank, it cannot be cashed or deposited to any other account.

Banking—credit unions

Many credit unions offer low- or no-fee checking accounts and free checks. Go to www.FindACreditUnion.com to find a credit union that is right for you. Most credit unions welcome spouses, children, brothers, sisters, and parents of the member. You will enjoy federally insured deposits and low-interest auto loans. And you'll earn higher than bank interest rates on your savings accounts.

Banking—direct deposits

Arrange with your bank or credit union to have your paycheck automatically deposited, your bills paid automatically, and your savings funded automatically from your checking account. With this type of arrangement you will be handling your money less, so you won't be as tempted to play games with the account. The national average bank charge for online bill pay is $.69 a month, which reflects the fact that most banks offer this service for free. Your bank will be able to answer all of your questions.

Banking—go local

Switch to a smaller, locally owned bank. The fee structure will likely be lower and some services will actually be offered at no cost, such as free checking and free checks.

Bill paying—envelope method

Use the envelope system to handle your household money. Once a month (or as often as you are paid), withdraw a sum according to your spending plan categories, and place that specific amount of cash into each envelope marked for that purchase instead of keeping it in your checking account. This method will really help eliminate the temptations to "just write a check" or use your debit card for this or that. For some reason, this system really keeps folks honest and forces them to spend only a set amount in each category. When it's gone, it's gone. This provides a great visual learning experience for children when they can actually observe their parents managing the money.

Bill paying—keeping track of due dates

To keep track of bills that are coming due, put the return portion of each bill in an envelope, address it, stamp it, and write the due date on the left-hand corner of the envelope. File the envelopes chronologically, and review them weekly. No more late fees.

Bill paying—pay the rent first

Which payment should you pay first when things are tight and something has to take priority? Pay the rent first. Typically, landlords act quickly if you don't pay on time.

Bill paying—pay twice a month

Get into the habit of paying bills twice each month, say, on the 1st and 15th. During the month as the bills arrive, follow this routine: Open a

bill and place the return portion in its return envelope and throw the rest away. Write the due date on the outside of the envelope and separate into two due-date piles: "1st of the month" and "15th of the month."

Boarders

If you have an extra room, consider taking in a boarder to help defray your costs. Post a notice at a local community college or corporation. Check with personnel offices at larger corporations in your area. Often they assist employees in locating affordable housing. Before you hand over the keys to your house to a stranger, check many references, get a credit report on the candidate, and have a written contract that includes Rules of the House.

Contingency fund in safe place

You need to have some of your contingency fund in small denominations of cash—$1,000 is reasonable, but any amount is good. Put it in a safe place outside of your bank, like a fireproof home safe or other similarly protected receptacle, known only to you and one other person. In the event of a natural disaster that cripples utilities and services, or if the economy experiences a worst-case bank holiday scenario, you'll want to have cash on hand. (A bank holiday is the temporary closing of a bank in the event that its obligations exceed its resources. It could also occur due to a natural disaster like a flood where the bank and all its ATMs are underwater and therefore will not work.)

Credit cards—approval by phone, so leave it at home

If you've always been convinced that you must maintain and carry a credit card "just in case of emergencies," here's what you can do to stop looking for emergencies: Write your credit card number, expiration date, and the credit card company's 800 number in your address book encrypted like "Aunt Penny," and then leave the card at home—frozen in a block of ice. Because you don't have it and you know it will be a hassle to make purchases without it, your urges to buy impulsively will be greatly reduced. But in case of a genuine emergency, you will have the phone number and information you need to get approval over the phone.

Credit cards—ask for a lower interest rate

If you receive an invitation to accept a new credit card with a remarkably lower interest rate, call your current credit card company and tell them about this competing offer. If you have a good track record with them, and they get the message that you just might leave in favor of the more attractive rate, you could receive an on-the-spot interest rate reduction. You'll wonder why you didn't call sooner. Remember, while the interest rate may be lower, the balance transfer fee may be huge. Read the fine print.

Credit cards—avoid annual fees

Credit card companies deny publicly that they waive annual fees, but insiders admit the practice is often used to save valuable customers. Squawk and you just might receive.

Credit cards—pay during grace period

Credit card interest is a terrible waste of money. Pay your bills in full every month during the grace period. If your credit card company charges a penalty or fee for not carrying a balance, cancel that card. There are plenty of no-fee companies who will be happy to have your business.

Credit cards—pay early in the month

Make credit card payments as early in the billing month as possible or make two smaller payments a month if you can't pay it all early. Most banks calculate interest on the average daily balance. The larger the payment and the sooner in the month you make it, the more

of it will apply to the principal. It may not be much savings at first, perhaps a buck or two, but savings grow month after month until the account is paid off.

Credit cards—pay with check system

Pay your entire balance during the grace period so you'll never incur interest charges. Whenever you use your card, follow this practice. On the same day, as soon as you walk into the house, write a check for the full amount of purchase and deduct it from your account balance. You spent the money so it is no longer available to you. It's gone. As soon as the statement shows up, mail the full payment immediately.

Credit cards—personal identification number (PIN)

Never write your personal identification number (PIN) on your debit or credit card or on anything that would readily identify what it is. Instead "embed" it in a phone number under a fictitious entry in your phone book. Example: If your PIN is 3614, make an entry of "Penelope 361-4000." Choose a PIN that can't be traced, and never select a number that can be derived from the contents of your wallet.

Credit cards—plastic surgery

If you are out of control with credit cards and want to create a real turning point in your life, invite a few close friends and relatives to celebrate your plastic surgery. They'll be so curious, you know they'll show up. Of course, you intend to cut up your credit cards, then make a personal commitment to no new debt.

Credit cards—refuse surcharge

If a store adds a surcharge to your bill for paying with a credit card, refuse to pay it. Credit card companies like American Express, Visa, and MasterCard do not allow venders to add a surcharge to credit card purchases.

Credit cards—register purchases in checkbook

To prevent month-end credit card statement shock and to also make sure you have set aside enough money to pay the balance in full when it arrives, record your credit purchases in your checkbook register in the same way you record your checks. In the first column instead of the check number, write something like "Visa" or "Credit" then deduct that credit purchase amount from your current balance. If you enter your credit card purchases with red ink, they'll stand out and it will be easy to reconcile the statement.

Credit cards—remove name from preapproved lists

One of the problems of paying off credit card debt is the number of preselected or preapproved credit card offers that begin arriving in the mail. In order to stop these offers, call 888-567-8688 or write to: Equifax Options, PO Box 740123, Atlanta, GA

30374-0123. Include your complete name, full address, social security number, and signature. Equifax is one of the three major credit reporting agencies. They will remove your name from the lists they provide and will also share your request with the other two nationwide credit reporting agencies, Experian and TransUnion.

Credit cards—safely dispose of applications

If you are not interested in preapproved credit applications or blank checks for an existing account that you receive in the mail, don't throw them in the trash. A thief who finds it can actually take out an account in your name and begin charging in your name. Always destroy applications by cutting them into bits and disposing of the pieces in two or three different trash receptacles. You want to make it impossible for the paperwork to be put back together. Thieves are getting very clever these days.

Credit cards—think before you carry one

Carry a credit card only if you keep the minimum balance at, or very near, $0. If you can't hold the rule, keep the card hidden in your dresser. Why? Because paying 18 percent to 20 percent on a monthly balance is crippling—a financial shot in the foot.

Credit cards—you only need one

Accept only one credit card and make sure it has no annual fee. There's nothing virtuous about having an assortment of credit cards. One is all you'll ever need. The only thing you can do with two cards that you can't do with one is owe more people more money.

Credit "repair" services

Avoid credit repair clinics or "specialists" who make promises to solve your credit report problems. There is no lawful way to repair a bad credit report or remove a bankruptcy from your file. Don't pay them a nickel.

Currency

Prevent newly minted paper currency from sticking together by placing bills front to front and back to back.

Customer service—call first

If you have a consumer problem, save time by calling and asking to speak to the service desk or manager. Explain your problem and ask what their procedure is for fast and effective resolution. If this is not satisfactory, have a clear idea of exactly how you would like the matter resolved.

Customer service—complaint letters

When writing a letter of complaint to a manufacturer or retailer, be clear, be bold, be neat, be brief, be courteous, be patient, and be thorough. Don't threaten; simply state the situation and ask for help in resolving your dispute. Give a date 3 or 4 weeks hence, at which time if you've not received satisfaction, you will

know to take the matter to the next level.

Customer service—document communications on a calendar

When requesting a refund, repair, or replacement, keep track of all communications on a calendar. Summarize phone calls and send a follow-up letter of understanding. Don't give up until you are satisfied.

Customer service—record a name, date, and time

Until a problem is completely resolved to your satisfaction, always ask for and write down the name and position of the person you speak with regarding a consumer problem. Also record the date and time of the call.

Customer service—return it for a refund

If you buy something that turns out to be faulty or unsatisfactory, don't stash it in a closet unless you have an unusual need for white elephant gifts. Return it. Get your money back or at least get credit toward a future purchase. With merchants so hungry for business these days, I think you will discover a generous return policy.

Education—audit a class or two

If you're not sure about a particular college or course, consider auditing a class or two. Even the most prestigious colleges and universities will allow you to take two or three courses without actually applying to the school. Inquire about the auditing fee.

Education—bartering

Whether it's an education for your children or for yourself, you may be able to barter for the tuition. Offer to clean the music teacher's house in exchange for piano lessons or work in the preschool office. Whatever you do well may be just what the private teacher, private academy, or university needs desperately.

Education—consider nursing or dental hygiene training

Become a nurse or dental hygienist. By majoring in one of these skills in your undergraduate program, you will have a profession that you can develop, which can also provide employment while attending medical or dental school. Becoming a nurse or dental hygienist in a shortage area or in the military may qualify you for student loan forgiveness.

Education—for seniors

Many colleges and universities across the country offer senior citizens the opportunity to take classes and earn degrees for free or at a considerably reduced fee. Proof of age (starting at 55 to 65) and state residency is usually required. These senior discount programs are often not publicized, so it is advisable to call the admissions office to inquire.

Education—reimbursement from employer

Go to work for a company that offers tuition reimbursement to its employees. There's nothing wrong with seeking employment with companies in locations and with policies that fall in line with your personal education goals.

Education—scholarships

Your time spent searching, researching, and applying for scholarships for yourself or your kids will be time well spent. Scholarships represent tax-free income.

Education—tuition for employees in higher education

Before you enroll at a college or university, find employment there. Employees are usually entitled to reduced, if not free, tuition.

Home business logo—tap local marketing classes

If you are starting a home business, check with your local community college or university. College art classes will design business logos as part of a class project, marketing classes will often help with brochures, and photography classes will take pictures.

Housing—building your home is a huge risk

Have your head examined before you attempt to build your own home. Unless you are a developer or professional contractor, you are in for a few surprises, not the least of which is that it will take twice as long as promised and cost twice as much as estimated.

Housing—buying, house-hunting photos

Use your digital camera or phone to snap pictures of each house you're interested in. Attach the photos to corresponding notes and information, and at the end of the day, rather than being confused, you'll have a clear record of exactly what you saw.

Housing—buying, interest on earnest money

When purchasing a home, make sure you will earn interest on your deposit during the escrow period.

Housing—buying, worst house in good neighborhood

If you're looking for a bargain, buy the worst house in a good neighborhood. You can always fix up a house, but you can't change the location.

Housing—buying or selling, document with photos

Take photographs both inside and outside of your house, and make them part of the contract along with a list of what stays with the property after the sale. This eliminates debate at the closing as to whether the dining room fixture was a crystal chandelier or a bare bulb.

Housing—buying or selling, win-win negotiation

When negotiating the purchase or sale of a home, always ask for more than you are willing to accept—even if that is beyond your level of expectation and you're sure they'd never agree. More than likely the other person will meet you halfway, in essence splitting the difference. That's what makes both of you winners. You get more than you ever dreamed possible, and they didn't have to give nearly as much as they thought you expected. It's called the "art of negotiation."

Housing—mortgage interest rate reduction

Inquire if the financial institution servicing your mortgage offers an interest rate reduction when payments are automatically paid from your checking account. Example: A credit union recently introduced a ¼ percent reduction for any member who authorizes automatic withdrawal.

Housing—mortgage principal prepayment, pay down

Pay more than your monthly mortgage payment in the form of a second *check* on which you have clearly written "principal prepayment." This is probably one of the best things you can do with extra cash. And you have no unsecured debt. You will pay down the principal more quickly, which will result in a tremendous savings of future interest.

Housing—mortgage principal prepayment, payoff

The One-Twelfth Trick. While your mortgage should be the very last debt you target for payoff, when that time comes, here's a slick way to do it. At the same time you make your regular mortgage payment each month, make a second payment that is equal to $\frac{1}{12}$ (one-twelfth) of one payment. Clearly mark this second payment as "Principal Prepayment Only." Do this every month and at the end of one year you will have made the equivalent of 13 monthly payments. This

simple trick will cut your payoff time by years and save thousands in interest.

Housing—renting, rent control

If you rent, find an area with rent control. If the law is in place, you might as well take advantage of it and enjoy the secure feeling that your rent will not be unreasonably increased.

Housing—selling, rent out before selling at a loss

If you are going to sell your home at a loss, try to hold off awhile and rent it out so you can take advantage of the tax loss when you eventually sell. Check with your accountant. If you can show it as an investment rather than a personal residence, you might be able to recoup some of the loss.

Insurance—auto, collision deductible

Increase the deductible on your auto insurance and save collision insurance. For example, if your insurance policy currently provides for a $200 deductible, meaning you will be required to pay the first $200 of any claim, increase it to $500 and your premiums will drop dramatically. Call your insurance agent to get quotes on various deductible amounts. Just make sure that if you do have a claim, you'll be able to come up with the deductible no matter how much it is. You'd be wise to have an amount equal to your deductible stashed in an interest-bearing account just in case, and then drive defensively to reduce the risk of ever having to use it.

Insurance—auto, collision for older vehicle

Eliminate collision insurance on an older vehicle. Depending on its condition, an older car may not be worth the expense of insuring for more than liability. Conventional wisdom says that if a car is worth $2,500 or less, drop the collision. You'd be better off putting an amount equivalent to

the collision premiums into an interest-bearing account and saving it toward another car. Of course you should never drive without the liability coverage required by the state in which you reside.

Insurance—auto, discounts for defensive driving course

Many states offer significant auto insurance discounts if the driver has recently completed a defensive driving course. Call your insurance agent and inquire if this applies in your state. If it does, sign up!

Insurance—auto, discounts for low mileage

Most insurance companies offer discounts to low-mileage drivers.

Insurance—auto, keep agent updated

Make sure your agent has all of the correct information including your teenage son's good driving record and 3 years' experience. All of these things might matter.

Insurance—auto, liability umbrella policy

Instead of carrying $1 million liability insurance on a single auto to be well protected when participating in car pools, insuring younger drivers, and so on, consider carrying a $1 million liability umbrella policy, which in most cases will cover all of your cars and your principal residence. The annual premium should be around $100 if all your policies are with the same company, if you have clean driving records and no inexperienced operators.

Insurance—auto, rate reduction for changed driving requirements

Be sure to let your auto insurance company know of any changes to your driving requirements, such as switching from driving to work to joining a car pool or not commuting to a job as you once did. Both of these events could

result in a significant rate reduction.

Insurance—don't buy too much

Make sure you have adequate protection but not excessive coverage, no matter what type of insurance you are considering. And by accepting higher deductibles, you can afford better coverage.

Insurance—don't make small claims

Too many small claims can lead to policy cancellations or premium hikes. Insurance companies think that someone who files frequently is heading for a serious accident.

Insurance—health, a must expense

Never be without health insurance. High deductibles with low premiums are recommended if you are and plan to remain healthy, because this type of coverage is for catastrophic events. One uninsured catastrophic illness or accident could wipe out everything you have saved and planned for.

Insurance—health, check at school

If your family can't afford full medical insurance for each member, consider the school accident insurance offered to each child at the start of the new school year. For as little as $10, your child or college student may be eligible for insurance that would cover the normal, but expensive, childhood accidents. Most kids' medical bills are the result of accidents (broken bones, damaged teeth, stitches, and other injuries), so this type of insurance makes a lot of sense.

Insurance—health, shop frequently

Shop for your health insurance coverage regularly. With many companies, the first-year premium is much less, so switching may not be a bad idea. If your employer offers a menu of coverage options, check them all carefully and determine which is best for your particular situation. Never cancel one coverage until you have another fully in place.

Insurance—home, discounts for security systems

Ask about homeowners' insurance discounts for security systems, smoke alarms, and good driving records. Always ask! The agent or company may not volunteer the information.

Insurance—home, mortgage: buy life insurance instead

Typically overpriced, mortgage insurance (not to be confused with private mortgage insurance called PMI, which is completely different) is like life insurance because it pays off your remaining mortgage balance in the case of your demise. But who says your spouse or heirs would want to apply insurance proceeds to pay off the mortgage, which may be the lowest interest debt you leave them? If you have this type of coverage, they'll have no choice. It is far better to buy regular term insurance. It's much cheaper and leaves your heirs with more options.

Insurance—home, mortgage: cancel private (PMI) coverage

Private mortgage insurance (PMI) is usually required to protect the lender against the possible default of a buyer who enters into a mortgage with less than 20 percent down payment. In most situations PMI can be canceled once the equity reaches 20 percent either by paying down the mortgage or the property appreciating in value. But it will not happen automatically. You must call and get the ball rolling. Expect to be required to prove the market value of your home and that you now have at least 20 percent equity. PMI is expensive, and you could be paying $1,500 or more each year in premiums. Do whatever you must to cancel it if you qualify. PMI does not protect the borrower in any way. It's for the lender all the way.

Insurance—home, renter's coverage a must

If you rent, buy a tenant's policy. This is a must. Landlords are not responsible for your belongings in case of disaster.

Insurance—home, replacement value for possessions

Add a replacement-cost rider to renter's or homeowner's insurance. It may cost a little more, but in case of a claim, you will be glad you added the rider. Without it, the company will depreciate the value of every item, and you will be a big loser.

Insurance—life, adjust when dependents change

Cut back on life insurance as your dependents become independent. Providing for a spouse alone costs less than a spouse and eight kids.

Insurance—life, avoid TV and mail offerings

Never buy life insurance from television or direct mail ads. This is a sleazy marketing ploy. The premiums are at least 400 percent too high for the coverage, and the exclusions are mammoth.

Insurance—life, for kids

Don't buy life insurance for kids. It makes absolutely no sense. Insure only wage earners (including stay-at-home moms), whose untimely demise would create a financial hardship.

Insurance—life, for singles

If you're single, buy life insurance only if someone is financially dependent on you and would suffer an undue financial hardship if your income were to suddenly disappear. Most singles have no reason to carry life insurance.

Insurance—life, travel coverage not necessary

Don't pay extra for travel insurance. Statistically, it is highly unlikely you will die in an accident, and even if you do, the basic life insurance you carry should be sufficient.

Insurance—pay premiums annually

If possible, pay insurance premiums annually. Avoid the added costs for monthly or quarterly billing.

Insurance—take higher deductibles

In essence, you partially self-insure by being willing to take the chance that you won't get sick, you won't crash the car, and you won't be burglarized. The higher the deductible, the lower the premium. The insurance company actually compensates the customer who is willing to share a great portion of the risk.

Investing—guidelines for beginning investors

As a beginning investor, any plan you consider should have all the following features or you run a great risk of failure: (1) The investment must be simple to understand and easy to follow. (2) It must take very little time to administrate. (3) It should not cause you stress or anxiety. (4) It must not change your lifestyle or cause

disharmony in your home.
(5) You must be able to handle the investment entirely on your own. (6) It must have the advantage of liquidity (getting your money back quickly in the event of an emergency). (7) It must work equally well for the person with very little to invest as well as the wealthy investor.

Investing—mutual fund instead of lottery tickets

Instead of throwing away $2 a week on lottery tickets for the next 50 years, invest that money in an aggressive-growth mutual fund. Don't even think of saying that such an investment is too risky. Investing your money in the lottery is the ultimate risk, and for all practical purposes carries a high-percent guarantee that you'll lose your money. Remember: The lottery is a tax on the ignorant.

Legal fees

If you hire a lawyer on contingency (a percentage of the settlement, plus expenses), make sure the expenses are deducted

from the total first. Example: Say the settlement is $15,000, and the attorney cut is a third plus $3,000 of expenses. Deduct the $3,000 first, and then pay the lawyer a third of the balance, or $4,000. If you pay the lawyer first, you'll have to pay a third of $15,000, or $5,000 plus the expenses.

Lending money—to friends and family

Don't lend money to people you know. If you decide a loan is in order, make sure you can consider it an outright gift. If you happen to receive repayment, it will be an unexpected bonus.

Lending money—when someone asks

If someone asks you for a loan, say you were just going to ask him for one. That usually ends the conversation.

Library fines

Avoid overdue fines at the library. Most libraries renew

books online or over the phone.

Phone—ask for credit for wrong long-distance dial

Always ask for credit immediately whenever you dial a wrong long-distance number. Don't be embarrassed. It's routine. Just call your service provider and make a very quick report.

Phone—ask for credit with long service interruptions

If your phone service is interrupted for more than 24 hours, ask for a credit.

Phone—block making long-distance calls

If your long-distance bill is really out of control, and you are determined to get that expense under control, take drastic measures. Instruct your phone company to block all long-distance calls. Now you will be able to place only local, toll-free, and 911 phone calls. And if you absolutely

must call long-distance, use a prepaid calling card, or check your long-distance minutes on your cell phone contract.

Phone—time your calls to save

Put an egg timer by the phone as a reminder to hang up before you talk yourself into debt.

Record keeping— business information

When you write a check to a company you haven't done business with before, jot down the address and phone number in your checkbook register so it's handy in case you need to check on your order.

Record keeping—documents in safe or freezer

Keep wills, insurance policies, and other important papers in a fireproof safe, or wrap them in plastic and put them in a sealed container in the freezer. They will be easily accessible and protected in case of fire.

Record keeping—documents on CD

Be prepared by scanning your family's important documents—birth certificates, passports, Social Security cards, insurance policies, property deeds, car titles, immunization records, pet medical records, school transcripts, business licenses, education degrees, and tax returns. Now burn the files onto two CDs. Keep one in a safe place and have a trusted friend or relative in a different state (your point person) keep the other disk.

Record keeping—documents tucked away

Roll your important papers and store them in cardboard tubes. They can be tucked away and will stay crease-free.

Record keeping—filing system for the family

Establish a color-coded family filing system. Use green folders for financial statements, red folders for kids' school papers, blue for car and home documents, yellow for medical papers, and orange for personal items. You'll know right away where your financial paperwork is.

Record keeping—filing system for sorting

Set up temporary finance files labeled "To be filed" and "To be tossed." In the first, place items that need to be saved permanently or long-term for taxes, and so on. In the second file, put dated material that can be tossed. Once a month, file the first and dump the second.

Record keeping—home contents on video

Film your home inside and out for insurance records. In case of a fire, you need to have evidence of the expensive wall coverings and decorator window coverings. While you are taping, narrate aloud, describing your home's contents in detail. Keep DVD in a safe-deposit box or transfer the digital files to a disk. Make sure the date is well documented. Film again every few years or when considerable changes are made.

Record keeping—wallet contents photos

Make a photocopy of everything in your wallet. Now if you lose your wallet, you'll have a record of the important information in it and can move quickly to have things replaced or canceled.

Record keeping—warranties

Buy a large, three-ring binder and a supply of plastic pocket inserts. Whenever you purchase a product, whether it's an appliance, lawn tool, or toy, staple the receipt to the owner's manual or warranty paperwork and file it away in one of the pockets. Now whenever something stops working or has a problem, you'll have the paperwork and all the information at your fingertips, including the customer service number. Or you could scan and retain these documents

electronically, as well. Always call—even if the warranty is expired—explain the situation, your purchase details, and then ask one simple question: What can you do for me?

Saving on expenses— discount for paying cash

Request a discount whenever you pay cash in a store that honors standard bank credit cards. Since they have to pay from 3 to 7 percent of the bill to the card company on a credit purchase, they should be willing to give you at least part of the difference in the form of a discount. It won't always work, but it's worth a try. If the owner or manager thinks you are going to use credit and at the last minute you inquire about a discount for cash, you'll be more successful.

Saving on expenses—discount on newspaper subscription

If you subscribe to a newspaper, check to see if discounts are offered for paying an entire year's subscription in advance.

Some papers offer a 10 to 15 percent discount. If you find you don't read the newspaper on the weekdays, change your subscription to Sunday only. You won't feel guilty, and you'll save a bundle.

Saving on expenses—garbage service

If neither you nor your neighbor regularly fill your garbage cans, ask if the family is interested in splitting garbage collection costs. Check to see if your city or county ordinances prohibit this. Many don't.

Saving on expenses—lunches out

Here's a reasonable and practical way to handle the high cost of eating lunch out every day. On Monday take $25 cash and put it in an envelope to be used only for your lunches. If it's gone before Friday, you'll have to pack your lunch.

Saving on expenses—mailing books

Use fourth class or "media mail" when shipping books through the US Postal Service. The savings are amazing.

Saving on expenses—mortgage escrow adjustment

Ask for a refund of any excess funds your mortgage lender is keeping in an escrow account. One woman discovered that her bank was collecting $100 a month more than necessary to cover anticipated property tax and insurance bills. When she asked that her monthly assessment be reduced to $\frac{1}{12}$ of the total annual bill, the bank quickly agreed and that reduced her monthly expenditure. She also received a refund for the more than $500 excess amount that was in the fund. You have to ask.

Saving on expenses—"won't be undersold" savings

Even though the store where you made a recent purchase doesn't advertise a "we won't be undersold" policy, always take a chance. If, say, the day after you make the purchase, you notice a sale by their competitor and the same item is offered at 50 percent off, take your purchase back—along with the competitor's ad—and simply ask what they can do for you. You'll be surprised what companies will do to keep a customer.

Savings—automatic deposits

Make arrangements with your employer to automatically deposit a certain percentage of your paycheck directly into your savings account and the balance into your checking. What you don't see you won't miss, and this is the most painless way to start saving.

Savings—bills instead of change

If you don't like dealing with change jars, commit to paying yourself a dollar every time you make a purchase. Think of it as charging yourself a service fee for shopping. You'll think twice about unnecessary stops at the mall and end up saving a lot in the bargain.

Savings—coupon savings back in cash

Many banks are opening convenient branch offices in major grocery stores. If this is true for the supermarket you frequent, open a savings account. Now when you buy groceries, write the check for the total before coupons are subtracted. Ask for your coupon savings back in cash (the equivalent of writing a check for more than the purchase amount, or using a debit card with cash back), and make a deposit to your savings account on your way out with that cash. Also, make a point of writing your check for more than the purchase by $5 to $10 if you can manage. Stash that cash in the bank as you leave too. It's a painless and convenient way to save.

Savings—create change to save

When you write a check for groceries, round it up and take the difference in change and deposit it each evening into a change jar you have at home. Example: If the bill comes to $33.02, write the check for

$34 and stash the 98 cents in change. You'll be surprised by how much change you'll accumulate in a year.

Savings—creative methods to save what you've saved

If you find yourself borrowing back the money you've determined to save, here are some tips for how to put some space between you and the stash: (1) Keep your savings and checking accounts in different banks; (2) open a passbook account, which will limit your access to the funds; (3) open your savings account in a bank in another city and make all of your deposits by mail; (4) establish an account that requires two signatures to withdraw.

Savings—don't spend coins

Collect loose change by making a personal rule not to spend it. Make it a habit to dump your pockets and purses every night into one collection receptacle. You won't miss the change, and you'll be amazed by how much you can save.

Savings—IRA contribution early in year

Try to contribute to your individual retirement account (IRA) as early in the year as possible. The difference between making your contributions each January 1 rather than December 31 of the same year could spell thousands of dollars of additional earnings in your account over the decades.

Savings—make payments to yourself after debt payoff

As you pay off a credit card or other loan, keep making the same payments into your savings account instead of sending them to the lender.

Savings—mileage reimbursements for a new car

Each month submit your expense report for the work-related miles you put on your car. Once you receive the reimbursement check, stash it into a special account for the sole purpose of saving for a new car. Usually the gasoline costs required to drive for job-related purposes can be absorbed into your regularly monthly spending. This is a great way to force yourself into a savings plan.

Savings—pay yourself

Once a month, or whenever you pay your bills, write a check to deposit in your money market fund or your savings account. If you can't start with 10 percent, start with less and increase the amount each month. Or use an automatic savings plan—let the bank take your savings out of your paycheck. You won't miss what you don't see.

Savings—reimbursements into savings account

When you are reimbursed for travel or other out-of-pocket expenses, save the money, and put it in your savings account instead of your checking account, where it will just disappear.

Savings—US savings bonds interest

Here's how to earn double interest. Buy US Series EE Savings Bonds on the last day of the month with money that has been earning interest in another account during the month. The bond starts accruing interest as if purchased on the first day of the month. Example: Buy a bond on June 30. When you receive the bond about 21 days later, it will be recorded as of June 1.

Savings—with kids

Open school savings accounts for your kids. Most banks offer these no-fee, no-minimum accounts for kids. Teach them how to fill out deposit slips and make their own deposits. These accounts usually have no minimum balances or service fees.

Social Security—know what you have

Call the Social Security Administration at 800-772-1213 for a "Request for Earnings and Benefits Estimate

Statement" or visit their website at www.SSA.gov. After you mail back the completed form, you will receive a statement showing all the money you have paid into Social Security as well as a personalized estimated monthly benefit upon retirement. If there are errors, such as they didn't credit you 1 year or they have you earning the wrong amount, they can be corrected but only if you report them.

Taxes—hardship extension, IRS Form 1127

If you have an undue hardship such as long-term unemployment, prolonged illness, disaster, or inability to borrow, and can't pay your federal taxes when they are due on April 15, call the IRS hotline (800-829-1040) and request Form 1127, "Application for Extension of Time for Payment of Tax Due to Undue Hardship." By filing this form, you will have until June 15 to pay without penalty. If the IRS says they've never heard of this form, be persistent. Insist on speaking with

a supervisor. It does exist, it is legal, and you have every right to file it if you qualify. This is different from the form "Extension to File Taxes" in which case you must still pay any taxes owing on or before April 15.

Taxes—lower your withholding

Don't give the Internal Revenue Service a free loan. If you receive a large refund each year, you're losing interest on the money. It pays to lower your withholding and bank the difference. Your employer's personnel office can tell you how to arrange it.

Taxes—prepare for tax deductible reporting

Keep a separate checking account for tax deductible expenses, and sort them every month by category, such as charitable contributions and medical and dental expenses. By year's end you'll be way ahead in the tax preparation hassle.

Taxes—property tax evaluation

Challenge your property tax bill. If the value of your property has declined, you might be entitled to a reassessment of your taxes.

Utilities—good customer perks

Usually if you have been a good customer of the utility companies (gas, water, electricity, phone) for at least a year, you can arrange to have your deposits refunded or credited toward your account. You may be able to get interest, too, if you ask.

Utilities—home energy audits

Request a home energy audit from your electricity or gas companies. Typically these audits are free and will help you discover where all that energy is going.

Word to the wise— choose to be content

Be content with what you have. As much as possible, do not spend your life scheming and planning to get more things.

Word to the wise— company ratings

Make sure you are dealing with a highly rated company of B+ or better. These days the smaller, lower-rated companies are dropping out regularly. Better safe than sorry.

Word to the wise— D-E-B-T reality

Convince yourself that unsecured debt is a four-letter word. As soon as you teach that to yourself, teach it to your children. Banish unsecured debt from your life.

Word to the wise— don't carry extra cash

Take along only as much money as you expect to need each day. Impulsive purchases are difficult to make when you have no dollars to spare.

Word to the wise—don't pay credit with credit

Never pay your credit card bill with a credit card. Just don't.

Word to the wise—keep a money diary

Keep a money diary by writing down every expenditure, no matter how small. Not only will you know where the money goes, but you will also automatically spend less because no one wants to write down lamebrain purchases.

Word to the wise—"on sale" doesn't guarantee savings

Myth: Buying things on sale is a great way to save money. Truth: Buying things on sale is a way to spend less money, but it has absolutely nothing to do with saving money.

Word to the wise—save money no matter what

Regardless of how much in debt you are or how little money you make, saving something consistently in a special place or account is going to change your attitude. Saving even a few dollars each week helps fill the emptiness that drives some of us to spend. Something of everything you earn is yours to keep.

Word to the wise—skip extended warranty coverage

As a general rule, extended warranty coverage on anything is a waste of money. Modern-day appliances, automobiles, and electronic equipment will operate well during the first year or 3, or whatever time the extended warranty covers. And most of these items come with some kind of a warranty anyway. You'd be better off taking that same amount of money and putting it into an interest-bearing account. That way when the item doesn't break down, you will not have thrown your money down the drain.

Word to the wise—spending rule of thumb

Stop spending money you do not have in your

possession—today. This means no charging on credit cards, no borrowing from friends or relatives. If that sounds too radical and impossible, agree not to incur any debt just for today. Taking it one day at a time is really much easier.

Word to the wise— start giving

Every life well lived should be giving back regularly; then that life will have meaning. When we are the neediest is when we should be giving the most. Financial bondage is a dead giveaway for an out-of-balance life.

Word to the wise—stop spending more than you have

Stop spending more money than you have. Consciously begin today to reduce expenses so that your outgo never exceeds your income.

Word to the wise—stop trying to impress others

Stop trying to impress other people. If you can stop spending according to demands put on your life by others (through peer pressure or the necessity to keep up), you will see a tremendous difference in the way you spend.

12

Outdoors and Garden

Barbecue—charcoal fire

To build a perfect charcoal fire for the barbecue, fill each slot of two or three empty cardboard egg cartons with briquettes. Set them in the barbecue, light the cartons, and you have a perfect charcoal arrangement with no lighter fluid required.

Barbecue—coals reused

After the food has cooked, don't let the coals burn themselves out. Scoop them up into an empty can and smother them by placing a nonflammable lid over the can. They can be used again.

Barbecue—fire up with a pinecone

For a fast, hot, and fume-free blaze, set a dry pinecone in the bottom of the barbecue. Build a pyramid of charcoal around it. Start your fire by igniting the pinecone.

Barbecue—propane check

Never sure how much propane is left in the barbecue tank? Make a streak down the side with a wet sponge. Moisture will evaporate from the upper, empty part more quickly.

Barbecue—vinyl tablecloth cover

Fold an old vinyl tablecloth in half and sew up the sides to make a cover for your outdoor barbecue grill.

Beach—bag for shells

Use mesh onion sacks for gathering shells at the beach. They're strong and they sift out most of the sand by themselves. When you get home, rinse the sack and its contents under an outdoor faucet, and you won't get a speck of sand in the house.

Beach—bag for wet suits

Take a large, resealable plastic bag to the beach with ¼ cup of baking soda inside. Use it to bring home wet suits. Just put them in the bag and shake. The soda absorbs moisture and helps prevent mildew and scary smells until you can get the suits properly laundered.

Beach—pocket on a towel

Sew a coordinating washcloth to a beach towel along three sides and use a Velcro-type fastener to close the fourth. Now you and your kids have an instant pocket for keys, coins, or suntan lotion.

Beach—sand-free radio

When you go to the beach, carry your radio in a resealable plastic bag. You can operate it without ever opening the bag. It will stay sand-free and completely dry.

Birds—bath

Now that you have a beautiful yard and garden, invite songbirds to splish and splash and entertain you. Pick up a green 12-inch-diameter drip tray—the kind used under a potted plant. Put the tray on the ground in a sheltered part of the garden, positioning rocks or small logs around the perimeter. Put a large rock in the middle of the bath to act as an island. Fill with water

and wait for the action. Flush
and replace the water every 2
to 3 days.

Birds—feeder

A milk carton makes a good
bird feeder. Cut out large windows on all 4 sides, leaving 2
inches at the top and bottom.
Poke holes through the top
of the carton, run a string
through the holes, and hang
the carton on a tree branch.
Add a dowel, stick, or skewer
for a perch. Fill the bottom
with bird food. Try decorating the feeder with adhesive-
backed shelf paper.

Birds—keep out of the fruit

Save dirty, yellowed, or torn
lace curtains to cover your
strawberry patch or raspberry
bushes to keep birds from
stealing the fruit.

Birds—nest-building material

Help the birds with their
spring nest-building chores.
Collect the lint from your
clothes dryer, tie it up in a ball

with string, and hang it in
your backyard.

Birds—treat

Smear a pinecone with peanut
butter and hang it from a tree
in your garden for a bird treat.

Boating—floating keys

Tie a couple of corks to your
key ring when you go boating.
If you accidentally drop your
keys overboard, they won't
sink.

Bugs and such—ants

Follow the ants' trail to their
point of entry into your house
and seal it with caulk. Then
find their nest at the other
end of their trail and destroy
it by pouring several gallons
of boiling water into the en-
trance, stirring it up, and pouring on more boiling water.

Bugs and such—ants, on hummingbird feeder

Ants can't climb up to a hummingbird feeder if you cover

317

the pole or cord with petroleum jelly or baby oil, reapplying every 2 weeks or after it rains. To keep ants out of the house, seal the point of entry with toothpaste, caulk, or masking tape.

Bugs and such—ants, spiders, and others

To prevent ants, spiders, and other bugs from entering your home or another structure, spray the foundation and the grout within a foot of the wall with a mixture of ½ cup ground lemon, including the rind (you can puree the lemon in a blender or food processor), and 1 gallon of water. Apply with a garden watering can. Not only is the weak solution versatile, it's mild, cheap, and environmentally safe.

Bugs and such—aphids

Mix 1 gallon water, 1 tablespoon vegetable oil, and 2 tablespoons Ivory Liquid. Spray on plants where aphid damage is evident.

Bugs and such—aphids, on roses

Add 2 drops of liquid dish soap to a quart of water. Pour into a spray bottle and spray plants periodically. This is especially effective on rose-loving aphids.

Bugs and such—bees, on hummingbird feeder

If you apply Vaseline to the feeding spouts of your hummingbird feeder, the bees will not bother it. The Vaseline makes the bees get stuck, which they don't like. The hummingbirds are unharmed by this sticky situation.

Bugs and such—cutworms, infestation

If your garden is infested with ants or cutworms, sprinkle used coffee grounds on the affected area.

Bugs and such—cutworms, shield

Remove the bottom out of an empty tuna can and sink the "ring" that's left into the soil around a young seedling. This will keep cutworms away from the plant.

Bugs and such—flies (bay leaves)

Crush bay leaves between your fingers, and then rub your fingers over your skin to repel gnats. Crushed bay leaves are good for repelling flies and mosquitoes too.

Bugs and such—flies (rubbing alcohol)

Rubbing alcohol makes a great fly and insect spray. The fine mist evaporates quickly and is not harmful to anyone but the pests. This doesn't necessarily kill them, but it anesthetizes the little guys, so once they're asleep, dispose of them quickly.

Bugs and such—flies (sweet basil)

Pots of sweet basil placed strategically around your patio, swimming pool, or doorway repel flies.

Bugs and such—flies on garbage cans

Sprinkle dry soap or borax into garbage cans after they've been washed and allowed to dry; it acts as a fly repellent.

Bugs and such—mosquitoes

Plant basil and pansies around your patio and house to repel mosquitoes. Mint planted around the house repels flies. Keep basil well watered so that it produces a stronger scent. Dried ground basil leaves left in small bowls or hung in muslin bags are also effective.

Bugs and such—repellent, all-purpose

Mix 1 clove garlic chopped, 1 small onion chopped, and 1 tablespoon cayenne powder to 1 quart of water. Allow to steep 1 hour, then add 1 tablespoon of Ivory Liquid. This all-purpose insect spray remains potent for only 1 week, so use it up.

Bugs and such—repellent, dryer sheets

A Bounce fabric softener dryer sheet rubbed over your skin or pinned to your hair will keep certain insects such as gnats away as you work in the garden.

Bugs and such— repellent, marigolds

It's true, marigolds really do discourage insects. No scary chemicals involved. Just plant these beautiful flowers among your vegetables for natural pest control.

Bugs and such—slugs, snails, cutworms, and grubs

Protect flowers and vegetables from slugs, snails, cutworms, and grubs by scattering lettuce leaves or citrus rinds around them. The pests will attach themselves to the food, which should be removed daily and replaced.

Bugs and such—wasps

In a pinch use hair spray to kill wasps. As long as you get some of the product on their wings, they'll go down.

Bugs and such—whiteflies, spider mites, mealybugs, cinch bugs, and aphids

Mix 3 tablespoons Ivory Liquid in 1 gallon water and mix well. Fill a sprayer with the soapy solution and mist the leaves of plants and bushes to kill these little pests.

Bugs and such—worms, on cabbage and broccoli

Here's a safe way to bust pests that bother your cabbage and broccoli plants! Dust the plants in late afternoon with baking soda. The mixture of morning dew settling on the soda will form an antiworm enzyme that won't harm humans. It will wash off easily with a little water.

Bugs and such—worms, on tomatoes

Worms won't bother your tomatoes if you plant a few sprigs of dill nearby.

Critters—cats, in the garden

To keep cats out of the garden, put fir boughs around shrubs or spray the area with a weak dilution of vinegar and water.

Critters—cats, in the window box

If your cat is digging in a window box, put pinecones around the plants. If the window box contains seedlings, staple screening over the top of the box until the plants mature a bit.

Critters—gophers and deer

Dog hair, available from a dog groomer, will repel gophers and other annoying furry pests. Human hair (get clippings from the local beauty salon) will repel deer, rabbits, and other garden invaders.

Critters—in garbage cans

Sprinkle a small amount of household ammonia in your outdoor garbage cans. Animals will be repelled by the strong odor.

Critters—rabbits

Sprinkle dried red pepper around the base of plants to keep rabbits away.

Critters—snails

Snails will turn around and go the other way rather than cross a protective border of sand, lime, or ashes.

Critters—snails and slugs

To keep snails and slugs out of your garden, sink pie pans into the soil so the rims are flush with the ground. Fill with beer. The slugs and snails will be attracted to the beer, which will be their final undoing. (This is a lovely object lesson for kids who think it's cool to drink beer!) Simply empty the pie pans when they get full.

Critters—squirrels, and attics

To keep squirrels out of your attic, get rid of any tree branches that hang over your house and outbuildings so the squirrels can't use them as ladders.

Critters—squirrels, and bird feeders

If your bird feeders are being pillaged by furry marauders, divert their attention with this simple ploy: Hang dried ears of corn, a favorite food of squirrels, from a tree some distance away from your bird offerings.

Florist-prepared plants

When you receive live floral plants in those beautifully wrapped containers, the wrapping materials may become deadly to the plant. The pot in which the plant is planted has holes at the bottom, but the foil or plastic wrapping prevents drainage. To eliminate this problem, hold the wrapping high, punch a hole in the center, tear outward, and with scissors carefully cut all around to within an inch or so of the edge. The overall appearance is left undisturbed, the water can drain properly, and the plant will be able to thrive.

Flower cutting

The best time to cut flowers is in the early morning while they still have some moisture from the cool night air and the morning dew.

Furniture—cleaning resin

Make a good lather with dish-washing detergent, household ammonia, and warm water. Sponge the lather on and wash gently. Don't use an abrasive sponge. For heavy stains, use a solution of bleach and water, but don't allow the bleach and ammonia to come in contact with each other. Restore the furniture's shiny finish by applying a coat of car wax.

Furniture—protecting plastic

The bright colors of outdoor plastic furniture, kids' gyms, and so on can fade from regular exposure to the sun. But you can prevent them from fading with a protective coat of car wax. The wax also repels dirt and grime, which makes for quick and easy cleanups.

Garden—temporary for kids and beginners

Make a temporary garden out of a plastic kids' pool. It's just the right size for beginners and children because it can be placed in the best light and can be disassembled and put away for the winter.

Garden hose—leather belt holder

Use an old leather belt to store your garden hose. Wind up the hose, slip the belt through the loops, buckle it, and hang it from a nail in your garage or basement.

Garden hose—old tire holder

Keep your garden hose rolled in an old tire. It will stay clean, dry, and ready to use.

Garden hose—sticking

To prevent the hose end from becoming attached to the spigot so tightly that you can't remove it without tools, rub a light coating of petroleum jelly on the garden hose nozzle and the spigot to keep them from sticking.

Gardening—cart

Use a child's plastic snow sled as an off-season garden cart. It glides easily over the grass for cleanup chores and is especially handy when it's time to lift and divide clumps of perennials.

Gardening—cleanup with denture cleaner or sugar

Two ways to remove garden soil from your hands and from beneath your fingernails: (1) Soak your hands in water in which one of those denture-cleaning tablets has dissolved. An added bonus: soft cuticles; (2) After a day of gardening, wash your hands with soap and water and a teaspoon of regular table sugar. The rough granules will scour your hands clean.

Gardening—cleanup with soap on a rope

Put a bar of soap in the toe of a pantyhose leg, tie a knot

over it, and tie the other end to an outdoor spigot. You can easily wash up after working in the garden.

Gardening—cleanup with soapy hands

If you don't wear garden gloves when gardening, coat your hands lightly with a mild liquid soap. The dirt washes off easily.

Gardening—compost bin

To make a compost bin, all you need are four wooden pallets (free, or really cheap, from stores or warehouses). Stand the pallets on their sides and wire them together into a square. When you need to remove compost, open one side like a door.

Gardening—fertilize with ashes

Ashes from a wood-burning stove or fireplace make wonderful fertilizer if you need to raise your soil's pH. Collect the ashes and scatter them around shrubs and bushes. Use ashes with caution, though, because applying too much can create serious soil imbalances. Limit applications to 25 pounds per 1,000 square feet.

Gardening—hosiery for tomatoes

Save old pantyhose, nylons, and tights for your garden. Cut them into long strips and use them to tie tomato plants to stakes or tomato cages. They are also great for tying other vegetables like string beans, cucumbers, and climbing plants to fences. Nylons are better than string because they "give" and don't cut off the plants' circulation the way string, wire, or twist ties do.

Gardening—melon pedestals

Set baby melons and cantaloupes on top of tin cans in your garden. The melons will ripen faster and be sweeter.

Gardening—photograph your hard work

Take pictures of your garden in bloom. This is a great way

to keep a record of what grew well and what plantings you particularly enjoyed.

Gardening—pickle juice for acidic soil

Work leftover pickle juice into the soil around an azalea or gardenia bush or around any other plant that needs acidic soil.

Gardening—tools, avoid rust with car wax

Prevent rust on garden tools by cleaning them with car wax.

Gardening—tools, avoid rust with petroleum jelly

To keep garden tools from developing rust, rinse and dry the tools, then coat the metal parts with a thin layer of petroleum jelly.

Gardening—tools, brightly colored handles

Paint your garden tool handles bright red so you can spot them easily in the grass or garden. If

your neighbor has taken notice of this terrific tip, you might want to select a color other than the one he chose.

Gardening—tools, cleaning with sand

Keep a bucket of sand sprinkled lightly with mineral oil in the shed or garage where you store your garden tools. When you're done using the tools, scour them with a bit of the sand to keep them clean and rust-free. The oil will leave a light protective coating on the blades to prevent rust.

Gardening—tools, gear hut

Get a large weatherproof mailbox, roomy enough to hold small garden tools and gear. Stake it in the ground in a convenient spot under a tree or near a hedge.

Gardening—tools, grips

Put a pair of kids' bicycle handlebar grips on the handles of your gardening tools to give yourself a firmer, more comfortable grip when doing yard work.

Gardening—tools, rust spots

Rub the rust spots with a new steel-wool pad soaked with soap, then dipped in turpentine. Finish by rubbing with a crumpled piece of aluminum foil.

Gardening—watering

Gardens need an inch of water a week. But how do you know how long to water to achieve that goal? Place a can, pot, or glass under your sprinkler and see how long it takes for the container to collect an inch of water. Once you have this information, install automatic timers on your watering systems. Watering less often for a longer period of time allows deep penetration and reduces the amount of water consumed.

Gardening—weeds, grass clipping prevention

Place grass clippings around plants to keep down weeds. The clippings also retain moisture and are a good source of nutrients.

Gardening—weeds, under carpet

If you want to set out vegetable plants but are overwhelmed by the immensity of the project because your garden is covered with weeds, try this unorthodox tactic: Take a large piece of old carpet and lay it over the garden patch. Make X cuts with a utility knife at the location where each plant should grow. Lift up the cut carpet flaps, dig a hole beneath, and sink the seedling. Water as usual and watch your plants grow. You won't have to worry about weeds because they won't be able to penetrate the carpeting.

Gates—seat belt those gates

While you're at the junkyard, pick up a few seat belts from discarded cars. The straps make great gate latches. Just nail one to your wooden gatepost and the other to your gate. If it is metal, attach both strips to the post, then pass one buckle end around the upright member on the gate and back to the other. Seat belts are weatherproof, easily installed, don't cost much, and never get out of alignment the way most conventional latches eventually do.

Lawn—cheap sod

If you have more time than money and need a new lawn, visit your local sod farm and purchase their "scraps," which are the odd-sized roll ends. You will have to patch them together, which takes time, but you can pick up these odd pieces at a tremendous savings.

Lawn—dog spots

To prevent those yellow dog spots in your lawn, feed your male dog a couple of table-spoons of tomato juice every day. This also works for female dogs, but not quite as well.

Lawn—mower care

If you won't be using your mower for several months in the winter, drain the gas and disconnect the spark plug. If you can't drain the gas, add a gas conditioner to the mower tank and your gas can to pre-vent the fuel from going bad.

Lawn—sawdust and seed

When seeding grass by hand, how can you tell if you've missed any spots? Mix fine sawdust with your seed; you'll be able to see the sawdust and the missed spots easily, and the sawdust will not adversely af-fect the new lawn.

Picnics—ants can't swim

Keep the ants away from the food on your picnic table by placing each table leg into a bowl or paper cup of water. Ants can't swim—they can't even float—so they'll leave your food alone.

Picnics—ants hate coffee

Spread dried coffee grounds or whole cloves around the pic-nic area. If you are on a solid surface, draw a white chalk line around the perimeter. For whatever reason, ants won't cross that line.

Picnics—basket cooler

Turn a picnic basket into a cooler by lining it with slabs of poly foam (from a fabric store) glued in place. As long as you pack items that have been thoroughly chilled, they will stay cool for several hours longer than in the uninsulated basket.

Picnics—flies

Keep flies from the picnic area. Put a vase filled with sprigs of lavender, mint, or elderberry in the center of the table. Be sure to rub the leaves frequently to release their scent.

Planting—bulbs in a hurry

Here's a quick way to plant 100 bulbs in less than 45 minutes. Instead of digging lots of holes for lots of bulbs, dig out the area you wish to plant to a depth of 7 inches. Spread the bulbs out evenly with their tips facing up. Add compost to the excavated soil; then shovel the soil lightly over the bulbs.

Planting—bulb markers

When you're planting bulbs in your garden and can't finish the project on that same day or weekend, stick wooden Popsicle sticks in the ground to indicate the exact location of each bulb. This way you'll know where to continue planting when you're ready to finish the job.

Planting—garlic

Every time you use a head of garlic, take the last three or four little cloves from the center, plus any that have started to show green, and plant them between other plants and shrubs in your flower beds. Plant each clove about ½ inch deep, flat end down, pointed end up. They will grow about 18 inches tall, and then they will start to dry out. This is the sign it's time to pull out a fresh garlic head. It takes about 5 months to get your first harvest. If you're always planting,

328

you will have plenty of garlic for yourself and others.

Planting—repotting

Drop a coffee filter in the bottom of a pot before repotting a plant. The water will drain from the pot, but the soil won't wash out with it.

Planting—root rehydration

Before planting bare root plants like roses and grapevines, make sure the roots haven't dried out. Unwrap the roots, remove any packing material, and soak the roots in tepid water for 6 to 12 hours.

Planting—seeds, germination test

Test old seeds to see if they're worth planting. Place 10 seeds on a dampened paper towel. Cover the seeds with plastic to keep them moist. Check the seeds after the germination time listed on the package has passed. If even some seeds germinate, you can still use the packet. Just sow the seeds more heavily than usual.

Planting—spacing

Mark the handles of your gardening tools with 1-inch increments. You will no longer need a ruler when planting or spacing plants, shrubs, or flowers.

Planting—square-foot system

Plant a garden and reduce grocery bills. Consider the popular square-foot gardening method, which requires very little time, space, and trouble. Check with your librarian or online for a how-to book.

Planting—trees with purpose

Plant deciduous trees (the type that lose their leaves in winter) on the south side of your house. They will provide summer shade without blocking winter sun. Plant evergreens on the north to shield your home from cold winter winds.

Plants—acid lovers

For beautiful azaleas, gardenias, and other acid-loving plants, add 2 tablespoons of white vinegar to a quart of water, and use to water these plants, occasionally.

Plants—no-drip watering

To keep hanging plants from dripping water, place a few ice cubes on top of the soil instead of watering with water. The cubes will melt slowly, releasing only the amount of water that the soil can easily absorb. By the time the cubes melt, the water will be warm enough not to shock the plant. This method is not acceptable for tropical or tender-leaf variety plants like African violets and orchids.

Plants—nutrition from boiled egg or pasta water

Don't throw out the water in which you've boiled eggs or pasta. The calcium and starches are great for watering houseplants.

Plants—portable when heavy

To transport a heavy plant or shrub, roll it onto a snow shovel. You can drag the shovel across the lawn without hurting your back.

Plants—seedlings, detergent scoop incubator

Save plastic scoops from laundry detergent boxes for planting seedling starters. (Of course, thoroughly wash the scoops before using.)

Plants—seedlings, grow lights

You don't need to buy an expensive grow light for your vegetable and flower seedlings. Regular fluorescent lights are just as effective, cost less, and last longer than fancy grow lights. If you combine one "cool white" with one "warm white" fluorescent tube in a standard shop fixture, your plants will thrive.

Plants—seedlings, plastic container hothouse

Those clear plastic containers with the lids attached that you get from a grocery store salad bar or corner deli make great mini "greenhouses" for seeds you start indoors. Fill the container with potting soil, add seeds, and water. Keep the lid down, and place it on a windowsill in direct sunlight until seedlings shoot through the soil.

Plants—seedlings, wagon hothouse

Baby's first wagon can be recycled as a hothouse for seedlings. Fill it with dirt, cover it with a piece of glass or Plexiglas, and move it into the sun.

Plants—trellis for support

Tie together plastic loops from six-packs of soda cans, attach to a fence or pole, and use in the garden as a support for climbing plants.

Plants—warm shelter

Cut off the bottom of an empty plastic water or milk jug and place over young plants to protect them from freezing.

Pool—aboveground repairs

If your aboveground swimming pool develops tears and cracks, patch them using bathroom caulking, smoothing it onto the damaged, dry pool surface. Leave it on overnight, and it will dry to a flexible, waterproof surface.

Pool—less slippery

Put bathtub anti-slip decals on the bottom of a kid's pool to make it less slippery.

Pool—towel rack

A folding clothes rack makes a great poolside towel rack.

Snow—shoveling

Spray vegetable oil on your snow shovel to keep snow from sticking.

Snow—sweeping

If only a small amount of snow has covered your sidewalks, sweep the snow away with a broom instead of shoveling it. The job will be completed more quickly and with much less stress to your back.

Surfaces—awnings

If your outdoor canvas awnings are faded and ugly, refurbish them by first cleaning them well and then repainting them with canvas paint.

Surfaces—concrete stains

Commercial cleansers such as Ajax and Comet work well to clean concrete that has been stained by mold or leaves. Sprinkle cleanser on the cement, add water, and scrub with a stiff broom. Allow to sit for a few hours, then rinse.

Surfaces—driveway oil stains

To remove oil stains from your driveway, sprinkle kitty litter on the stain and "scrub" with a brick in a circular motion. Repeat for stubborn stains.

Surfaces—fake flagstones

Instead of using expensive flagstones for garden paths, use salvaged pieces of cement, which you can find at apartment complexes or city streets where sidewalks are being replaced. They create the same rustic effect when randomly placed and edged with thyme or other greenery.

Surfaces—icy wooden deck

If your wooden deck gets icy in the winter, sprinkle it with cornmeal. This provides traction and a snack for the birds when the ice melts.

Surfaces—ivy in bricks

To get rid of ivy rooting in cracks and mortar of bricks, cut the vine away, wait for the suckers that cling to the brick to dry out, then simply brush them away.

Surfaces—washing bricks

Wash bricks with a mixture of household bleach and

water—a 50/50 mix for heavy deposits, a weaker mix for lighter ones.

Swings— rope burns

To keep kids from getting rope burns while playing on a swing, put foam handlebar grip pads over the rope. They can be adjusted for height.

Tablecloth—for outdoors

When entertaining outdoors, use a clean, bright beach towel for a tablecloth.

Terra-cotta pots—cleaning

The white rings on the outside of terra-cotta pots, caused by minerals in the water, can usually be wiped away with white vinegar.

13

Pets

Cats—canned food at room temperature

Always let canned cat food come to room temperature before serving. Cold food straight from the refrigerator can upset a cat's stomach.

Cats—dried food, not canned

Feed your cat dried food instead of canned. It is cheaper, neater, and more convenient. It also lasts longer, is less likely to spoil when left in the cat's dish, and even helps clean the cat's teeth. Cats with special conditions should be fed according to a veterinarian's instructions.

Cats—kitten training

Discourage a kitten from scratching furniture by placing pieces of aluminum foil on upholstery and around table and chair legs. The sight and sound will frighten her off.

Cats—litter box cleaning

Use hot water and liquid dishwashing detergent to clean litter box surfaces. Avoid using chlorine bleach for cleaning.

Fumes can be created through a chemical reaction between the bleach and residual ammonia in a litter box after it has been emptied.

Cats—litter box liner

Line the bottom of the kitty-litter box with ¼ inch of baking soda to prevent odors.

Cats—litter mat

Put a sisal mat or a piece of some other material that has a deep pile in front of the cat's litter box. Now litter won't get tracked all over the place. Once a week, simply shake out the mat.

Cats—litter substitute

Shredded paper makes a wonderful substitute for kitty litter. You can either use the shreds from an office or shred your own newspaper. It is much better than the litter because it absorbs waste and odors better, doesn't need to be replaced as often, and is free.

Cats—scratching pads

If your cat prefers the furniture to his scratching post, try placing carpet samples throughout the house. For some reason, many cats prefer them.

Dogs—beef jerky trick

When you open a bag of dry dog food your pet is not terribly fond of, put a few pieces of beef jerky in the bag and leave them. They will slowly diffuse a pleasant odor that may make the food more appetizing to your dog.

Dogs—bells and walks

Hang a bell on your doorknob. As you are about to take your pet for a walk, ring the bell. Soon, the dog will associate going for a walk with the bell and will ring the bell himself when he needs to go for a walk.

Dogs—burrs off coats

To remove burrs from a dog's coat, soften them by applying

a few drops of mineral oil or shampoo, then comb them out easily. Mineral oil is cheap and available at drugstores.

Dogs—collars made of leather belts

The next time one of your leather belts wears out, don't throw it away. It will make a great collar for your pet. Just cut it down to size and punch a new hole.

Dogs—house-training puppies

Nothing makes puppies urinate more than being cold. Fix their bed in a warm spot, and they'll have fewer accidents.

Dogs—pooper-scooper

Don't toss out the cardboard French fry container next time you eat fast food. Instead flatten it and save it for your next dog walk. When Fido leaves his mark, pull out the container, pop it open, and scoop up the mess. Transfer to the plastic bag you also carry with you, and drop the whole thing into the nearest trash can.

Dogs—puppy repellent

Mix ¼ cup oil of cloves, 1 tablespoon paprika, and 1 teaspoon black pepper. Pour into a small container with a tight-fitting lid. Label and keep away from children. Dab this repellent on furniture legs, carpets, and other items you want your puppy to stay away from. The scent will diminish over time, so reapply until training is complete.

Dogs—stop the chewing on paws

To cure a dog of chewing on her paws when she gets bored, paint the spot she likes to chew with oil of cloves (available at drugstores).

Dogs—treats

Forget those expensive dog treats! Fill a small plastic container with dry dog food and give your dog a bite-size portion for a snack or reward. It's better for your dog's health and a great way to give pets on a restricted diet a treat too.

Dogs—water with ice cubes in summer

During hot summer days fill your dog's water bowls with ice cubes. They'll have nice cool water throughout the day.

Fleas—dip

For an effective flea dip, boil orange and lemon peels in water. Cool the water and use it for a pet rinse or dip. Smells nice and fresh. You can also slice citrus and rub the fruit into the dog's coat. The bugs will keel over from the smell.

Fleas—keep off pet's head when bathing

When bathing a dog or cat, first lather up a ring of shampoo around the animal's neck to help keep fleas from running to the pet's head while you are washing its body.

Fleas—they hate vinegar

When bathing your pet, add 1 cup vinegar to the bathwater. Also, buy a spray bottle; fill it with 2 parts water and 1 part vinegar. Spray your pet daily, before his morning walk, to both prevent and eliminate fleas.

Fleas—they hate yeast

To prevent your pet from becoming a flea magnet, rub some brewer's yeast (available at the grocery store) into his coat before you let him outside.

Food—ant deterrent

If ants are getting into the pet food, put the dog or cat bowl into another shallow bowl that has water in it.

Food—hold the onions

If you choose to make your own pet food, never use onions. Onions are toxic for many animals.

Food—kitten and puppy feeder

Feed a litter of newly weaned kittens or puppies from a muffin pan. Weaker babies won't have to compete with stronger ones for food.

Food—scoop

Cut an empty plastic water or milk jug on the diagonal from top to bottom and use as a scooper for pet food.

Hair—in washing machine

After laundering pet bedding, you may discover a lot of pet hair remaining in the bottom of the washing machine. It's not easy to wipe out, so do this: Allow the machine to dry out, then use your vacuum hose to remove all of it easily and quickly.

Hair—on furniture and pillows

Remove pet hair from upholstered furniture and pillows quickly and easily by running a damp sponge over them.

Hair—use a steel-wool strainer when bathing

When bathing animals, place steel wool in the drain to keep hair from clogging the drain.

Murphy's Oil Soap for skin

Use Murphy's Oil Soap to soothe your pet's dry, itchy, or flea-allergy skin. It is gentle and all-vegetable. Follow the directions on the bottle for dilution. Murphy's Oil Soap is especially good for Shar-peis, as this breed has a lot of skin problems. This product can be found in the grocery store in the furniture polish and laundry section.

Odors from accidents

Here's an effective cleaning solution to remove odors from pet accidents: Add 2 tablespoons citronella oil (from the drugstore) and ½ cup rubbing alcohol to 1 gallon water. Use this as you would soap and water to clean floors, patio areas, sleeping quarters, and so on that have been affected by pet odors.

Vaccinations and flea control at pet supply stores

Instead of running to the veterinarian's office to have your pets vaccinated or treated with flea-control programs, call a local pet supply store. Many are now offering low-cost vaccination clinics. You could save at least 25 percent off the prescription costs and avoid paying an office and exam fee.

14

Repairs and Maintenance

Air conditioner—clean filter

To clean an air conditioner or humidifier filter, take the foam filter out of the grill and soak it in a solution of equal parts white vinegar and warm water. If you clean the filter regularly, an hour of soaking will be plenty. Just squeeze the filter dry when it's clean, and then place it back in the air conditioner.

Air conditioner or radiator—disguise

To hide an under-the-window radiator or air conditioner when not in use, hinge together three 30-inch-high window shutters to form a folding screen.

Appliances—chip touch-up

The nasty black chip on any white home appliance, porcelain sink, ceramic tile, or even your white car can be quickly repaired with a liquid correction fluid like White-Out or Liquid Paper, available at office supply stores. Carefully paint the chip, and it will dry in just a few minutes.

Appliances—keep small repair parts together

When repairing appliances, line up small parts on masking tape to keep them in order and to prevent their mysterious disappearance.

Appliances—preserve finish

To preserve the finish of your washer, dryer, and other appliances, wax them with car wax twice a year.

Balcony safety

If your home or vacation spot has widely spaced posts on an outdoor balcony, get a roll of plastic webbing for repairing lawn chairs and weave it between the posts to protect anyone or anything from falling through.

Bucket measurements— no more guessing

Mark pint, quart, and gallon measurements on a bucket with red fingernail polish to make sure you never have to guess on the measurements.

Carpet and rugs—renew for bathroom

Don't throw out bathroom rugs that have lost their rubber backing due to multiple launderings. Slip a piece of rubber shelf liner under the mat. That will keep it from slipping and extend its useful life.

Carpet and rugs—repair bleach spots

Color in the bleached-out spot in your carpeting (which often occurs near a bathroom where bleaching products have splashed or dripped) with a nontoxic marking pen in a shade as close as you can find to that of the rug. This is exactly what a carpet professional would do if you called for repair.

Caulking—smooth

For the smoothest finish, run an ice cube over fresh caulking to shape it and get rid of lumps.

Ceramic tile—change color

If your kitchen or bathroom is suffering from outdated avocado green or some other 1970s colored ceramic tile, and you don't choose to replace it at this time, do this: Purchase a product like Fleckstone (manufactured by Plasti-kote), available at home improvement centers. It is a multihue, textured spray paint sold together with a clear acrylic topcoat that, when applied as directed, produces "new" tile that can be cleaned with a damp sponge. Even if it takes five kits to do the job, you'll spend around $50, and that sure beats remodeling.

Circuit breakers

Never switch on two or more circuit breakers simultaneously. Turn them on one at a time, and pause slightly after each to prevent a power surge.

Closet rod—fix sagging

To fix a sagging wooden closet rod, buy a length of ½-inch galvanized pipe and a length of ¾-inch thin wall PVC piping, both the same length as your rod. You can get these at your local home improvement center. Slip the pipe inside the PVC and slide the PVC into the existing rod brackets. (You can remove the printing on the PVC with rubbing alcohol.)

Closet rod—improve glide

If hangers don't glide along the clothes rod, rub it with waxed paper or a candle.

Doors—aluminum like new

Make aluminum doors (or window casings) look new by rubbing a ball of aluminum foil back and forth across the pitting.

Doors—cushion slamming

To cushion the bang of a door that has a habit of slamming

shut, glue ⅛-inch-thick pieces of foam rubber along the stop.

Doors—improve sliding screen door action

Sliding screen door lost its smooth gliding action? Rub an old candle along the bottom metal track of the door's frame. It will work like new again without a drippy, oily mess.

Drains—completely stopped up

If a drain is completely stopped up, don't try to clear it with chemical drain cleaners. They may bubble back up into the sink or tub and cause permanent damage to the finish of the fixture. If there's only a moderate clog, pour boiling water with a few teaspoons of ammonia down the drain, wait a few minutes, then plunge.

Drains—preventing clogs

Pour ½ cup washing soda (not baking soda) directly down the drain, then slowly and carefully add 2 quarts boiling water. This weekly preventive maintenance will ensure that clogs will never be a problem.

Drains—sluggish

To clear a sluggish drain, pour 1 cup baking soda into the drain followed by 1 cup white vinegar. Allow to sit overnight. In the morning, flush with a kettle of boiling water. Plunge the drain a few times with a plunger. This is an excellent maintenance tactic to keep drains running well.

Drawer—sticky

To remedy a sticky drawer, rub the sides with a candle.

Furniture—scratches on wood

Make your own inexpensive cover-up for furniture scratches: Mix instant coffee and water into a thick paste and apply it to hide nicks and scratches on dark wood furniture.

Furniture—uneven legs

If a furniture leg is uneven, try buttons of different sizes under the leg until you find one that makes it even. Use hot glue around the button edge and position in place.

Grout—clean and whiten

Use white shoe polish—the kind with an applicator top—to clean, whiten, and brighten stained tile grout. Simply apply the polish, wipe the tiles with a damp cloth, allow to dry, and buff.

Grout—paint over the gray

If the white grout on your tile has become gray and grimy, that's a fairly good sign the grout was not sealed, in which case there is no way to make it completely white again. But you can paint it white, using an oil-base paint. Ask at your local paint or home improvement store about which type to use. Do this only if the tiles are glazed (sealed); any paint that gets on them can be wiped off with a dry cloth. If paint gets on unglazed tiles, it will be absorbed, leaving the tiles looking even more unsightly.

Hair dryer revival

If your once-trusty hair dryer sounds like it's gasping for its last breath or turns itself off midsession, check the intake vent before you toss it out. When those air holes are clogged with hair or dust, the unit overheats, and its built-in safety mechanism turns off the motor. To clear the air holes, run a vacuum over the clogged holes.

Hot glue—items stuck together

Items stuck together with a hot-glue gun can often be pried apart if heated with a hair dryer. You may also heat a thin-bladed knife from a hobby or art supply store, then carefully work it between the two items.

Insulation rebates

Many utility companies give rebates for this type of home

improvement because it conserves so much energy. As a bonus, you'll save a lot of money on heating and cooling costs.

Keyholes—no more fumbling in the dark

Brush keyholes with luminous paint, and you won't fumble for the lock in the dark.

Ladders—protect your aluminum siding

Place a pair of athletic socks on the top ends of an extension ladder to protect aluminum siding from the ladder's sharp edges.

Leaks—ceiling

If you notice water leaking through the ceiling, immediately hammer a 16d nail through the Sheetrock to allow the water to drain before it damages the plaster or drywall. Later, after the leak is repaired, all you'll need to cover the emergency repair is a dab of Spackle and touch up paint.

Leaks—faucet wisdom

A faucet leaking 60 drops a minute wastes 113 gallons of water a month. That's 1,356 gallons a year down the drain. Better to fix the leak right away.

Leaks—roof

If your roof leaks, control that leak by tacking a string into the roof sheathing where the water comes through. Place a bucket under it. The water will run down the string into the bucket rather than down your ceiling.

Leaks—toilet

To find the water leaks in your home, try this test: Turn off all running water in the house. Find your water meter and take a look. Is it still moving? Chances are you have a water leak, and chances are even better it's your toilet. Put a few drops of food coloring into the toilet's tank. If without flushing, the color shows up in the bowl, it's leaking all right. Get a toilet repair kit at the home repair center. This is a very simple do-it-yourself repair.

Lighting—extracting broken bulbs

If an electric bulb breaks off in the socket, follow this simple procedure: Turn off the power to the fixture by either unplugging the fixture or turning off power at the main service panel. Cut a potato in half, and push one of the halves into the broken bulb piece. Turn the potato, and the broken piece will come right out.

Messy job—when answering door or phone

When you're painting or doing other messy jobs around the house, keep a couple of plastic sandwich bags nearby. If you have to answer the door or the phone, just slip your hand into a bag to avoid spreading the mess.

Nailing—hold nail with a comb

The best way to hammer a very small nail into the wall is to place the nail between the teeth

of a tiny comb, hold the comb to the wall, and hammer away.

Nails—rust-free

Prevent nails from rusting by placing them in airtight jars with a little WD-40 or oil.

Nails and screws—use heat

To keep the wall or plaster from splitting or cracking when hammering in a nail, drop the nail into a pot of hot water for 15 seconds, remove, then carefully hammer it in. To remove a stubborn screw, pass a lighted match over the end of the screwdriver; the hot tip will then twist out the screw.

Nuts—for sockets

Find a nut to fit each socket of your set. Glue the nuts in a row in a tool tray. Now store each socket on its own nut, and it will stay secure and in place.

Nuts, bolts, and screws—loosen

If you don't have penetrating oil and need to loosen a nut,

screw, or bolt, use vinegar, lemon juice, or hot pepper sauce instead. All of these products contain acid that attacks minerals and rust.

Painting—around door hardware and window edges

Before painting a door, coat the knobs, locks, and hinges with petroleum jelly. Afterward, use a cloth to wipe off the jelly and any paint that may have been spilled. Use this method on window edges as well.

Painting—avoid drips on your hands

Push a paintbrush handle through a slit in a sponge. It'll stop the drips from running onto your hand.

Painting—barrier for splashes on face

Cover your hands and face with a very thin film of petroleum jelly before you start painting. Paint splashes will simply wash off.

Painting—baseboards

Borrow your kid's skateboard when painting baseboards. Sit on it and roll along as you work.

Painting—catching can drips

Glue a paper plate to the bottom of a paint can to catch drips. Before you open the can, apply several dots of glue from a hot-glue gun to a plate. Position the can on the dots and let sit for 5 minutes. Or place a small amount of paint on the paper plate. It's much more convenient than using newspaper because when you pick up the can, the plate goes along.

Painting—citronella to repel insects

A few drops of citronella oil added to a bucket of paint will keep mosquitoes and other flying insects away from a fresh paint job.

Painting—don't waste paint if delayed

When tackling a painting job you may not be able to

complete in 1 day, don't waste the paint in the rollers and brushes by cleaning them. Simply wrap the brushes or rollers tightly in plastic wrap and store them in the freezer. Remove them from the freezer a little while before you start painting again, and you can pick up right where you left off.

Painting—gentle scraper

An old, metal kitchen spatula is perfect for scraping up softened paint remover and paint. Regular paint scrapers have sharp corners that make it all too easy to scratch or gouge the wood.

Painting—how much paint is left?

Mark the level of paint on the outside of the can so you can tell how much paint is left without reopening the can.

Painting—keep brushes soft

Keep paintbrushes soft by giving them a final rinse in water containing a bit of liquid fabric softener.

Painting—no doors painted shut

Fold a couple of sheets of newspaper over the top of the door. You won't be able to paint the door shut—no matter how hard you try.

Painting—nonslip outdoor steps

When painting outside steps, add a bit of fine sand to the paint to create a nonslip surface.

Painting—picture hook markers

Replace picture hooks with thumbtacks before you paint a wall. Paint over the tack, then remove it once the wall is dry. Now you can rehang pictures in exactly the same spot, using the same hole for the hook.

Painting—scraping paint from windows

To quickly scrape the dried paint from windows, use a single-edged razor blade that you dip into a solution of liquid soap and water. The blade will glide along and the job will take little time and effort.

Painting—soften hard brushes

Soften hard paintbrushes in hot vinegar for a few minutes. Then wash them in soap and warm water and set out to dry.

Painting—stairs

If you need to paint the stairs while living in your house, do this: Paint every other step. Let those dry thoroughly, mark them with a piece of masking tape, and then paint the rest. Taking the steps two at a time during this renovation should give the family some great exercise.

Painting—storage

Store partially full cans of paint upside down. The paint will form an airtight seal, extending its useful life.

Painting—strain lumpy or debris-filled paint

If paint appears lumpy or contains debris, stretch a pair of pantyhose over the top of a clean bucket and strain the

paint by pouring it through the hose into the bucket.

Painting—window frame trick

Before you begin painting window frames, cut strips of newspaper, dip them in water, and press them onto the glass close to the frame. When the paint dries, moisten the newspaper with a damp sponge and peel it right off. Presto! No messy windowpanes to scrape clean after the painting is done, and no sticky tape to remove.

Pipes—frozen

First open the faucet to release pressure from thawing water. Then apply heat with a hair dryer, heat gun, or heat lamp, starting at the faucet side of the frozen area.

Pipes—prevent freezing

If a particular pipe in your home freezes regularly, allow the corresponding faucet to drip ever so slightly when subfreezing weather is predicted.

Reassembling wisdom

Before you take something apart to fix it, take a picture so you can see how it fits back together. To help you remember how to reassemble it, place each part in the correct sequence onto the sticky side of a piece of duct tape.

Refurbishing wisdom

When you finish refurbishing a room in your home, write down this important information on a piece of paper and tape it to the back of the switch plate: the brand and color of the paint, how much it took to paint the room, how many rolls of wallpaper were required, and the circuit breaker number that serves this room. You'll be happy to find the information the next time.

Roof repair

If you have a loose or missing roof shingle, slip a piece of sheet metal or builder's felt (tar paper) over the damaged area and under the shingle above it. Hold it in place with dabs of roofing cement.

Rubber mallet—make your own

Cut an X in an old tennis ball and put it on the head of a hammer to make a rubber mallet.

Sanding—in tiny or hard-to-reach spaces

Use an emery board to sand small or hard-to-reach areas like shutter slats or drawer runners.

Sandpaper—longer lasting

To make sandpaper or emery paper last longer, back it with masking tape. The tape helps keep the paper from tearing or creasing while you are working and doubles or triples its longevity.

Saw blade storage

Store circular saw blades in old record album jackets.

351

Scissors—sharpen

Sharpen scissors by cutting several times into 220 grit sandpaper. Turn the scissors over and repeat to sharpen the bottom blade.

Screwdriver caddy

To make a great screwdriver caddy, tightly coil a roll of corrugated cardboard and stuff it into a 2-pound coffee can. Poke all your screwdrivers between the corrugations.

Screws—anchor in plaster wall

Here's how to anchor a screw in a plaster wall: First make the hole by driving a nail into the plaster. Plug the hole with fine steel wool. The screw will go in firmly—and stay.

Screws—holes in wood

If a screw hole in wood furniture becomes too large to hold the screw, try this: Remove the screw and pack the hole with toothpicks and wood glue. Wait for the glue to dry, then trim the toothpicks even with the surface. Re-drill the hole, and replace the screw.

Spray cans—keep nozzles clear

Hold a spray can of anything upside down to clear the nozzle between uses. While the can is completely inverted, spray a few times to clear the passage.

Squeaks—hinges

Lubricate the pin on a squeaky hinge with petroleum jelly instead of oil. You won't need to worry about drips on the floor.

Squeaks—stair steps and floors

Both squeaky stairs and floorboards can often be silenced temporarily with talcum powder. Work the powder into the cracks and wipe away the excess. Repeat as necessary.

Stain—storage

Store leftover water-base stain in a thoroughly cleaned ketchup bottle with a flip-top lid. You'll be able to dispense exactly the amount you want with no mess. Be sure to label the bottle with the exact contents.

Staining and refinishing—clean sanded surfaces

Dampen a rag with rubbing alcohol to clean sanded surfaces prior to applying stain or finish.

Stud location in walls

Studs are the vertical wooden supports behind your walls. They're handy for hanging pictures and such because a nail or screw is more likely to stay in place when it's been driven into a stud as opposed to just the drywall. To locate the studs in a wall, find a light switch or electrical outlet in the room and take the plate off. If you peek in there, you might be able to see a nail or screw from one side of the box going into a stud. Switches and outlets are almost always initially installed against a stud for stability. The stud is 2 inches wide, so visualize and mark the center of that stud. Sixteen-inches from that mark in either direction should be the center of its neighbor. And so on around the room. Note: Some new homes have studs 24 inches on center.

Toilet replacement

Before forking out the big bucks to purchase a toilet or sink, check with a local plumbing contractor. Many times they have used items that are in perfect condition because they were removed from new homes when the homeowner wanted to upgrade or change the color.

Tool protection for small tools

Staple a pocket protector to your workbench so you can keep track of those really small tools that have a way of disappearing.

Vacuum hose clog

To dislodge a vacuum hose clog, first turn the vacuum off and unplug it. Unwind a metal hanger and, leaving a slight hook on the end, slide the hanger into the hose, hook the blockage, and pull it out.

Vinyl floor tile removal

To remove a vinyl floor tile, aim a hair dryer set on medium at the tile's corners and center. Heat will cause the adhesive on the underside of the tile to become moist and sticky. Slowly work a putty knife between the floor and the tile to pry it loose.

Wallpaper—bubbles

Remove bubbles and blisters in wallpaper by cutting an X into the wallpaper with a very sharp razor blade and regluing the paper.

Wallpaper—grease spots

Remove a grease spot from wallpaper by rubbing baby powder into it. This serves as an absorbent.

Wallpaper—moisten and smooth prepasted paper

If you're working with prepasted paper, use a plant mister to moisten it. A handheld squeegee is a great tool for smoothing prepasted wallpaper quickly and evenly.

Wallpaper—papering around outlets

When wallpapering over outlets, first insert childproof electrical outlet plugs. When you cut through the paper, you won't get a shock.

Wallpaper—preparation

Two days before you plan to wallpaper, reroll the roll of paper the opposite way. The paper will be flat, and the job will go faster.

Wallpaper—removal

To remove wallpaper, start by cutting several crisscrosses in each panel of paper with a utility knife so the wallpaper remover or steam can seep into the cuts and help loosen the paper.

Wallpaper—squirt gun as tool

Keep a child's squirt gun handy when wallpapering. It's perfect for dampening corners that have dried out or didn't get quite wet enough the first time around.

Wallpaper—vinyl

If vinyl wallpaper is too tightly curled, you can relax it with a hair dryer set on warm. Hold the dryer 6 to 8 inches away, and wave it back and forth over the paper.

Walls—hanging pictures on wallpaper

To hang pictures on wallpaper: Cut a notch in the paper, bend it back gently, then drive the nail into the wall. If you remove the nail later, you can simply glue the paper flap over the hole, and there won't be an ugly blemish on the paper.

Walls—removing clear tape

Remove clear tape from walls by warming it slightly with a hair dryer.

Washing machine maintenance

Take care of your washing machine, and you'll add years to its useful life: To unclog hoses and flush out all the minerals and all the gummy buildup, fill the machine with hot water (no clothes), pour in 1 gallon of distilled white vinegar, and allow to run through an entire cycle.

Water heater maintenance

Perform water heater maintenance twice a year, and you'll get many more years of service from it. Turn off the power to the water heater at the circuit breaker and drain the sediment from the bottom of the tank. In areas with hard water, draining is best done every month.

White glue—soften in bottle

To soften white glue in a plastic bottle, place the bottle in boiling water for a few seconds until the glue softens. If it's in a glass bottle, run hot tap water over the bottle for a minute or two, then place the bottle in simmering water. Or simply add a bit of white vinegar to the amount of glue

355

you're going to use and stir with a toothpick.

Windows—cracked

If a window cracks in your house, protect yourself and the sash frame until you can replace the glass by taping the crack with packing tape or adhesive-backed weather stripping. But don't count on this temporary fix to hold for very long.

Windows—match storm windows and screens

To match storm windows and screens to the correct windows, draw a diagram of the house and number each window frame. Use a permanent marker to write the same number on the corner of the appropriate storm window or screen. Attach the diagram to the garage or basement wall, and you'll never have to guess which window or screen goes where.

Windows—paint worn mini-blinds

Instead of replacing worn metal mini-blinds, paint them.

Wash them with soap and water in the bathtub, rinse thoroughly, and dry completely. Carefully spray-paint them. Selecting the same or similar shade will make the job easier.

Windows—painted shut

Don't use a screwdriver to try to pry open a window that has been painted shut. Instead, move a pizza cutter back and forth in the stubborn groove.

Windows—screen patch

To repair a small tear in a window screen, cut a square patch a little larger than the damaged area. You can buy screening at the hardware store. Unravel and remove a few strands of wire from all four sides. Bend the wire ends over till you can slip them through the screen. Then bend them farther to hold the patch in place.

Windows—spring-clean windowsills with paint

Instead of trying to scrub windowsills clean each spring, just paint them. It's faster, and the results are much better.

Wood—refinishing

To identify the type of clear finish on wood so you can refinish it, touch the finish with a cotton ball dampened with nail polish remover. If the cotton ball sticks or the finish softens, it's varnish, lacquer, or shellac. If there's no effect, it's polyurethane. The best tool for removing old finish from carvings and other hard-to-reach areas is a natural bristle paintbrush with the edges trimmed to a stubby length.

Wood—staining

Softwoods like pine, poplar, and fir may absorb stain unevenly. To test for firmness, press your thumbnail into the wood. If it leaves an indentation, it's a softwood. Seal all softwoods before staining by coating with a wood conditioner.

15

Shopping

Auctions

Stretch your dollars by buying things such as building materials or appliances—even gifts—at auctions. Learn how to be an impeccable inspector, because all sales are final.

Bartering

Whenever possible, trade goods or services instead of money: haircuts for typing, babysitting for landscaping, or housecleaning for electrical work.

Buy in bulk—protect savings

Buying in bulk may not always be a money-saving activity if your family unconsciously consumes more when they see large amounts of anything. Somehow that feeling of using just a little vanishes when the shampoo, for instance, is in a quart-size bottle. To counteract this problem, have small containers for laundry soap, shampoo, cereal, and so on. Fill them from the large bulk container, which is stored out of sight. Besides seeming that there isn't an unlimited quantity of anything, the small containers are easier to handle, and the chances of slipping and pouring out too much are lessened.

Buy in bulk—with a partner

If you are single and want to take advantage of bulk buying, find a shopping partner—someone with your same situation—and pool your shopping needs. Two-for-one is a real waste if the second item goes stale before it can be used. But with a partner, each gets one for half price.

Buy used—consignment store, buying

High-quality, previously owned clothes are sold for as much as 70 to 85 percent below the price of a similar item that is new. Shop well, and you will find unbelievable bargains.

Buy used—consignment store, buying and selling

Make money and save money at a consignment store. If you take in used clothing (men's, women's, and children's) that is in good to excellent condition, the owner will resell the items and send you a check for a percentage (usually 50 percent). These shops are also a great place to hunt for wonderful bargains. Find a consignment shop in an upscale neighborhood, and you've got it made.

Buy used—garage sale map

Before checking out garage sales, make a special garage-sale map. Start with a map of your local community and cover it with clear contact paper. Using a grease pencil, mark the locations of the garage sales you want to visit this weekend. Now you can design a logical route to make the best use of your weekend time. Erase the marks after you attend each of the sales.

Buy used—thrift shops

Check out thrift shops, but never buy just because you've found a good bargain.

Compulsive shopping— $100 bill trick

If you find yourself shopping compulsively—buying stuff on credit that you neither need, really want, nor can even afford—try this rather unconventional tactic: Tuck away a $100 bill in a very secret place known only to you. In the future, whenever you get the urge to purchase something or feel overcome by a case of the "I wants," tell yourself, *OK, but you'll have to go home and get that $100 bill*. For some reason the urge will pass quickly. Knowing you can if you want, but you choose not to, has a wonderful preventive effect. Try it.

Compulsive shopping— go on a diet

Break the compulsive shopping habit. Don't carry credit cards with you, put yourself on a cash diet, and throw away all junk mail, such as mail-order catalogs, without even opening it.

Contracts—avoid buyer's remorse

Think about a contract for 30 days before you sign. Any purchase that requires your signature probably requires payments. You just might have a change of heart, and even if you don't, you will be confident in your decision after 30 days and will hopefully avoid buyer's remorse.

Coupons—ask for help

When a great sale or coupon offer sends you to an unfamiliar store, don't spend a lot of time searching for the item. Remember, the store wants you to wander around so you'll just happen to pick up all kinds of other things. Instead, when you enter the store, ask an employee for the exact location, make your purchase, and get out of there as quickly as possible.

Coupons—doubling or tripling

Find a market that will double the coupon's value. This practice varies throughout the country, but if you have good coupons, make sure you find a way to double them. Some stores even triple them on certain days.

Coupons—in envelope with grocery list

Save business reply envelopes from your junk mail and use the back for grocery lists. Your coupons will fit nicely inside the envelope, and you won't have to worry about losing them.

Coupons—photo album organization

Organize your coupons in a small photo album. You can organize the coupons by store or category and can easily flip through it to find the ones you want. The album will fit neatly into a purse or bag.

Coupons—smallest size purchase

If you have a qualified coupon, you'll usually save a higher percentage of the purchase

price by buying the smallest size.

Coupons—speed up checkout

If you're a couponer, make sure that before you get to the store you use a highlighting pen to mark the expiration date on each coupon you intend to redeem. Your checker will be happy and so will everyone waiting in line behind you.

Coupons—Sunday newspaper extras

Ask your newspaper delivery person if you can pick up any leftover sets of coupons that remain once the Sunday newspapers are stuffed and put together. Most will gladly comply because there's that much less for them to manage.

Coupons—use only if really saving money

Use coupons only for items you would buy even if you didn't have the coupon and only if it is truly a savings. Check other brands that might be on sale or are already cheaper. Manufacturers often offer coupons as incentives on new products. But you're not saving anything if you buy something that was not on your list.

Damaged or floor model goods—discount

Always ask for a reduction or discount if the item you desire is marked or scratched or is the floor model. You're not complaining, whining, or being obnoxious. You're negotiating, and that's smart.

Electronics—buy gently used at repair shops

Before buying a new television, stereo, or other piece of electronic equipment, check with a good repair shop. Many times, excellent-quality merchandise has been abandoned, and the shop will sell it to you for only the cost of the unpaid repair bill.

Factory direct—buy seconds and overruns

If you have factories in your area that manufacture things you regularly use, call to see if they have factory outlets where they sell seconds and overruns. Try the local newspaper for roll ends of newsprint. It makes great picnic table coverings, gift wrapping, and all kinds of crafts. Paper factories often have toilet paper and other paper goods available. Don't confuse factory outlets of this type with outlet malls that are more retail than discount.

Generic or store brands

It's amazing how many brand-name products have a generic counterpart—everything from grocery items to prescription and over-the-counter drugs. You'll be surprised how close they are to the expensive brands. Think this way when buying clothes as well. Take a little time, and before you make that whopping purchase at Nordstrom, sneak into

Walmart and see if they don't have a very good generic.

Groceries—avoid the first day or two of the month

Avoid shopping on the first day or two of the month. Some stores have been known to raise their prices during the time that government aid and Social Security checks come out.

Groceries—bag your own for easy unloading

Bag your own groceries so you can group items together to match the way your kitchen, pantry, refrigerator, and freezer are arranged. You'll save a lot of time putting things away.

Groceries—buy ahead

This will cut down your trips to the grocery store and will often save 50 percent of the unit cost. Reorganize your kitchen and pantry. Find places outside the kitchen to store dry and canned goods.

Repackage large amounts into small units.

Groceries—cooler in your trunk

Keep a cooler in the trunk of your car. You can stop for groceries without having to go straight home afterward.

Groceries—discontinued products

Today's grocery stores carry only those items that move well to maintain their profit margins. Watch for product shelf labels with either a line drawn through the price code numbers or the letter "DC" or "Discontinued" written on them. By purchasing these "unadvertised" specials, you will often find savings of at least 20 percent or more on your register tape.

Groceries—don't shop when hungry

Never shop when hungry. You will be compelled to buy everything in sight, regardless of what's on your list.

Groceries—ethnic foods

Purchasing certain items at ethnic markets can often result in remarkable savings. It's best to go into any new store with a good idea of what a comparable product would cost elsewhere. Just because the Asian market offers spices, water chestnuts, bean sprouts, and bamboo shoots, for example, doesn't necessarily mean they'll be sold at a bargain compared with the cost at your discount grocery.

Groceries—generic and store brands

Some store-brand grocery items are exactly the same as the more expensive brand-name version. By law, certain items, such as aspirin, baking soda, cornstarch, honey, molasses, peanuts, pecans, salt, sugar, unbleached flour, and walnuts, must be exactly the same content and composition, regardless of packaging or quantity gimmicks. Always buy the lower-cost generic brands when buying these items.

Groceries—haul in with a trash can

If you find it difficult to carry all of your groceries at once and end up making numerous trips from the car to the house, buy a trash can with wheels and load your groceries into it. You can just wheel it right into the kitchen.

Groceries—lists, arrange by store layout

Arrange your shopping list according to the general layout of your supermarket. You'll save steps and cut down exposure to impulse items.

Groceries—lists, make them when you're hungry

Make your grocery-shopping list at home when you are hungry. You will be more creative and thorough.

Groceries—loss leaders, rain checks

When the supermarket sells out of the loss-leader items (those items the store has priced below their costs to get you into the store), always ask for a rain check so you can still buy them at rock-bottom prices when supplies are replenished.

Groceries—loss leaders and sales, menu planning

Take full advantage of the store's loss-leader products, and design your weekly menus around the weekly grocery store sale ads.

Groceries—meat for the freezer

When you purchase meat that you intend to freeze, slip it into one of the free plastic bags from the produce department before you put it into a resealable plastic freezer bag. This way you can reuse the expensive resealable storage bag again and again without having to wash it out or worry about bacteria. There is no need to label the bag because you'll be able to see the label through the plastic.

Groceries—meat near sell-by date

The marked-down price of meat that has a sell-by date

that will expire soon can be dramatic. The meat is still good, but if you can't use it on or before the expiration date, freeze it immediately and use it within 3 months.

Groceries—meat pricing

When buying meat, bear in mind that an expensive lean cut may be more economical than one that requires you to throw away excessive bone, gristle, or fat.

Groceries—milk and produce runs

When you need to make milk and produce runs between your regular major shopping trips, but you are tempted to turn the trip into an excuse to stock up on impulse items, make a precise list and engage the services of an errand runner, such as a responsible teen.

Groceries—perishables in no-spoil quantities

When shopping for perishable foods, buy only amounts that can be used while they are still good. Buying in larger quantities just because you get a low price is no bargain if you end up throwing part of it away.

Groceries—price book

Keep a price book that lists the prices of regularly purchased items at a variety of grocery stores in your area. Refer to it when you see specials or ads to determine whether or not it's really a bargain.

Groceries—price by volume

When you buy iced-tea, lemonade, or fruit-juice mix, figure cost not by weight but by the per-quart yield the whole container will make. Packaging on these types of items can be very deceiving.

Groceries—produce by the bag

Buy produce in a bag for the best value. Watch out: Often the bruised and spoiled fruit will find its way into the bottom of a bag. Pick out the best bag and the heaviest one. Weigh a few before you decide.

Groceries—produce straight from the farm

Find a farmers' market. You can buy locally grown fruit and vegetables at great prices. Some areas hold these markets only in the warm months; in other areas they're held year-round.

Groceries—produce weigh-in

Prepackaged produce must have a minimum weight as printed on the packaging. Not all potatoes are created equal, however, so a 10-pound bag may weigh 11 pounds, and a 1-pound bag of carrots may weigh 1.5 pounds.

Groceries—products shelved high and low

When grocery shopping, look high and low. Usually you'll find the less-expensive store and generic brands at the bottoms and tops of the shelves. The higher-priced name brands are conveniently located at eye level—yours and your children's.

Groceries—reduced prices

Search for bargains in the day-old baked goods, dented can, and meat-that-is-about-to-expire bins. You have to be careful, but as long as the cans are not bulging or leaking and the end dates meet your approval, go for it. Also, look for generic and off-brands for additional savings.

Groceries—shelf-life expert

Become a shelf-life expert. Buying in bulk will do you no good if you end up throwing most of it away due to spoilage. Some things last indefinitely, while others spoil, even if frozen, after a certain period of time.

Groceries—shop during off-hours

Shop midweek and during off-hours. Typically, store sales and double- or even triple-coupon savings occur midweek. Also, there's less distracting hustle and bustle early or late in the day or at meal-time, which allows you to do a more efficient job of shopping.

Groceries—shop for less than 30 minutes

Plan ahead and know what you're going to buy so your grocery-shopping trips will be short and sweet—less than 30 minutes if at all possible. If you linger longer, it will cost you. Market surveys indicate that shoppers spend an extra 50 cents each minute for every minute over 30 spent in the supermarket.

Groceries—shop in smaller stores

Many large grocery stores do not have the best prices. Check the smaller independent markets in your area and do some price comparisons. They may have fewer choices, but they may also have lower prices and shorter checkout lines. Many small markets also accept manufacturers' coupons.

Groceries—shop less often

See how long you can go between grocery-shopping trips. Start by doubling the time between trips. If you go to the market every day, stretch it to every other day. Once a week? Shop after 2 weeks next time. You'll waste less, use less, and spend proportionately less.

Groceries—shop only with cash

Grocery shop with cash only. You will be a much more careful shopper knowing you can't go over your limit because you don't have a checkbook, debit card, or credit card to fall back on.

Groceries—shop the perimeter

Concentrate on the perimeter of the grocery store rather than the center aisles. Around the outside is where you'll find healthier food with the least packaging and processing: produce, meats, fish, and dairy.

Groceries—spices and herbs

When purchasing spices and herbs, first check your health food store. Many carry spices and herbs in bulk quantities, and you can measure out and purchase as much or as little as

you like. Don't buy more than you know you will reasonably use in the next 6 months.

Groceries—stop impulse buying

When you pick up an item that is not on your grocery list, place it in the child's seat of the shopping cart. Just before checking out, reevaluate the budget-breaking items and make yourself put all of them back except for one item. That's your reward for controlling your impulses in the grocery aisles.

Groceries—vacuum sealing

If you buy large quantities of staple items, consider investing in a vacuum-sealing machine. But don't buy one unless you're sure you'll use it.

Impulse buying—count the cost

Ten dollars here, 20 bucks there doesn't seem like it will make much difference in the long run. But if you spend $20 on impulse items each week, that's $1,040 a year. Little things do matter, and when it comes to spending impulsively, they matter a lot.

Impulse buying—let someone else care for "your" stuff

A little attitude change will allow you to thoroughly enjoy lovely things but leave them in the stores. Let someone else dust, polish, and care for them. You can visit "your" stuff whenever you like and change your mind without consequence!

Impulse buying—shop only by plan

Stop shopping. Shopping often means strolling through the mall when you have nothing particular in mind to buy, simply looking for great bargains and things that happen to strike your fancy. That is a very dangerous thing to do. I'm not suggesting that you never again buy anything, but instead that you spend only during a planned act of acquiring the goods and services you need and not make

spur-of-the-moment, impulse purchases.

Impulse buying—shop only with cash

Retailers are keenly aware of the statistics that prove you will spend at least 30 percent more if you are in the store with a credit card, debit card, or checkbook. The last thing they want is a customer who carries cash. Why? Because the cash buyer is cautious and less impulsive.

Impulse buying—shop when you're short on time

Do essential shopping when you don't have much time. If you have too much time to browse, you'll be tempted to buy impulsively.

Impulse buying—use a wish list

If you struggle with the "I wants," create your own wish-list system. As you think of things you want, write them on your wish list and date the entry. Then keep your wish list with you at all times. The rule is that you must leave the item on the list without purchasing it until it has been on there for 3 months. Periodically review your list, especially when you add some new gadget to it. Surprisingly, your level of need for most of the items diminishes to the point that you'll no longer even want it. Any item that remains after 3 months indicates that the item deserves further consideration.

Impulse buying—wait 24 hours

If an item costs more than the amount you set ahead of time, wait 24 hours between the time you make a decision and actually make the purchase. More times than not you will change your mind, which means you will have avoided a needless purchase.

Layaway plans

Many stores offer layaway plans. This is a great way to purchase something over a period of time without incurring debt. As long as the store holds the merchandise until you make all of the payments, it's not a debt, because you can change your mind and get a refund. Layaway forces you to save for things before you purchase them.

Limit your shopping time

Is it hard for you to stick to a time limit when shopping? Buy a small oven timer and set it to the desired time you wish to spend shopping. Stick it in your pocket or purse, and when the timer goes off, it's time to go home. Or you could set an alarm on your cell phone or watch.

Mail-order shopping

If you love mail-order shopping and find yourself going nuts with the orders even though you've been disappointed in the past with all the junk you ordered that you neither wanted nor needed, here's a tactic to help curb the urge and actually trick yourself: Take great pains and enjoy every moment of studying your favorite catalogs and websites. Fill out the order form or load up your "shopping cart," being careful to select all the items you love the most and in all the colors and sizes you desire. When you're done, "save for later" or prepare the form for mailing, write the total amount on the outside of the envelope, and then purposely set it in a place you will see it often. Leave it there for a full week. By the time the week has passed, give yourself a little test: Without opening the order form or catalog, or returning to the website, can you remember what you ordered? Probably not, so it doesn't matter anymore. Throw it in the trash.

Major purchases—plan carefully

A major purchase deserves careful planning. Break down the cost of the item into a monthly sum you can put aside over a period of time. Example: If you want to buy a new sofa, put pictures of the one you like on your refrigerator and in your checkbook. Determine the amount you will spend and how much you will put into a special account for this purpose each week or month. If your goal is firmly planted in your mind, you won't feel deprived when you give something up to keep making those savings deposits.

Major purchases—save first, spend later

Instead of putting larger purchases on credit, save first. Once you have enough cash, make the purchase. Amazingly, by the time you save up the money, you may change your mind a dozen times. You might even decide you no longer need or want it.

Off-season clothes—stock up

Seasonal items (such as swimwear, coats, and boots) are often cleared out at phenomenal prices, so if you can handle the thought of buying snow gear in the spring, go for it.

Sales—beat the rush

If a sale starts on Thursday at 9 a.m., there's a good chance that if you walk in on Wednesday afternoon, you'll get the sale price.

Salespeople—get friendly

They usually know when things are going to go on sale. Ask, and then be willing to wait.

Scanners—beware

Many retail stores equipped with checkout scanners have store policies that say you get the item free if the price is scanned incorrectly. Stay alert and watch the prices being scanned. If you see something that doesn't look right, speak up. Curiously, each year overall scanner errors in this country register in the millions of dollars, to the benefit of the retailer.

Subscriptions—share

Cut subscription costs by using the buddy system. Find a friend or relative who enjoys a similar magazine or newsletter that you do. Each of you pays half the cost and shares the publication when it arrives each month. Enlarge your group to five: Subscription rates are split four ways, and the fifth person receives the issues last. Instead of participating in the price, the fifth reader becomes the librarian—cataloging, sorting, and storing the publications for the group.

Wholesale

Look through the wholesale listings in your local Yellow Pages or online for items that you buy frequently or in bulk, such as pet food, paper and party goods, and garden supplies. You'll find that many wholesalers sell their wares to the public but don't advertise.

Work in retail

If you are looking for a job, either primary or one to augment your present income, consider the advantage of working in a retail store, then carefully choose the store. By selecting one in which you already shop, not only will you make extra money by receiving a paycheck, you will also almost always receive an employee discount on the products you would be purchasing anyway. A 30 percent employee discount is not unusual. And remember, that's 30 percent off the lowest sale prices, too, which can translate to some healthy bargains.

16

Travel and Entertainment

Air travel—airport quiet spots

If you need to find a quiet place in an airport to either sleep or work, but you don't belong to one of those expensive elite clubs, go to a gate where the plane has just taken off. It will be deserted for a while, and when another scheduled flight moves in on you, find another location where a plane has just departed.

Air travel—airport rental cars

Car rental companies with desks in the airport are generally more expensive than off-site renters. It costs these companies a lot of money to lease airport desk space. And guess who gets to make up the difference?

Air travel—bereavement fares

Most airlines offer reduced fares in time of bereavement. When you call for a reservation under these circumstances, explain your situation and ask for their bereavement fare. Don't be offended if a cooperating airline requires verification of funeral arrangements.

Air travel—book the first flight of the day

Book the first flight of the day. When flights are delayed, they affect other connections. The earlier you leave, the more options you have. Avoid taking the last flight of the day if you must be at your destination the next morning. If that flight is canceled, you're stuck.

Air travel—booking problem

If you are dealing directly with the airline reservation desk and are unable to book the flight you want, hang up and call a second time. If you get a different ticketing agent, you may get what you want.

Air travel—don't fly immediately after dental surgery

Never fly if you have had dental surgery within the past 12 hours. The change in air pressure will cause severe pain and possibly bleeding.

Air travel—insurance for lost luggage

If your luggage is lost and it isn't recovered, each airline has a limit of liability up to a certain amount of the depreciated value of the bag and its contents. If your loss exceeds their limit, your household insurance policy may pick up the difference. Check with the airline for their limit of liability.

Air travel—itinerary information attached to luggage

Write the dates of your stay and where you want lost luggage to be delivered in the city you'll be visiting. Attach this abbreviated itinerary to the outside of your luggage.

Air travel—lost luggage claim and receipt

If your bag does not show up on the luggage carousel, make sure you fill out a claim form and get a receipt before you leave the airport.

Air travel—make your luggage look unique

Checked bags frequently go astray because they look alike and someone might walk off with one that looks like yours. Buy brightly colored luggage, put a colorful luggage strap around your bag, or use neon-colored stickers to make your bag stand out in a crowd. Tacky luggage is also a less likely candidate for theft.

Air travel—rebook by phone, not in airport

You're at the airport when you learn that your flight has been canceled. Don't rush to the ticket counter where you will have to wait in line with everyone else on the canceled flight. Use your phone and call the airline's reservation number. Ask to be rebooked on the next scheduled flight.

Air travel—reduce chance of delays

When booking a flight, remember that the more times you land, take off, or change planes, the more you increase the chance of delays. If you can't avoid making connections, look for a flight that has stopovers at small airports. Reduced traffic reduces delays. Allow at least an hour for connections.

Air travel—remove luggage tags from previous trips

Remove all luggage tags from previous trips to avoid confusing the baggage handlers and scanning devices.

Air travel—save with layovers

An airline flight that makes a stop between your departure city and your destination can sometimes be significantly cheaper than one that makes no stops. You may have to spend an extra hour or two on the ground, and you risk additional delays, but the savings may be worth it.

Air travel—seating, don't wait for check-in

Arrange for your seat assignment when you book a flight.

377

If you wait until you check in, you're less likely to get the seat you want. Some airlines won't assign seats more than 30 days in advance, so check back on their website periodically.

Air travel—seating, strategy for one

When only middle seats are available, ask the gate agent to put you in the empty seat between two people with the same last name. Chances are good you'll get that aisle or window seat when they ask if you'd like to switch so they can sit together.

Air travel—seating, strategy for two

When two people are traveling together on a plane with three-abreast seating, one should request an aisle and the other a window. This maximizes the chances of the seat in the middle remaining empty. If someone does sit there, and you want to sit next to your companion, just ask the person if they'd like the window or aisle instead of the annoying middle seat.

Air travel—skip curbside check-in

Skip the curbside luggage check-in facility if at all possible and go directly to the ticket counter. Your luggage is more likely to be handled correctly, and you won't be expected to tip. If you must use airport curbside check-in, remember these are airport—not airline—employees. Double-check their work, especially the three-letter destination code on your bags' tags. If you want to see your bags at the other end of your trip, tip these handlers.

Air travel—when diverted flights cause delays

If a flight is diverted, causing departure delays, most air carriers will give you a meal voucher. If you need to stay overnight because the airline has a problem, most will pay the hotel bill plus the cost of ground transportation. But you must ask, so don't be timid.

Air travel—willing to be bumped

If you wouldn't mind getting bumped from your flight

because you have the time and could use the voucher that most airlines offer as an incentive for taking a later flight, let the gate agent know that you are willing to give up your seat if needed.

Car travel—backseat organizer

A shoe organizer hung over the back of the front seat can hold small toys, crayons, and other loose items in the car.

Car travel—drive someone else's car

Consider driving someone else's car. Auto-transport companies (listed online) are often looking for good drivers to move cars from one part of the country to the other. Typically you pay only for gas, and they'll even get you started with a full tank.

Car travel—learn with audio books

If you are like most people, you drive about 15,000 miles each year, which expressed in time equals about a college semester. Use the time spent in the car listening to books on tape or self-improvement tapes.

Car travel—take business and truck routes

If you prefer leisurely car-trip vacations, take the business or truck routes through cities. You'll find good motels that aren't near the interstates. These places can be very nice and quite inexpensive.

Hotels—group security

When checking into a hotel, get a hotel business card for each family member to carry in case of accidental separation.

Hotels—save on rates

On any given day, hotels can have many different rates depending on occupancy. If possible, call the hotel desk instead of the 800 reservation number. Ask about weekend rates, holiday and seasonal specials, or discounts for affiliations you might have, such as the Automobile Club of America.

Hotels—suite instead of two rooms

If you need more than one hotel room on vacation, a suite is usually cheaper than two rooms. An efficiency suite will save you even more, allowing you to cook a few of your own meals.

Libraries—interlibrary loans

Call your library to see if you can borrow that book you've been tempted to buy. If they don't have it on hand, ask for an interlibrary loan. Even small libraries belong to large networks of libraries, and chances are very good they'll be able to get that book for you and in less time than it would take for them to acquire it for their own shelves.

Movies—wait for DVDs

All but the biggest blockbusters are available on DVD 3 months—sometimes even sooner—after release. Your patience will pay off.

Outings—attend rehearsals

If tickets to a special concert or local play are out of your price range, ask if you can attend a rehearsal.

Outings—be a bowling league sub

Sign up at your local bowling alley to be a league substitute. For a nominal fee you will be able to bowl in the place of an absentee league member.

Outings—college entertainment

Local colleges often show movies in a setting that's better than some small theaters and at a much lower cost. What's more, live theater, student film shows, and guest speakers can often be seen for free.

Outings—community events

Most cities have community-sponsored entertainment during summer months. Many churches and colleges have free performances during holidays. Make it a habit to check the paper, library bulletin boards, and your community's website for local events.

Outings—ice alternative

When preparing for a family outing or vacation, fill an empty plastic water or milk jug ¾ full with water, freeze, and then place in a cooler. It will keep your food items cold longer than a block of ice will, there's no mess as the ice melts, and if the jug is clean, you'll have fresh drinking water.

Outings—kids at the mall

Load the kids in the car and drive to the biggest mall around. Make the rounds of the "hands-on" toy stores, such as FAO Schwartz or the Disney Store. The stores where kids are always welcome have wonderful play areas.

Outings—perks for volunteers

If you enjoy cultural events or visiting local museums and theaters, volunteer as an usher, ticket collector, or to fill some other position. In exchange, you will probably receive free or reduced admissions. Ask about the policy ahead of time.

Outings—stargaze

Get a book about constellations from the library and arrange a starry-night outing to identify constellations. Bring a thermos of hot chocolate and a great big, cozy blanket.

Packing—avoid leaks in suitcases

Make sure the bottles of shampoo, lotions, and makeup in your suitcase don't leak all over your clothes. Store liquids in zip-type bags.

Packing—business information on luggage tags

Put your business address and phone number on your luggage tags. Your home address and information may suggest to potential thieves that your house will be vacant. Make sure to put the same information inside each piece of luggage too.

Packing—care for stains on the road

Pack a laundry stain pretreatment in your luggage, and use it on stains before they can set. This way, stains will wash out easily once you're home and do your laundry.

Packing—clothespins for drying clothes

Toss some clothespins into your suitcase. They'll turn any hanger into a makeshift clothes dryer.

Packing—earrings kept safe

Pierced earrings won't get lost if you poke them through a handkerchief or cotton sock or into a bar of soap.

Packing—hair dryer for ironing needs

A hair dryer can double as a travel iron. Dampen the creased garment and spread it on a flat surface. Set the dryer on medium-heat and hold it in one hand while smoothing the fabric with the other.

Packing—keep suitcase smelling nice before you pack again

Store an unwrapped fragrant bar of soap in a suitcase to prevent musty odors from forming during storage.

Packing—list for going and coming

Toss the checked-off packing list you used to prepare for the trip into your suitcase. Use it to recheck when gathering everything at the end of your stay.

Packing—lost luggage readiness with a companion

When traveling with a companion, each of you should pack some clothes in the other's luggage to lessen the impact if one bag is lost or detained.

Packing—make photocopies of wallet contents

Whenever you travel, make two photocopies of everything

in your wallet (credit cards, driver's license, medical insurance card, passport, and so on). Put one copy in your luggage, and leave the other at home.

Packing—organize small essentials for hotel room

To keep everything organized when you pack for a trip, group all the small essentials into large zip-type plastic bags. When you get to the hotel, put your bedside bag (travel alarm clock, flashlight, night-light) on the night table; the toiletries bag (powder, deodorant, toothbrush, hair essentials, makeup) on the bathroom shelf. Everything's together, easy to use, ready to go in a moment's notice, and you probably won't leave things behind.

Packing—shampoo for your clothes

Don't bother packing laundry detergent. Shampoo is great for washing blouses and underwear. Caution: Shampoos formulated for oily hair are more alkaline and should not be used on delicate fabrics like silk—they can cause fading.

Packing—small bag for stop on the way

If an overnight stop is on your car-trip itinerary, pack a small bag with one change of clothes for each family member and basic toiletries. Instead of unpacking the whole car, all you'll need to take into the motel is one bag.

Packing—travel with tape

When traveling, always take a roll of clear tape. It removes lint, seals bottles, and even temporarily mends cuffs and hems. Duct tape works well, too, particularly where stronger mending is needed, like for shoe repair or suitcase patches.

Packing—wrap pants around mailing tube

Roll slacks around a mailing tube to keep them from wrinkling in your suitcase.

Restaurants—don't order fish on Mondays

The worst night to order fresh fish in a restaurant is Monday. Most restaurants don't get fish deliveries over the weekend, so Monday's fish special is Friday's delivery.

Traveling—with maps and disappearing ink

A disappearing-ink marking pen, available at the fabric store, is great for marking maps. In a day or so, your marks will fade, and your map is all ready for the next trip.

Traveling—with medications

If you are taking medications when you travel, take an extra watch and keep it always set on home time. You'll never have to wonder when to take your medicine.

Traveling—with pets

Have a special ID tag for any pet traveling with you. Include the name and phone number of someone who can be contacted and will be able to get in touch with you if your pet is lost while you're on the road.

Traveling—with remedy recipe

Do-it-yourself remedy for traveler's . . . uh . . . (how do I say this delicately?) dysentery: In a glass mix 8 ounces fruit juice, ½ teaspoon honey, and a pinch of salt. In a second glass mix 8 ounces purified water and ¼ teaspoon baking soda. Alternate sips from each glass until you've finished both.

Vacations—avoid tourist site crowds

Before visiting popular tourist sites, call ahead to find out when the tour buses usually arrive. Dozens of tourists arriving at the same time can flood attractions with crowds, which can result in long lines and shoddy service. Buses usually run on fixed schedules, so you should be able to count on the information you receive.

Vacations—camera prop

Fill a small fabric bag with dried beans or rice to keep in your camera bag. When you want to take a time exposure and need to hold the camera very still, simply set the beanbag on a steady surface, place the camera on the bag, line up the shot, and shoot. The camera stays perfectly still because it is securely cradled on the beanbag. This is also a perfect solution for when you want to get into the photo too. Just securely position the camera on the beanbag, set the timer, and run like crazy.

Vacations—factory tours

Many interesting factories offer formal or informal tours. Call the chambers of commerce for a list of all the factories that offer tours in the cities you will be visiting on your next family vacation. While you're at it, keep a list of the ones in your own area. Typically, these kinds of tours conclude with free samples of the factory's products. I know what you're thinking: Few, if any, banks offer tours.

Vacations—involve the whole family in planning

Involve the whole family in vacation planning, particularly the kids. Letting them participate helps them put to use their geography and history knowledge. Saving the money first and then deciding how it will be spent demonstrates to your kids the principles of economy and good money management. If everyone has a voice in making the big decisions, the result will be far less grumbling and a lot more cooperation.

Vacations—new bulbs for lights with timers

Before you go away on vacation, put new lightbulbs in all the lamps connected to timers. You want to be sure that when the timers go on, so will the lights. Save the lightbulbs you replaced for using when you'll be home.

Vacations—peace with kids

At the start of a trip give each child a handful of dimes. If they ask "How much farther?" or any other tiresome questions, they forfeit a dime. Let them keep what's left.

Vacation—plants

Before leaving on vacation, put your plants in a small, plastic children's swimming pool. Fill the pool with about 3 inches of water. The plants will survive for at least 1 week. Make sure the pool is in an area that will not get direct sunlight.

Mary Hunt, award-winning and bestselling author, syndicated columnist, and sought-after motivational speaker, has created a global platform that is making strides to help men and women battle the epidemic impact of consumer debt. Mary is the founder of Debt-Proof Living, a highly regarded organization consisting of an interactive website, a monthly newsletter, a daily syndicated column, and hundreds of thousands of loyal followers. Since 1992, DPL has been dedicated to its mission to provide hope, help, and realistic solutions for individuals who are committed to financially responsible and debt-free living.

As a speaker, Mary travels extensively, addressing conferences, corporations, colleges, universities, and churches at home and abroad. A frequent guest on radio and television, she has appeared on dozens of television shows, including *Dr. Phil*, *Good Morning America*, *The Oprah Winfrey Show*, and *Dateline*.

Mary lives with her husband in Orange County, California.

These 7 simple rules will change your life!

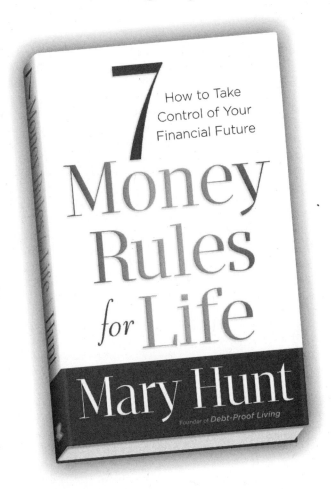

These days most of us need some help managing our money. Mary Hunt's simple rules will move you from financial uncertainty to financial confidence!

Revell
a division of Baker Publishing Group
www.RevellBooks.com

Available Wherever Books Are Sold
Also Available in Ebook Format

Teach your kids to have a healthy relationship with money and build a strong financial future.*

*Even if you still have a lot to learn.

Mary Hunt can show you how.

Christmas—with no debt, less stress, and more joy!

Mary Hunt shows you how to assess your situation, commit to no new debt, and think creatively about gifts.

What Is Debt-Proof Living?

It's a great big wonderful website offering help and hope to anyone who wants to learn how to manage their money more effectively. If you want to get out of debt—or stay out—and learn how to live below your means, Debt-Proof Living is the place to be. It encompasses many elements:

A lifestyle

Debt-proof living is a way of life where you spend less than you earn; you give and save consistently; your financial decisions are purposeful; you work toward your goals by following a specific plan.

A system of personal money management

Debt-proof living is a specific method that makes it possible to debt-proof your life.

A newsletter

In continuous publication since 1992, the DPL newsletter is now published in an online format available to all members of this website.

A website

DebtProofLiving.com is the home of the debt-proof living brand. It is primarily a member-only website with features ranging from money management tools, articles, resources, community forums, consumer tips, recipes, and more.

Visit DebtProofLiving.com today!